Unlikely Ways Home

Doubleday

NEW YORK

LONDON

TORONTO

SYDNEY

AUCKLAND

Unlikely Ways Home

REAL-LIFE

SPIRITUAL

DETOURS

Edward L. Beck

PUBLISHED BY DOUBLEDAY
a division of Random House, Inc.
1745 Broadway, New York, New York 10019

DOUBLEDAY and the portrayal of an anchor with a dolphin
are trademarks of Doubleday, a division of Random House, Inc.

Excerpt from *Traveling Mercies* by Anne Lamott appears
courtesy of Pantheon Books.
Excerpt from "The House of Belonging," in *The House of Belonging* by
David Whyte. Copyright 1997 by David Whyte. Reprinted by permission of
the author and Many Rivers Press.

Book design by Gretchen Achilles

Library of Congress Cataloging-in-Publication-Data

Beck, Edward L., 1959–
    Unlikely ways home : real-life spiritual detours / Edward L. Beck—
    1st ed.
        p. cm.
    1. Religious biography.   1. Title.
    BL72.B43 2004
    204'.092'2—dc22
    [B]

                                                            2004043819

ISBN 0-385-50858-1
Copyright © 2004 by Edward L. Beck
All Rights Reserved

PRINTED IN THE UNITED STATES OF AMERICA

JULY 2004
First Edition

1   3   5   7   9   10   8   6   4   2

FOR ROBERT,
always likely

In memory of
EDWARD SEAN O'NEILL
(1947–2003)
and
MARCO GARCIA
(1983–2003)

AUTHOR'S NOTE

The following stories recount the experiences of real people. A few (in four of the twelve chapters) have asked that their names and circumstances be altered to protect their anonymity. Some events depicted have been reconstructed within the generally accepted boundaries of creative nonfiction. The views and opinions expressed by the people in the stories do not necessarily reflect those of the author.

[Our pastor, Veronica,] sings to us sometimes from the pulpit and tells us stories of when she was a child. She told us this story just the other day:

When she was about seven, her best friend got lost one day. The little girl ran up and down the streets of the big town where they lived, but she couldn't find a single landmark. She was very frightened. Finally a policeman stopped to help her. He put her in the passenger seat of his car, and they drove around until she finally saw her church. She pointed it out to the policeman, and then she told him firmly, "You can let me out now. This is my church, and I can always find my way home from here."

And that is why I have stayed close to mine—because no matter how bad I am feeling, how lost or lonely or frightened, when I see the faces of the people at my church, and hear their tawny voices, I can always find my way home.

—ANNE LAMOTT, *Traveling Mercies*

This is the bright home
in which I live,
this is where
I ask
my friends
to come,
this is where I want
to love all the things
it has taken me so long
to learn to love.

This is the temple
of my adult aloneness
and I belong
to that aloneness
as I belong to my life.

There is no house
like the house of belonging.

—DAVID WHYTE, "The House of Belonging"

CONTENTS

Unlikely Ways Home

Before the Stories

"RELIGION IS SO BORING," a friend of mine said as we sipped an overpriced Cabernet Sauvignon in a trendy midtown Manhattan bar that he had chosen. We were on our way to dinner and a critically touted Broadway play that *I* had chosen. Not up for a weighty conversation about religion or, worse, an argument where I got testy "defending the faith," I tried to ignore his comment.

"Those are really interesting lights over the bar, aren't they?" I said.

"I mean, take the sermons, for example. God, *I* could do better."

"Guess you don't want to talk about the lights," I mumbled into my paper-thin wineglass.

"And the Mass and all that ritual," he continued, ignoring my illumination segue. "The same thing week after week. No offense, I know it's what you do with your life and all, but man, you guys are gonna keep losing people unless you can make this stuff more interesting."

As a matter of fact, losing people had indeed been on my

mind after having just witnessed one of the worst scandals ever to rock the Roman Catholic Church. As a priest in that same Church, I can vouch that the ignominy of it even prompted some disillusioned clergy to consider leaving.

"And how do you propose we make 'this stuff' more interesting?" I said, finally hooked and curious as to what my baiting friend would suggest. (I had learned from past experience to trust his instincts. What he may have lacked in book smarts, he made up for in street wisdom.)

Just then a cocktail waitress in a barely legal miniskirt crouched down to place our bill on the low brushed-pewter table. As she walked away, her rear-end practically visible, my friend's eyes followed her to the bar.

"Now, take that," he said. "*She's* interesting."

"Here we go," I said. "You initiate a serious conversation about religion and then, with your limited attention span, you leap to sex before we can get one minute into the conversation."

"No, I'm serious," he said. "Look at her, man. *She's* spiritual. Didn't you notice the way she lit those candles over there before? Almost reverently, like it was the beginning of Friday-night Sabbath or something. Maybe she's Jewish."

"No, I didn't notice," I said, convinced that he was reaching for anything to make his carnal attraction somehow spiritual.

"And then the way she smiled when she came back after giving us our drinks, asking us if we were *happy*."

"She meant with your *drink*," I said, annoyed. "It wasn't some Aristotelian query about the state of your soul."

"Don't use those big words with me," he said. "See, that's the trouble with you guys. Unless someone is on their knees praying in a church, reciting all that mumbo-jumbo and jumping through your pious hoops, you don't think they're religious or spiritual."

"That's not what I said. All I'm saying is that her smiling and lighting candles is no indication of her spiritual prowess."

"Now who's getting sexual?" he said, laughing. "Trust me, I'm on my third wife. I know about these things. No, really, I'm sorry. Then what is an indication of spiritual *prowess*?"

I hesitated, not knowing quite how to respond. What *did* I think made someone spiritual?

"I suppose how she's dealt with things in her life," I finally said. "What she cares about and why. Whom she loves. How she's handled the tough stuff. What the ground of her being is, her center."

"Whoa. You can tell *you* do this for a living. So, you kinda mean her life story and shit like that?"

"Yeah, I guess so," I said, somewhat hesitantly. "But more important, if she perceives God as part of that story."

"Isn't that kind of what the Bible is about?" he asked, somewhat surprising me. (He had sideswiped me with similar retorts ever since I had met him in my first parish assignment as a priest.)

"Yeah, a lot of it is," I conceded.

"Well, I betcha, if you asked her, she'd have a life story of how she became a cocktail waitress and why she seems so happy doing it."

"I'm sure she would," I said, "but what would make it *spiritual*?"

"All the stuff you just spouted off," he said. "The things that matter to her. I'm sure the 'ground of her being,' as you say, isn't in this bar, but she sure seems to bring it here."

"And if God's not a part of any of it for her?" I asked.

"You mean *your* notion of God. What about *her* notion? I know she probably has one. Most people do. Whether they call it a higher power or whatever, it's in there somewhere."

With our dinner reservation awaiting us, we left without ever finding out if our cocktail waitress indeed had perfected the lotus position, but my gadfly friend had piqued my curiosity. While I was hardly convinced that the cocktail waitress was living proof of spirituality run rampant in the watering holes of New York City, maybe my drinking buddy had a point. Surely the waitress *did* have a story, and I began to wonder what it was, and if perhaps she did perceive a spiritual dimension to her life.

As a priest I've heard many "spiritual life stories," some of them quite unorthodox. I've met spiritual people who never would call themselves religious and religious people whom some might not identify as spiritual. (A friend of mine says, "The pious novena mumblers are the first ones to nearly run you down as they speed out of the church parking lot.") So then, are there any criteria for being "spiritual?" What role, if any, does institutional religion play in one's spiritual journey? And is it ever too late to nurture the soul dimension of our lives?

Questions of that sort were the genesis of this book. I wanted to give voice to some of the stories that I've been told. They intrigued me and seemed worth retelling because the paths traveled in them appeared unlikely. I found myself thinking, *I doubt I could've ever found God that way*. But then I realized that often people say the same about my own circuitous spiritual path. Working on Wall Street and in the New York theater were hardly apt prerequisites for entering a monastery and becoming a priest. But then again, maybe they were. Aren't all of our paths unlikely in some fashion, thus rendering them *more* likely?

Whether they appear to you as likely or unlikely, the stories in the following pages cover a wide breadth of experience:

—a topless dancer who finds her way out of a bar and into an unexpected venue; and a soldier in Hitler's army who, years later, feels called to be a Roman Catholic priest.

—a firefighter, himself the son of a retired firefighter, who is killed in the World Trade Center; and a wayward son who is nearly the death of his parents.

—a gay couple who find God in one another; and a family of eight who tries to find God in loss and absence.

—a young man betrayed by a priest he trusted; and an African-American government employee who never imagined he would become a priest.

—a rabbi's daughter who must learn to say good-bye to her father; and another daughter who discovers how to say hello to her mother.

—an incarcerated felon who finds God behind bars; and a married couple who struggle in their own kind of prison.

Soon after the tragic losses at the World Trade Center on September 11, the *New York Times* began running their Portraits of Grief series in which the paper succinctly told the life stories of people who had died in the attack. Small black-and-white photos of the victims, usually smiling, frozen in a happier time, accompanied the short bios. The series quickly became one of the most popular the *Times* had ever run, winning a Pulitzer Prize and eventually spawning a book in which all of the stories were gathered together.

Why the unprecedented popularity of such a straightforward undertaking? After all, the stories were told with no great literary flourish or vaunted hyperbole. Rather, they were simple stories of ordinary lives as told by family members who loved and missed the featured victims. Yet their stories captured the heart of a nation. Why? Because we care about one another's stories. We see our own lives reflected and wonder how we would cope in similar circumstances. A haunting melody lingers in our heads: "What's it all about, Alfie?" We want to know.

The stories in the following pages help us to answer that question by providing a peek at how others have answered it. While their stories are unique, we will no doubt recognize aspects that we share in common. And although not all of the people we will meet are overtly religious, all do perceive a spiritual dimension to their lives. As they wrestle with the question, *What's it all about?*, we may find ourselves contemplating answers that heretofore we have not considered.

While institutional religion may be losing members, spirituality continues to enjoy a high profile and is gaining adherents. Books abound on the topic, workshops have waiting lists, and select retreat centers are engaged years in advance. A *USA Today* Gallup poll in January 2002 found that while almost half of Americans appear to be alienated from "organized religion," 50 percent still considered themselves "religious"; 33 percent said they were "spiritual but not religious"; and only 10 percent said they were "neither spiritual nor religious."

The cultural evidence seems to support the statistics. In addition to their aerobic and Pilates classes, gyms offer yoga and meditation sessions. Business executives are meditating together before power meetings that will determine the fate of multimillion-dollar deals. Athletes pray before taking the field, pop stars thank God for their successes, and politicians appeal to "faith-based initiatives" to promote their agenda. And there may even be some cocktail waitresses who center themselves with calming mantras before attending to their parched patrons.

While some of the above testimonies to thriving spirituality might seem a bit superficial (After all, do we really care if a scantily clad Britney Spears thanks God for her mind-boggling success?), it is indisputable that God matters to all sorts of people. Whether finding their way through the New Age movement, in a twelve-step program, by way of a huckster televangelist preacher, or by affiliation with religious traditions that span millennia, all seekers have something in common—faith seeking understanding which, incidentally, is the traditional definition of theology proffered by Saint Anselm, archbishop of Canterbury, in the eleventh century. It would seem that in more recent centuries spirituality has been wrested from the exclusive stronghold of institutional religion, only to be embraced by people from all walks of life who have their own story of faith to share.

If you are one of those seekers who perceives an alternate reality to your life, a dimension greater than human reason can ascertain, perhaps you will glimpse a bit of your numinous journey reflected in the following stories. And perchance that inkling of recognition will prompt you to explore further your own unique path, heartened by the realization that you have companions along the way. To paraphrase C. S. Lewis, we tell stories to know that we are not alone. So then, the stories . . .

CHAPTER ONE

Leaky Roofs

HE WAS THE KIND OF GUY that she usually avoided; she was the kind of girl he always fell for. Bill was standing by the window of his dorm room as Madeline was hurrying across the university quadrangle. Something moved inside him.

"The sun was hitting those red curls in just the right way, like a fiery frame on a perfect picture." His infatuation is visible even today, thirty-seven years later, as he recalls that moment in the quadrangle, remembering how the overflow of her glowing hair rested gently on the upturned collar of her peacoat.

"She looked off-the-boat Irish," he says, "with a small upturned nose and skin the color of milk. I said to my roommate, Brian, 'Hey, who's *she*?'"

Bill says that Brian jumped up from the bed. "Oh, yeah," he said from the window, somewhat disappointed. "I've seen her before. Cute, huh? I think her name is Margaret, or something like that. I saw her with some girlfriends at the two-for-one last week at Mickey's. She seemed to hang out with her friends most of the night."

Bill ran out the door and down the two flights to catch up

with Madeline, who was racing to a political science class that had begun ten minutes earlier. "Hi, how are you?" said Bill, breathless behind her.

Madeline turned to see a guy she recognized from around campus. She remembered watching him and his friends throw some freshman into a university pond outside the science building. A few times she had noticed him towing his bulky lacrosse gear to practice. He wasn't her type. She liked bookish guys, ones who used words that sent others to the dictionary and who wore cardigan sweaters worn thin at the elbows.

"Hi," she said, and turned around and kept walking.

"Um . . . I'm Bill. Bill Fagan. I don't think we've met before, but I'd love to change that." Bill now stood in front, blocking her way.

Madeline rolled her eyes, unimpressed by the unoriginal line. She had come from a small New England town outside of Boston and was used to more passive men, ones like her father and brother, who preferred discussing the relevance of Thoreau in the computer age to chatting up chicks. The men Madeline knew moved through life with a hint of repression. The man standing in front of her didn't seem to be that kind of man. But she was now seeing Bill close-up for the first time.

"He had those turquoise eyes," she says, "with long black lashes that seemed to tickle his eyebrows. He was pretty startling, I have to admit." He wore an oversized sweatshirt with a large "A" on the front. It hung loosely on his well-built frame, the hood forming a high collar around his handsome, slightly pock-marked face. "It's funny, though," says Madeline. "What I remember most is that he smelled of baby oil."

They were in their second year at a prestigious Catholic university in the South. Bill was the product of New England prep schools, but lacked the highbrow intellectual air of many of his classmates. Madeline had heard stories of the escapades of Bill and his frat buddies. Rumor had it that they rallied weekly in their dorm to show the Southern boys how beer was really supposed to be drunk. Hardly something that would impress Madeline.

"Look, I'm really late for class," Madeline said, "and I don't get most of what this professor talks about anyway, so I really have to run."

Bill says he knew he was getting the brush-off, but refused to take the hint. "Okay, sure, but how about tonight or tomorrow? I could just stop by to say hello."

AND THAT'S JUST WHAT HE DID—for the next two years—a lot of hellos, and too many good-byes. Bill and Madeline became smitten lovers: studying economics and the required theology courses together; eating the bad cafeteria food at a private corner table; taking long hikes in the ambling hills surrounding the university; and falling asleep together in each other's dorm room long after curfew.

Bill learned that Madeline was a part-time reporter at her hometown local paper during summers. He liked the pride she took in her small town—one, she was quick to point out, that tourists traipsed through each fall to marvel at the renowned rainbow foliage.

She told Bill she once broke a story about a textile mill that she discovered was pouring gallons of industrial toxins into the pristine waters of a river that ran through the center of town. Simultaneously, a medical student doing research had revealed occurrences of unusual cancers in town children. The *Boston*

Globe picked up the story from the wire and put it on their front page, making Madeline somewhat of a local celebrity. Bill could see that she was a woman drawn to a noble cause.

And Madeline began to see that Bill wasn't as vacuous as at first she had assumed. One winter afternoon she spotted him in the university chapel kneeling in the first pew with his head bowed, and it wasn't even Sunday. She wondered how often he did that, and what he was praying about. He looked peaceful and childlike. Two days later she was surprised to hear him say that he usually avoided the weekly drinking soirées in his dorm, fearful they could threaten future job interviews in the real world.

"I'd always leave before it got too crazy," Bill says now. "I was intent on being successful and rich and was pretty damn sure, even back then, how I was going to do it."

Madeline admired his mature discretion in not allowing college pranks to ruin an ambitious life plan. Maybe she could learn to love a man like this.

Turns out, she did. Six weeks after graduating from college, Bill and Madeline married in a traditional Catholic church wedding just outside of Boston with Bill's roommate, Brian, as best man and Madeline's sister, Carey, as maid of honor. The newlyweds said, "I do," before witnesses and God, and they meant it forever.

MANY TIMES I HAVE HEARD THEM TELL the story of their meeting. Sometimes the details change—a few are added, others left out—but passion is always evident (in the telling). It is as if that magical moment lives again for them, as it seems to for rapt listeners. Perhaps the headiness of that passion helps to make up for some of the heartache that followed later.

Although I first met them long after they had married, I felt connected to them from the beginning. They introduced themselves to me outside of church after a Sunday Mass at which I had presided, and they invited me to go sailing with them that afternoon on their thirty-five-foot schooner, named *Waterview*. Before the sun had set that day, beyond the choppy blue waters, they had shared with me much of the sacred story of their life together.

SOON AFTER THE WEDDING they moved into a small farmhouse in the western hills of New Jersey. They describe it as a "handyman's special," an erroneous choice since Bill could barely negotiate a hammer.

"It was so funny," says Madeline, "because he didn't even know the difference between a Phillips and a regular screwdriver, and here we were in this dilapidated shack that needed a lot more than a screwdriver. For the first six weeks, when it rained, we hung buckets from the ceiling with rope to catch the water dripping in. One bucket was right over our bed and after a bad night storm, we woke up to water streaming from the sides of the bucket onto the lace duvet cover that my grandmother had given us."

"Never mind the lace duvet cover," says Bill. "How about streaming onto *us*. We didn't sleep the rest of the night because the bed was so wet. And when I had to get up to pee, I slipped on the floor and fell right on my ass. I was black and blue for weeks." They laugh.

When Bill and Madeline speak of those initial years, they hint that the early struggles somehow strengthened their marriage. "They helped produce that indissoluble bond you hear so much about," says Madeline. "Kind of like the way gold gets tested in fire. And that leaky roof became a kind of metaphor for our marriage. We fixed it together. I just didn't realize that we'd have to keep on fixing it."

IT WAS A LONG COMMUTE to work for Bill, who had gotten a job as an assistant to a well-known investment banker in a popular New York brokerage firm. Not able to pass up employment with a firm many of his classmates coveted, he commuted four hours, round-trip, while Madeline stayed home and wrote freelance articles for local newspapers and writing journals. She became pregnant six months after they were married.

"I had so looked forward to having a child, though we hadn't planned on it quite that soon," says Madeline. "But we couldn't have been happier. Maybe a little concerned that we weren't too stable financially. Both our families said they would help us though, so I said some prayers and trusted that God would see us through."

A boy was born just as the new roof was being completed. Two more children followed in consecutive years, another boy, then a girl, and then a miscarriage. They always said they had four children. Madeline wrote less and got involved with her children's school, substitute teaching there when necessary, while Bill worked his way up in the firm more quickly than any associate had in its seventy-five-year history. And he came home later and later.

"I gave up trying to keep meals warm for him," says Madeline. "And most nights I gave up hope that he'd be there to keep me warm either. I started to feel so lonely, and . . . angry, I guess. And then I'd feel guilty because I knew how hard he was working to make our life what it had become. But I started to hate what it had become. It wasn't only his working later and never being around. It was that even when he was home, he wasn't really here, mentally. I began to feel that I finally had the leak-free, showpiece house I'd always wanted, but that now my marriage was broken."

Bill and Madeline agree that they stopped communicating about anything significant. He worked all the time, and when he came home, he was too tired for meaningful conversation, a tiredness Madeline perceived as disinterest—and maybe more. Their lives became centered on the children, with Madeline picking up the slack from Bill's absence. They'd talk about the children's needs when Bill could find the time, but they neglected their own. It began to take a toll.

"I always felt that I was working so hard for a purpose," says Bill. "But after a while I just forgot what that purpose was. Then when the money started rolling in, it was like an aphrodisiac or something. I couldn't get enough of it. And no matter how much I thought I wanted to be home with Maddy and the kids, I convinced myself that being at work was more important. I really did believe I was doing it all for them."

Sunday was the only day Bill didn't work. "That was one commandment I was intent on keeping," he says with a hint of pride. They went to church as a family and usually then to brunch at a local diner, where people often commented on the beautiful family that, to the casual observer, seemed on its way to realizing the coveted American dream, whatever that was supposed to be.

Madeline first began to pray for guidance in church at Sunday Mass. She'd steal glances at the man at the end of the pew, their three children between them, and she'd wonder who that man was. "I'd ask God to help me, to help me *find* Bill again, to make him care about me again, to make him want to be home with me again. I just couldn't understand what had happened. He seemed so different from when we'd met. I prayed to understand what had changed so drastically."

The starry-eyed guy from the university quadrangle who had wooed her with his Irish charm and sharp wit had become someone she hardly knew. At one time warming her with a peerless smile and gentle hands, his love for her now seemed frozen in his absence and lack of touch.

"I began to feel as though we were living a sham," says Madeline. "Everyone would say to me, 'What a lovely family you have,' and we were a lovely family, but I wasn't feeling that love. I mean, I loved my kids and I guess Bill did, too, but he seemed somehow dead inside, and I was also becoming that way. I wasn't sure he loved anything except being at work. He'd fly off the handle about the stupidest, littlest things—when he was around to fly off the handle. I felt like I was doing it all alone, and that he was just bringing home the paycheck for me to keep it all going. I didn't have a partner anymore. His firm had the partner, and I had a sugar daddy. I had everything I'd ever wanted, except him. God, I resented it."

Madeline says that out of desperation her conversations with God became more frequent. When she would express to God how she was feeling, her resentment seemed to lessen and she mustered strength to continue. "It was as if God was saying, 'Just hold on. You'll get through this.' So I held on."

RESENTMENT TURNED to something else the September night that Bill came home late and quietly slipped into bed beside Madeline. "I was, of course, awake," says Madeline. "I was about to say something to him, when I smelled a new cologne. I couldn't place it at first."

By this time, they had moved from the farmhouse into a large Tudor-style home with six bedrooms and an added wraparound porch that didn't quite fit the architecture of the rest of the house. Swings, which the kids loved, hung from hooks on both sides of the house; the landscape was peppered with seventy different varieties of trees planted by a local horticulturist whom Madeline had met in her spinning class at the YMCA. The back of the house was built into the side of a hill that formed an external green wall that gently sloped toward the remaining five acres of property. The Fagan family had finally arrived.

"I nuzzled up to him, as if I wanted to cuddle," she says, "which must have surprised him because that hardly ever happened anymore. What I really was doing was trying to get a better smell. And then it hit me that no man would ever wear that scent."

She describes it as "sweet and trendy, like the smells that waft from *Vanity Fair* and *Cosmopolitan* magazines when you peel back the glued pages." It was, without a doubt, a women's magazine smell.

"I began to feel sick by the putrid scent of it. I was so angry and sad all at once. I couldn't believe it. But I just lay there. I didn't know what to do or say. I remember the Timex alarm clock ticking softly, consistently, on the nightstand beside our bed, and thinking to myself, 'What did I do that drove him to this?'"

MADELINE'S FIRST INSTINCT was to question her own culpability for Bill's affair, sadly not an uncommon response when one is confronted with the betrayal of a spouse. She said that many women friends in similar circumstances questioned their own responsibility for the infidelity of their partners. "How willingly we are seduced into blaming ourselves," she says. "My primary question was why wasn't *I* good enough?"

In retrospect, Madeline supposes that there were other signs that Bill was cheating, but she didn't want to see them. There were the secretaries who seemed to last only a year, sometimes just a few months—all pretty, none too bright. Perplexed by the high staff turnover, Madeline asked Bill about it once.

"Don't any ugly girls apply for a job at your firm? And why do these women seem to stay only a few months? It seems like every time I call your office, another girl answers." At the time she didn't know that most of the other partners had had the same secretary for years. It was only Bill's office that played musical chairs.

He shrugged off her comment and dismissively waved his hand at her. "Madeline, you are letting your active imagination get the better of you again," he said.

Then there was the diminishment in their sexual intimacy. Sure, he was around less and working hard, but even when he was home and they went to bed early, he didn't seem interested in making love. It was always "The kids might hear" or "I have to get up early" or even the tried and untrue "I have a headache."

"You know, most married couples don't have sex all the time," he said one night when Madeline pressed him on it. "It's normal for it to wane after a while. Haven't you heard that from any of those women you have lunch with? What, do they do it with *their* husbands every night?"

"Bill, six months is a lot different from every night. It's been *six* months. Is something wrong?"

But there never was anything wrong. He claimed that it was all in Madeline's head. She didn't understand the pressures he was under. He was working so hard for them, and all she did was complain. She tried to tell herself that maybe it *was* in her head, but it became harder to convince herself of that as he drifted further away.

And now, as he lay beside her with the unmistakable scent of another woman clinging to his sleeping body, there was no convincing herself any longer. "I knew that sex decreases as a marriage progresses," says Madeline. "It even gets a little boring, the same old thing. I mean the act, not the spouse." She smiles. "But this was different. And I even started to blame my religion, maybe because I didn't know who or what to blame. Catholicism seems to leave so little room for creativity in sex, so who wouldn't get bored? It says we can do it only one way and not be committing a sin, so who wants *that* on your mind every time? It becomes easier just to go to sleep.

"And then I started to make excuses for him. I remembered reading that men cheat more than women because it's in their nature to. That they have this instinct to sow their seed in as many places as possible to perpetuate the species. The article made it seem that it's unnatural *not* to cheat. So maybe he was just a victim of his nature, I thought.

"Then I began to question whether God cares about our sexual habits at all. Maybe the Ten Commandments are just human decrees promulgated to maintain some kind of balanced sociopolitical order, more our creation than God's. I just didn't know what to think anymore. I wanted some explanation or justification, but I was having trouble finding it."

Two months passed before Madeline could say anything to Bill about her suspicions. She continued to feel numb and confused, unable to shake the thought that perhaps his infidelity was partially her fault.

"I kept thinking that when a marriage goes on the rocks, it's both partners who put it there. Like in *Cat on a Hot Tin Roof* when Big Mama is blaming Maggie for the problems in her son's and Maggie's marriage and she says that 'when a marriage goes on the rocks, the rocks are right there,' and she points to the bed.

"Maybe I wasn't giving Bill what he wanted. I thought, I must have done something to cause this, too. I kept asking myself, why wasn't I enough for him? I tortured myself for weeks, and when he kept coming home later with even less-convincing excuses, I knew I couldn't take it anymore."

Madeline began to pray to God in a more visceral way for solace. Raised Catholic, she had always found her religion to be formal and removed from her. She had gone to church on Sundays, more or less had kept the commandments, and had tried to adhere to most of what the Church taught. "Except when it seemed so inane that I couldn't possibly bring myself to follow it." (The prohibition against birth control fell into that category.)

But now she began to pray in a way she never had before—not just in church, but also in the car, in the bathroom, in the supermarket, while drying her hair—heartfelt pleas that came from the deepest part of her.

"I told God that if this marriage was a sacrament that He had blessed, then He'd better do something to save it, because I couldn't. I didn't want to walk away from it, but I couldn't stay on my own. I think for the first time I prayed with my guts rather than my head. I had no choice. It just happened. I had no one else to turn to. I'd find myself driving to pick up the kids with tears streaming down my face and I'd be talking out loud to God. I wanted to know what I should do. I asked if God had a *will* for me, for us, in all this."

Bill will never forget the night Madeline confronted him with her suspicions. As usual, he had been working late and came home to a quiet house with the kids long ago sent to bed. A bright light was shining from the doorway of the den. When he walked over to put out the light, he saw Madeline lying on the sofa in her paisley nightgown, looking out the window into the darkness, her reflection visible in the sparkling glass lit by the overhead light. Bill also saw his reflection as he stood in the doorway, and in a moment he knew that something was radically wrong. When Madeline turned toward him from the window, he saw that her eyes were red and swollen, and her face drawn and pale as chalk dust. She stared at him without speaking.

"At first, I thought that something had happened to one of the kids. I couldn't imagine . . . I said, 'Maddy, what is it? What's wrong?'"

"Everything is wrong Bill, everything," she finally said. "And I can't do this anymore. Unless you're willing to sit down with me, here tonight, and talk about it and come clean about *every-thing*, then I can't stay here anymore." She began to sob. "I never thought I'd walk away from our marriage, but I can't live like this. I *won't* live like this. And I won't allow our children to either."

"Maddy, what in the world are you talking about? Have you gone mad?"

"Bill, don't bullshit me. Not anymore," she screamed. "I know. I know it all. I know about the women. I know about your late nights at work. I know about those calls on your cell phone that you ignore whenever I'm around. I know, Bill. And if we're to have any chance at all, you have to tell me. I have to hear it from you. And you have to tell me why."

Bill moved toward her and sat on the end of the sofa.

She pulled her feet toward herself and wrapped her knees with her arms, her nightgown becoming a protective tent. She rocked herself from left to right as tears wet her knees through the flannel.

"I wasn't exactly sure what to do at that moment," says Bill. "I thought about denying it. I thought about convincing her that this was all in her head. But to tell you the truth, I was tired. I was tired of the lies, tired of the sneaking around. Just tired. It wasn't even enjoyable or exciting anymore. Part of me was so relieved that it was finally over, that I'd been discovered. I was actually glad. And even if she decided to leave me now, at least it was finished. I couldn't stand the in-between anymore."

BILL CAME CLEAN that night. Although he knew it was hard for Madeline to hear about the frequency of his infidelity and to absorb the graphic details of his betrayal, she never stopped him from continuing. Her tears flowed silently; her eyes beckoned him to go on. It felt like a purging for both of them. And when Bill was finished, Madeline had one question: "Why?"

"I couldn't really tell her why," he says, his eyes filling up. "I'm not sure I knew myself. I'm still not sure I know. What I did tell her was that I still loved her, and that I wanted to stay married to her for the rest of my life. I know that sounds strange in the midst of everything I was saying, but it was true. I felt at that moment that now our marriage had the possibility of being stronger than ever. If only we could get past this part. If only she could forgive me and help me, help us, to get past this part, we'd be okay. And I knew that God wanted that, too. I can't tell you how, but I just knew."

* * *

BILL SAYS THAT THE DISCOVERY of his infidelity opened the door for him and Madeline to talk about other problems in their marriage, too. Although realizing it was hardly an adequate excuse for his straying, Bill told Madeline that he hadn't felt appreciated by her for some time—that she gave all her free attention to the kids. "I felt like all I ever got was your leftover, tired self." He also told her that she didn't take any interest in the things he liked. "Couldn't you just sit and watch a football game with me once in a while? Would that have killed you?"

Previously, Bill had avoided speaking about these things. Knowing the minefields, he had tiptoed around them, finding it easier not to talk about issues he knew would cause eruptions. But then the feelings went underground, the resentments built, and eventually they exploded in unexpected and hurtful ways. Both were left wondering, *Where did that come from?*

Bill also suggested that the discovery of his infidelity produced more than mere better communication. He felt that his marriage could be "stronger than ever" if they could surmount the hurt.

"I know that many wouldn't agree," he says. "They think you can never come back from lying and infidelity. After all, I've read that 65 percent of couples divorce after an affair is found out. But I believed that if she could really forgive me, then something else was possible. Of course, that's what I wanted, since I'd caused the suffering. That may be years of Catholic theology speaking, but it's also what I truly believed and hoped."

When he and Madeline went to a marriage counselor, for the first time Bill began to acknowledge some of the reasons for his infidelity. The woman therapist, who had been recommended by friends who had struggled in their own marriage, was intent on Bill's expressing why he had been unfaithful.

"Bill, if you can't talk about it here," she said, "you'll never talk about it."

And so he did.

Madeline sat and listened, wondering how she could have missed so much of a man she thought she knew so well. "After he talked about all that stuff about him getting my leftover, tired self," she says, "and me not watching football with him, which I thought was ridiculous, then he starts talking about his fear of getting older. And I sat there and wanted to shout, 'Don't you think I have that fear, too? But it doesn't mean I sleep around with every Tom, Dick, and Harry!' I couldn't understand how sleeping around could've made him feel younger."

"It wasn't just feeling *younger*," says Bill. "It was feeling that I could actually still be attractive to these women. In some way, they seemed to care about me. I didn't love them, but I loved the fact that they wanted me. And I just wasn't sure you did anymore.

"It was like in that movie, *Moonstruck*," he continued, "when Olympia Dukakis's character says that men cheat because they're afraid of death. It's like we can feel younger if other women still want to be with us. Like it's not all over for us. I can still have an orgasm. I can still make someone happy."

"Yeah, *yourself*. How about making *me* happy, Bill? I always still wanted you. For God's sake, how could you not have seen that I wanted you home with me and our kids? You just didn't seem to care about that—or anything else, including sex. Little did I know that you didn't want sex with me because you were having it elsewhere. Jesus. What was more important?"

While the therapist helped them find out what was more important, Bill and Madeline began a spiritual journey that proved to be the real source of healing in their relationship.

Madeline had already begun praying fervently to God, but now Bill found himself drawn to prayer as well. While he, too, had been raised Catholic, he had stopped praying once he began having affairs. "I just couldn't look at God because I wasn't sure how God was looking at me." Bill started looking again. He would stop at St. Elizabeth Ann Seton Church in lower Manhattan at lunchtime and sit in front of the Blessed Sacrament for an hour.

"I gave up lunch, but I began to be fed in another way. I knew I'd really hurt Maddy, and I knew it was going to take a lot for her to forgive me, but I also knew that she was going to, because the love was that strong. I'd sit and ask God to show me the way, to show me how to make it better again. I said that I was sorry, and I promised to do anything He told me."

BUT, SURPRISINGLY, it was Madeline who was told to do something. She had taken a neighbor's son to the park near their house on a bright spring day many months after her confrontation with Bill. The daffodils had begun to poke their heads through the rain-softened ground. She missed these forays to the park, which she once had made with her own children. Her neighbor Joan was receiving chemotherapy for breast cancer and appreciated Madeline's offer to take Joan's son, Jason, outdoors when she was too tired to do so. Madeline was sitting on a bench beside a cloudy green pond while graceful white swans floated by. Jason played kickball with two other boys who were being watched by their nannies.

"I was praying about Bill and me and the whole mess. Praying for the grace to let my feelings of anger and resentment go. I was ready to be done with it. And as I was admiring the beauty of these swans, I somehow remembered being told that they mate for life. I started wondering how long they'd been together and whether they had any baby swans. One of them was nuzzling his head in the wing of the other, cleaning her, or kissing her— I'm not sure which.

"And then I remembered hearing that even though they stayed together for life, they weren't always sexually monogamous. They had an occasional slip, so to speak. I have no idea why I thought of that then. It came to me from nowhere. But I knew I was meant to be there at that moment. I know it sounds weird, but it was the grace I'd been praying for. Because I thought, if with all of that beauty, these swans could put up with the ugliness and still get through it, and be floating past me now with such grace and dignity, then I could get through it, too. And I knew right then that I had to forgive Bill. That I had to give him and *us* the chance to start again. I knew that forgiveness was the missing piece. And, of course, it was God, not the swans, who gave me that, but I had to wait my turn. That was the day I was finally ready to receive it."

THAT NIGHT SHE TOLD BILL about the swans in the park. He couldn't understand how such an ordinary occurrence, involving birds no less, had made such a difference in Madeline, but he could see that it had. And he didn't dare question it.

"We were in bed that night," he says. "I was feeling the same unease I'd been feeling for months. We hadn't slept together. We'd held each other a bit, but that was all, and even that felt uncomfortable. And when I turned out the light that night, after reading a bit, I quickly kissed Maddy good night, and then I turned on my side. And out of nowhere, she just put her arms around me from behind. I knew immediately that it was different this time. She really held me, for the first time in years, I think. And I started to cry, couldn't stop." He begins to cry. "And she just held me the whole time as I sobbed. My pillow was as wet as it had been the nights when our roof leaked at the farm-house. And that night was the real beginning of repairing the marriage that you now see."

THE REPAIR WAS NOT IMMEDIATE and the results are not impene-trable. "Forgiving doesn't mean forgetting," says Madeline. She still wonders occasionally who is calling on Bill's cell phone and about whether his excuses now for being late are always true. But she's learned to live with the doubts and not let them cripple her or her new appreciation for the newly buoyant man she met in the quadrangle those many years ago. She has a lot of her old husband back, and she trusts that this time it's for good.

Today, it's hard for one to see those repaired cracks in Bill and Madeline's marriage. I recently visited them at their summer home at Hilton Head and watched them play with their grand-children at the water's edge of their expansive property. During dinner they laughed about the time Bill fell in the pool of water beside their bed in the farmhouse. They held each other on a porch swing that faced a setting magenta sun as brilliant as any I have seen. And they retired that night to a master bedroom built to face another sun, one whose first rays would greet them the next new morning.

NOT ALL COUPLES MAKE IT through the way Madeline and Bill did. (And to think that it was *swans* that made the difference. Go figure.) Success stories are nice to hear—and tell—but many marriages end in failure, in divorce and bitterness, in a refusal or inability to move beyond seemingly insurmountable obstacles. I know some Catholic couples whose marriages have failed and who are plagued with guilt about divorcing, aware that it is contrary to Church teaching. But they see no other way. The marriage has died. It is no more. *They* are no more.

While the Church's answer to such couples is to possibly annul the marriage, some are hesitant to say their marriage never existed. Annulment doesn't feel quite right to them. They worry about what that says to and about their children, the products of a love that had existed for a time. And so they are left with the dilemma of either never marrying again or "living in sin" with their next spouse. Neither alternative is appealing. Many live the "in-between" of not feeling accepted by their Church, yet not wanting to live without it. It is a pastoral problem that many feel the Church has yet to address adequately. (Although some priests have proffered a resolution by privately suggesting to couples that they follow the Church teaching that prompts them to act according to the dictates of their informed consciences.)

But couples who do make it through, like Madeline and Bill, are witness to something powerful and real: a love that is stronger than failure, perhaps even stronger than death, as the Song of Songs says. Such couples give hope to those who struggle in the midst of heartache that seems endless and irreparable. They remind us that forgiveness may be renewing and life-giving. And they show us that our leaky roofs can sometimes be repaired—and perhaps made even stronger.

CHAPTER TWO

Hitler's Army Priest

"C'MON, ANTON. SING US A GERMAN HYMN," the other priests cajoled. Embarrassed, he shook his head and looked at his shoes. Sitting on a wooden chair in the first row of the conference room, with his hands resting on a cane that he held loosely between his legs, he looked childlike, innocent.

"Anton, at least offer the benediction in German," one of the priests said.

"*Nein,*" he said quietly, shaking his head. "Let the good Father begin the conference. Stop such nonsense."

His English was good, but heavily accented; he sounded like the German tourists I remember meeting in southern Spain when I studied there as a college student.

"Anton, would you like to offer the prayer in English before we begin?" I finally said, attempting to rescue him from his overzealous confreres. I guess it wasn't much of a rescue.

"No, thank you." He looked up at me with gray eyes, shielded by wire-rimmed glasses that seemed to fit his face perfectly, as if they'd always been there.

I was in Minnesota leading a priests' retreat—gutsy at my age, since often I'm still the youngest in the room at such clerical gatherings. Forty-two of them had convened for five days at St. John's University campus in Collegeville. I was supposed to inspire them, or teach them something they didn't already know. *Right*.

I skipped the prayer and began the conference. Anton slept through most of it, really boosting my confidence.

Later, I parked myself next to him at dinner in the refectory. We were in a large, red, brick building that formerly was the seminary for the diocese and now is used to house theology students and groups such as us. The corridors were long and shiny, like bowling alleys.

"Mind if I join you?" I said, already placing the napkin on my lap.

"No, I'd be delighted," said Anton. His stomach domed toward the table, betraying a few too many strudels.

The other priests at the table were busy conversing about a golf game they had scheduled for the next day during their free time. I was tempted to make a remark about "retreating from the retreat," but I resisted. Instead, I sat enraptured as this eighty-year-old priest, while cutting his ham with utmost precision, began talking about his life. By the end of the meal, I was asking him if we could meet again . . . and then again.

ANTON SCHULD WAS BORN in Biebrich (now part of Wiesbaden) on November 7, 1923, four days before Hitler was arrested in Munich after a failed attempt to overthrow the regional government there, a prelude to the takeover of the national government. The "Beer Hall Putsch," as it came to be known, was Hitler's attempt to oust the Weimar government of Friedrich Ebert and establish a right-wing nationalistic one in its place. During his imprisonment, Hitler wrote his opus, *Mein Kampf*, a chilling forecast of what was to come in Nazi Germany. In 1923 one dollar was the equivalent of four billion marks, an economic disaster that would set the stage for Hitler's unlikely ascent to power ten years later on January 30, 1933. Anton was nine years old that year, a year when his country was changed forever.

"People just fell for him," said Anton. "They were out of work, and he promised to get them jobs. He had this fascinating way of talking. He said, 'Give me four years and you will not recognize Germany.' Well, that was certainly true, but for unimaginable reasons."

Anton remembers changes at school, his first indication that Germany would indeed be different. A banner was strung across the entrance that read "You are nothing. The nation is everything." Flags with swastikas were hoisted each morning, as the students were required to sing Nazi propaganda songs. At ten years old, all children were expected to join the "Hitler Youth Movement." Although Anton and his brothers were initiated into the group at school, his father would not permit them to attend the meetings or to wear the uniform.

"The youth used to march on our house shouting slogans," said Anton, "because they knew we weren't at the meetings. When my father made a move to go to the door one night as they were shouting in the street, my mother barricaded it with her body, knowing he would say something that would get us all in trouble."

The Hitler Youth met on Sunday mornings at eight o'clock, a deliberate attempt to prevent the children from going to Mass or services. Not caring if the elderly practiced their religion, the Nazis let the churches remain open, but they wanted the youth for themselves, for the future of a Germany where the state trumped God.

The synagogues were another matter. They simply burned down many of them, but, interestingly, the one in Biebrich, though vandalized, remained standing.

"When we *were* forced to attend certain Hitler Youth meetings on Sundays, we simply went to Mass earlier, at 6:30 a.m." said Anton. "My father always thought he was outsmarting the Nazis."

All of the schools were "public," but each week for two hours the priests, ministers, and rabbis taught religion in the schools. One day, soon after Hitler took over, Anton walked into his classroom and saw that the crucifix that had hung in the front was gone; the children were told that the clergy would no longer be coming to the school to teach their "propaganda." Later that night at dinner, when Anton told his parents what had happened, his mother said, "It's a bad omen. This isn't good."

Months later Anton was walking home from the market with his father, a tall man with a gentle face and thinning hair that, according to Anton, "he tended to very carefully." Although the family used to kid him about it, much of this jesting had diminished of late. After all, these were serious times. It was becoming difficult even to buy food, as Anton and his father had just discovered at the market.

"Papa, why are they wearing those patches on their clothes?" asked Anton as they neared their home. Anton remembers that people wearing yellow stars and pink triangles pinned to their jackets were passing him and his father, who hesitated at Anton's question.

"The Jewish people have to wear the yellow stars now, Anton," his father said somberly. Gone was the ebullience he had exuded at family gatherings when he played his flute with abandon as his brother Tony accompanied him on the accordion.

Gone was the quick smile that Anton had always seemed able to coax readily.

"But why?" asked Anton. "Will my friends Sander and Marx have to wear them, too?" They were two Jewish boys from Anton's class—the *only* Jewish boys in the class.

"Probably, Anton."

"But why, Poppa?"

"Because we have a madman running things now," his father said impatiently, grabbing Anton by the shoulder. "But never repeat that. Do you understand me?"

"Yes, Poppa," Anton said, startled by his father's forcefulness. "But what about the pink triangles?" he ventured to ask, albeit more meekly.

"They're for other people, Anton. Just other people. No more questions. The less you know the better. It's safer that way."

ANTON AND SOME CLASSMATES began meeting with the parish priest in the basement of the parish house for religious instruction. Encouraged by his devout Catholic parents, Anton enjoyed the classes on the Bible and his faith. Father West, a stout man with a deep voice and round spectacles, commanded everyone's attention with a simple glance. Although he had been warned by the Nazis to tone down his rhetoric or risk the consequences, threats never seemed to alter Father West's passion for speaking the truth. Anton remembered one class in particular.

The blackboard loomed in the middle of the room while the children sat on the floor on some cheap pillows that were strewn about randomly. Father West seemed particularly agitated that day; his usually pallid complexion was a flushed pink. He had been pacing around the perimeter of the dank basement, when usually he would have been greeting the children and some of the parents dropping them off. When the students were seated and settled, the priest walked to the blackboard, his black cassock billowing behind him, and picked up the chalk. He drew a cross and, next to it, a swastika (a "hooked" cross), and turned to the class of hushed students. His face grew even redder.

"*This* is *our* cross," he said as he pointed to the Christian symbol and hit the chalk against the blackboard. "*This* is not," he said angrily, crossing out the swastika with such force that the blackboard lurched backward on its shaky wheels. "And that is our class for today. Meditate on it well." He left the room as the students parted for him like the Red Sea.

Often after such meetings, the Hitler Youth waited outside the church to beat up the youth who had attended the church meetings. Anton and his friends would have to climb up the back wall of the church garden to escape them. One night as the students were leaving the church, they noticed that the Hitler Youth had smeared the church with black painted swastikas. Father West handed out pails with soapy water and helped the students clean off the slurs. "Little bastards," Anton heard West mutter as he threw soapy water against the red brick.

Anton and his parents noticed Nazi spies standing in the back of the church on the following Sundays, sometimes taking notes during the priest's homilies. One Sunday Father West began speaking about the boycott of Jewish merchants. Germans had been told not to buy from the Jews. The Nazi Party would photograph people buying from Jewish merchants and hang the pictures outside of the courthouse to brand the buyers as disloyal. Nazis also passed out propaganda tracts that Anton remembers termed the Jews "maggots that bleed our nation, sucking out our blood," maintaining that the economy was failing because Jews controlled the money. Father West spoke against such slander.

"We are Christians," he said, as the Nazis hovered in back of the church. "Love and compassion is our Gospel. Recognize your Christian dignity. Jesus, a Jew, is our *true* leader. Let us never forget that." Within days Father West was removed from the rectory in the dead of night and never heard from again, presumably sent to one of the camps for political prisoners.

Tensions at home began to mount as well. One night Anton's uncle Tony came to the house and said jokingly, "I don't know, Karl. I don't see the Fuehrer's ("leader," Hilter's preferred title) picture hanging up. What kind of German loyalist are you?"

"I wouldn't put his picture in the toilet," Anton's father spat back.

"Karl, are you crazy?" Anton's mother said in a loud whisper, dropping a plate into the sink and running to close the window that faced the street. "What if someone heard you say that? Do you want to get us all killed?" Her hand was shaking as she pointed at him. Karl left the room without saying anything.

Anton's parents had been arguing since the Nazi takeover. Karl had refused to join the Nazi Party, something that was asked of all Germans. He worked for the city, but because of his refusal to join the party, any hope of promotion was dashed. The Schulds were struggling economically, as were many of the German citizenry, and Anton's mother, Mae, worried about how to feed her three boys, considering their welfare more important than any superficial political allegiance.

"Karl, what's the difference?" she said to him one night after dinner. "So you join the party. It doesn't mean you have to believe in what they stand for. Our boys are hungry. They are going to our parents and begging them for a piece of bread. Isn't that more important than your damned idealism?" She turned away from him as Anton and his brothers grew silent.

Karl threw his napkin onto the table and leaned forward so that his tie dipped into the sauerbraten gravy in his plate. "How can you say such a thing, Mae? We are a Catholic family. If we do not live what we believe, then none of it matters. The boys will be fine. We will all be fine."

Mae turned back to face him with tears in her eyes. "What if they take you away like Leo (Karl's sister's husband, Leo, had been taken away for opposing the Nazi Party)? What will we do then?"

"They will not take me away. Hitler will not last long."

IN 1941, when he was seventeen years old, Anton was attending business administration school and, after classes, apprenticing with a business that was working for the military copying war design plans. The war had begun two and a half years earlier. As the bombings became more intense, sometimes it was difficult for Anton and his co-workers to make it home at night. No street-lights were allowed during the war. Even a small escape of light from a window could result in a fine. With explosions erupting, Anton and the other workers would grope their way through the pitch-dark city, wearing only fluorescent buttons for identification. At the sound of sirens they would rush to the nearest cellar and stay there until the "all clear" signal sounded. Sometimes that meant spending the night in the cellar.

One afternoon SS officers rounded up Anton and all other young men his age to address them in the middle of a public square. Although there was a draft in place for young men once they turned eighteen, the Nazis were intent on recruiting willing boys for the SS to fight in Hitler's army even earlier.

"Who of you will fight for the Fuehrer and our nation?" asked an unusually fat officer. "Step forward if you are willing to be a man and defend our nation."

No one moved.

"Are all of you cowards?" the officer roared, lifting his rifle in the air. He walked down the line of frightened youth, stopping at Anton. "What about you, young man? You look healthy and strong. Don't you want to serve your leader?"

Anton looked at the ground.

"Pick your head up. I'm speaking to you." The soldier was inches away from the boy's face.

"Answer me."

"No, sir."

"No, *what*?" the soldier demanded.

"No, sir, my father would not give permission to serve in the SS," said Anton. (At that time, parents were required to give permission for any child under eighteen to serve in the SS.)

"We will see about that," the officer growled. "Step back."

Although Anton worried that his comment might endanger his father, before long it was a moot point. A few months after the roundup, just days after Anton turned eighteen, a draft card (without postage) arrived in the mail. (Anton remembers it lacked postage because a drill sergeant, whom he encountered later, would laugh when the boys collapsed from exhaustion because of the strenuous training and say, "I don't care if you die there. It doesn't even cost me a stamp to get another one of you.")

The draft card read, "You are to report for basic training camp in Utrecht, Holland, on April 1, 1942." No one was unaffected by the news. Anton's mother cried and disappeared into the bedroom. His father sat at the kitchen table with his head in his hands and said, "You will do what you must." The parish priest walked with Anton in the church garden and said, "Go, Anton, or they will execute you. But you must not do anything immoral or against your conscience. And in this war, that will be a difficult."

The three months of basic training in Holland were grueling, with strenuous exercise, formation drills, and military maneuver practices. The motto drilled into them was the same for every soldier: "Be absolutely obedient to orders, without questioning." After basic training, Anton was sent to school to learn Morse code, and then to San Brieu, France, which was occupied by Germany at the time. Interestingly, the soldiers' quarters there were a former seminary that, after the war, was converted back to a seminary. The Germans put in a heating system while occupying the buildings, and years later Anton met a priest who had been trained at the seminary who thanked him for putting heat in the place. "We would have frozen in that building if it weren't for you delicate soldiers," he kidded.

While at San Brieu, Anton and his unit had a particularly tough sergeant, who drilled them until many collapsed. Not far from the camp, a house of prostitution was provided for the "needs" of the German soldiers. The German military actually guarded and took care of the whorehouse. (Anton says that this was considered a service to the town as well, because it prevented the rape of the local women.) One night the soldier on duty took ill, and Anton was called to replace the sick soldier. After standing guard all night, Anton returned to the base with no time to perform the usual ablutions before fall-in. It was an omission not unnoticed by the persnickety sergeant.

"Soldier, what's the matter with your face?" the sergeant asked snidely.

"My face, sir?" said Anton.

"Yes, it seems dirty. Could it be that you disgrace your unit by showing up in this line without even having washed?"

"No, sir," said Anton. "But I had no time to shave, sir."

"Why not?" the sergeant screamed.

"I had duty last night at the cat house, sir. Hans got sick. I just got back."

The sergeant smiled and stepped back. "Well, then you can stay in your own house for a few days and learn some proper hygiene. Fall out, soldier."

Anton was grounded for a whole week for his one-day-old stubble.

To ensure their safety, the German soldiers were not permitted to go to public places outside Germany, including churches. Since no chaplain was provided to attend to the spiritual needs of the soldiers in Anton's unit, each man cultivated his own faith, if he had any.

"I prayed a lot on my own," said Anton. "I really needed God at this time. I was so conflicted being in the war. I knew I had to defend my country. I was a German, after all, and I had friends who were dying, being killed by the Allies. But I could never get it out of my head that I was also serving a madman, as my father had said. Somehow I knew even then that there was something evil about Hitler, though I could've never imagined the extent of it at the time. I prayed for guidance and perseverance. And I prayed to make it out alive."

At the time, Hitler was helping Mussolini retain control of North Africa, but with diminishing success as the British began to make headway. Anton and his unit were moved to southern France because the Germans feared the Americans would invade there. When that appeared unlikely, the unit was moved once more and began the journey to North Africa to help the failing effort there. In the middle of the night, Anton's unit was put on a train from southern France, through Rome, to southern Italy to make the passage to Africa. Things were not good in Italy.

"Kids, little children, began storming the train," said Anton. "They were so hungry. They cried out, *'Pane, pane,'* and we threw some bread from the train, but it wasn't much. We didn't have that much ourselves. It was sad."

By the time the unit reached Mount Vesuvius, just north of Naples, it was Christmas, 1942. Christmas had always been an important religious holiday for Anton and his family in Germany. He was feeling melancholic as he heard the Christmas carols rising on the night air from the nearby village on Christmas Eve. Someone had found a Christmas tree and the soldiers placed it near the latrine. A soldier shared cookies that his family had sent from Germany. Children began appearing again, begging in the camp. *"Pane, pane . . ."* The soldiers, moved by their plight and pleading eyes, gave them most of the cookies.

"Then old people came asking for our potato peels," said Anton, shaking his head and pausing, with tears welling up in his eyes. "Dirty potato peels, and they just shoved them into their mouths like starving animals."

Anton awoke on Christmas Day with a compelling desire to go to church. "I just needed to be there." In Germany he had always been happiest in church—singing, praying, and listening to words that stirred the deepest parts of him.

"It always felt right to me there," he said. "I've always prayed to the Holy Spirit and, in Germany, we always sang a lot. It just lifted my spirits. And they sure needed lifting in Italy."

At midmorning, Anton snuck over the fence of the camp. Soldiers were laying communication cables in the frozen lava of Vesuvius. Anton managed to avoid being seen by them and made his way to the village Catholic church. Once arriving, he removed his hat and walked into the darkened nave. No Mass was in progress, but there was a sprawling manger arranged under a statue of Mary by a side altar on the right of the church. Hundreds of candles illuminated the corner of the little church, as the baby Jesus lay surrounded by figurines of Mary and Joseph, an angel, shepherds, and countless animals, all expertly carved out of olive wood. Anton knelt in the straw that overflowed onto the step beneath the altar railing and prayed.

"I cried in that church that day," he said. "I was homesick, tired, discouraged. But as soon as I walked in that church, I was overcome with peace. I prayed to the Holy Spirit. I prayed for my family, for my friends who had been killed . . . and for the enemies who had been killed, too. It seemed such madness to me, the whole thing. But somehow I knew that morning that I was going to make it through it. That there would be life beyond here for me. Christ had been born for me. And I hadn't done enough for him yet."

It was the only time Anton went into a church during his time in the German Army. A few days later, he was put on an Italian destroyer launched from Sicily, bound for the city of Tunisia, but because of the constant attacks by the British, they were diverted, and docked in Bizerte. The next day the unit hitchhiked to Tunisia, the last stop for Anton as part of the German Army.

Tunisia was the first place where Anton saw real combat. He and his unit were fighting the British Eighth Army on the front lines while the Americans were positioned just south of them.

"Tunisia was an interesting place," said Anton. "It was the only time I was ever in a mosque. What was really interesting was that the German officers were the ones who told us to take off our boots and to show respect when we entered it. I was surprised that they even cared. As I stood there watching the men bend over, touching their heads to the floor, a part of me knew we were all the same. We pray, we worship because we have to. It's part of the way we're made. So, I prayed in the mosque. Probably to the same God."

His prayer didn't prevent him from having stomach problems in Tunisia, however. Apparently, the spicy cooking of the Arabs didn't agree with him. That, combined with the searing heat, caused him to faint one day on the front line. Soldiers carried him to an Arab hut where they gave him water and some shade.

"It was always hard to know though if they were really Arabs because they moved between the British and us," he said. "Sometimes the Germans and the British would dress up like Arabs in order to spy. But we liked the Arabs. They fed us sweet bread boiled in oil. They would dart in and out of our foxholes saying, 'Gush, gush.' That's what they called the bread."

In the tent the Arabs put cool rags on Anton's head and slowly gave him boiled water that had cooled. When he was sufficiently revived, Anton and Hans, a soldier friend, left the tent, only to discover that the British tanks had broken through the front line. Anton and Hans were now *behind* British lines and needed to escape quickly if they were to avoid being captured.

"But we were so thirsty," he said. "The sun was scorching. And Hans and I knew of this spring we had drunk from not far from where we were. And even though we knew it was a risk, we needed water."

They made their way to the spring, and as they bent over the edge to drink, British soldiers began shooting at them.

"But we kept on filling our canteens," said Anton. "Funny how the water was more important than being shot at."

Their thirst slaked, Anton and Hans slipped into a deep wadi that hid them from the view of the approaching British. They huddled there quietly for about a half hour, after which they began discussing plans to get themselves back to their unit. Suddenly Anton heard rustling above him and looked up to see a revolver staring him in the face.

"You, get out, c'mon," said a young blond British soldier, who looked even younger than Anton.

Though their English was almost nil, Anton and Hans understood the soldier's command. He was standing on the brink of the wadi, motioning with his gun for the surprised German soldiers to climb out of their discovered lair. Their African tour in the German Army had ended. Anton and Hans were captured about one hundred miles southwest of Tunis on April 25, 1943, which just happened to be Easter Sunday.

"They were actually very nice to us," said Anton. "They put us in a jeep and offered us cigarettes, and brought us back to their camp, which had barbed wire around it and a few guards standing at the entrance. We slept outside in the open, under the stars. I remember that first night, looking up and thinking that my parents and brothers in Germany were looking at the same sky. Somehow, it helped me get to sleep that night."

Interrogations began the next day. Anton was brought to the tent of a British officer. When Anton walked in, he clicked his heels at the officer.

"Don't you know how to salute an officer?" the British officer said in German, obviously not happy. "*Don't you?*"

"I only know how to salute a German officer," replied Anton.

"Go outside again, and come in and salute me the way you salute a German officer. *Now.*"

When he went back in, Anton clicked his heels again, and raised his right arm, extending it straight from his body until his hand was slightly above his head. The officer reluctantly accepted this German salute, believing that it was the only one Anton knew.

In basic training Anton and the other soldiers had been drilled to give only their name, rank, and serial number. So that's what Anton did, much to the dismay of the frustrated interrogating official.

"I also just acted real dumb," said Anton. "I could never tell them that I was in the signal corps, because then they'd never leave me alone. Bad enough we already had to change the Morse code messages every few hours because they kept figuring them out. So I just kept saying the same thing in German and my dumb expression finally got me off the hook."

A few days later Anton was transferred to Bone, a town in northwest Tunisia, and then put on a French freighter from Bone to Oran, west of Algiers. The three-day boat ride nearly broke Anton. The prisoners were so crowded together that they couldn't move. Positioned among them were large food cans with a sickening smell that served as latrines. Hungry though he was, Anton couldn't eat the biscuits and corned beef that were served to them because of the stench. Just as well, because when they hit rough seas, many men began vomiting, including the guards stationed above, who vomited on Anton and the prisoners lying on the deck below.

The prisoners disembarked at Oran, and as they were marched from the boat, Algerians and Moroccans threw flowerpots at them and motioned with their fingers that they would cut their throats if given the chance. Not exactly friendly territory for the confused German prisoners.

"Thank God, we were turned over to the Americans here," said Anton. "They treated us much better. We actually had only two guys to a tent then. It was like being in heaven. It really was. And they fed us real food. One American soldier said to us, 'If you still have any food from the British, throw it away. A dog shouldn't have to eat that shit.' My tent partner and I stayed up half the night talking and speculating on what would come next. We didn't know it would be a boat ride that would change everything."

Within days they were put on American transport convoy ships bound for the United States. The zigzagging the ships had to do, to avoid the U-boats positioned in the surrounding waters, extended the ride for three extra days.

"The thing I remember most about the trip were the lice," said Anton. "The boat was infested with them, at least the prisoners' part of the boat. We would search each other's body parts for lice each day, under arms, between legs, and crush them when we found them. I've never itched so much my whole life."

Large brawls among the prisoners began when the American soldiers would flick their used cigarette butts into the crowd of huddled prisoners. Anton smoked his last cigarette on this ship.

"I couldn't believe that guys were so addicted to those things. I saw guys trade their wedding ring for *one* package of cigarettes. Can you imagine that? I could always take them or leave them, so that day I decided to leave them."

The other event from the voyage that Anton remembered vividly occurred the night a German soldier friend had to relieve himself. While the American ship had bathrooms, a vast improvement over the large, stinking buckets on the French freighter, a guard sat watch at the bathroom to monitor activity. Josef, a slight German prisoner who limped due to a wound he had sustained in battle, awoke in the middle of the night and made his way to the bathroom with his full bladder, only to find the American guard asleep at the door. Rather than wake the guard, Josef simply opened the door to the bathroom, but he startled the sleeping soldier, who shot Josef dead. Although it was an accident for which the Americans later apologized, it reinforced Anton's suspicion that "prisoner of war" was also a dangerous status.

"You must remain faithful," said a fellow prisoner lying on the floor next to Anton the night of the unfortunate shooting. The prisoners had finally settled down again, though whisperings about the fate of Josef buzzed the floor.

"Faithful? What do you mean?" asked Anton as he looked at the soldier, who had a Bible sticking out from underneath his makeshift pillow of rolled-up clothing.

"Do not get discouraged, even at Josef's death. God will not abandon us."

Not having yet considered God's abandonment, Anton turned to go to sleep with the prisoner's words reverberating in his head. They would not be the only words of Helmut that Anton would remember.

By the time the ship docked in New York City, Anton was more than ready to place his feet on terra firma. The prisoners were told not to look left or right as they disembarked, a command, Anton assumed, to ensure that the prisoners not recognize where they were. But there was no hiding the fact that, with its tall buildings and dizzying energy, New York City was the port of welcome. The German prisoners and their clothing were successfully deloused with a special soap, and then the prisoners were placed on a Pullman train to a camp in Aliceville, Alabama, making Anton and his fellow prisoners the first prisoners of war to reach these shores.

The German prisoners were treated well in Aliceville. They

were fed adequately and given clean barracks in which to sleep. Although there were fifty men in each barracks, and they slept on threadbare cots, it was a vast improvement over the ships. And there were bathrooms—huge ones, with hot showers in which Anton often lingered. He even played cards with his comrades while sitting under the shower.

Helmut was assigned to the same barracks as Anton, and he kept his Bible under his pillow there, too. After an evening card game of skat, a favorite of the German prisoners, he approached Anton near the washroom.

"I need your help here," said Helmut.

"My help?" said Anton. "What help can I give you?"

"I've seen you pray. I know God is in your life. We must work to make sure God stays in the lives of our fellow soldiers."

Anton was perplexed by Helmut's words. *Where had he seen him pray? How could he help with God?*

"I don't know what you're saying," said Anton.

"We need to hold prayer services here for the soldiers. I'm going to study to be a Lutheran minister after the war. I could use your help."

There was no chapel in the camp for the prisoners because, according to Anton, the Americans assumed the German soldiers were all Nazi agnostics or atheists. One American officer had actually said, "I thought you Germans worshiped the gods of nature or something like that."

"I will help you," said Anton finally, though he wasn't sure why he agreed.

Helmut and Anton began conducting prayer services for the soldiers using Scripture reading and extemporaneous praying, with some of the gatherings lasting up to two hours. Anton admired Helmut's sincerity and his deep faith, observing that

Helmut's Bible was his most prized possession, dog-eared and worn, but seemingly a living Word in Helmut's life. He treated the men with compassion, listening to them late into the night. He cared for them, more than some of them cared for themselves.

When later they were transferred to the camps in Fort Dix and Bridgeton, New Jersey, Helmut and Anton continued to minister to the prisoners, though here chaplains were brought in to say Mass and hold services in an empty barracks, thanks to the continued prayers and requests of Helmut and Anton. Anton said that one priest chaplain was a bit naïve though, as demonstrated that Easter Sunday when he had invited a buxom woman with blond ringlet curls to the camp to sing religious hymns for the Mass. It was the only time Anton saw the barracks full for Sunday services, and a good number of the soldiers weren't even Catholic.

A week later it was another kind of singing that highlighted the tensions that existed. The German prisoners were singing songs as they marched to the camp. In the midst of the patriotic German songs, a group of prisoners began singing an anti-Jewish song, favored among the Nazis: "Wish that the Jews would march again through the Red Sea, and this time the waves consume them. Then the world would have peace . . ."

A few of the Jewish guards who spoke German surely understood. But the tensions were not only between the Americans and some of the more nationalistic Nazi soldiers, but also among the varied group of German soldiers themselves. German Communists, Nazis, and German soldiers who were not sympathetic to the Nazi Party all mixed together—or didn't. When the Nazis raised a flag with a swastika on Hitler's birthday, the Communists pulled it down before the Americans could.

"I was offended when news reports called us all Nazis," said Anton. "It simply wasn't true. But it is easier for us to just categorize groups of people, because then we don't have to really learn anything about who they really are. We still do it."

Anton had many jobs at the camp, but for the most part he worked in the fields, cutting trees, cultivating and harvesting crops such as spinach, washing lima beans, and canning red beets. There was a Heinz ketchup factory forty-five minutes from the camp at Bridgeton that benefited from the bushels of tomatoes that the German prisoners sorted out and bottled as ketchup. In addition to the fields, Anton repaired roads and worked in the officer's mess hall as a waiter. One morning, while serving the kind and courteous General Peterson, Anton heard news of the German defeat at the Battle of the Bulge, a turning point in the war. He knew, as he eavesdropped on the American officers' conversation, that the war would soon be over.

While the war did indeed end shortly afterward, the expected liberation of the prisoners was slow in coming. In fact, once the war ended, the Americans saw little reason to adhere to the conditions of the Geneva Convention, and took the gloves off. Some began treating the German soldiers with disdain as news of the atrocities in Germany began filtering back. When Anton was transferred to Kilmer, New Jersey, from Fort Dix, food rations were meager and the tensions high. American soldiers were being shipped home from Europe and were sent to some of the camps for reentry. Anton worked in the mess halls, feeding the returning soldiers, but did not himself have enough to eat. It was here that he met Major Smith, "Smitty" as they called him, a man who would indeed be a major catalyst in Anton's life.

"He became like a father to many of us," said Anton. "He used to always say, 'Give those prisoners more food,' like somehow he knew how hungry we were. Our own guardian angel."

Anton got to know Major Smitty because Anton, Helmut,

and Walter, a fellow prisoner, were the representatives chosen to plead the prisoners' concerns at the American headquarters in the camp. Anton and Helmut had a sympathetic ear in Major Smitty, who allowed them to increase church services for the prisoners, and gave Helmut, an expert carpenter, permission to furnish a small chapel on the base.

One day Anton was alone praying in that chapel when a soldier came in. Anton heard the door close and turned to see the soldier kneeling in the center aisle. As Anton returned to his own prayer, the soldier moved to the pew behind Anton.

"May I confess my sins to you?" the soldier asked. He looked troubled, somehow desperate.

"To me?" said Anton. "Why no, I'm not a priest."

"I know," said the soldier, "But I want to tell you anyway. Could I tell you my sins and have you pray with me?"

Anton was taken aback, not knowing what to make of this unusual, yet humbling request. He hesitated.

"Well, I suppose you can tell me," Anton finally said. "But I can't give you absolution or anything."

"That's okay. You will give me more than that simply to listen to me."

The next day Helmut was sitting on a coal box outside, studying and reading his Bible. He had already begun his seminary studies via readings. Anton sat next to him, eager for one of their many theological discussions.

"Why aren't you a seminarian, too?" asked Helmut, out of the blue.

"Because I've never thought of it," responded Anton, surprised by Helmut's question.

"Well, you should," said Helmut.

"No, I don't think so," said Anton. "I have to go back to my

old job when I get home, help make some money for my family.
Germany will be a mess when we return."

"You should begin your studies to be a priest," said Helmut
more insistently. "That will be the best thing you can do for your
family, and for many others. I see it in you."

Anton allowed the thought for the first time.

"I'll think about it," Anton said finally. "I won't say no."

"I REALIZED IN THE CAMP how much there was a need for God,"
said Anton. "Helmut's naming it gave me permission to finally
consider the priesthood. I don't think I ever felt worthy before
that. And that soldier asking me to hear his confession seemed to
confirm that maybe others saw something in me that I didn't see
in myself. I loved my Church. Jesus was central for me. I prayed
to the Holy Spirit constantly. And I'd just lived through a war that
I knew was going to require a lot of healing. I began to think
maybe this was a way I could be of service."

FINALLY, ONE YEAR AFTER the war had ended, Anton and his fellow prisoners were put on an American Liberty ship to Europe
from Camp Shanks in New York. They landed in Le Havre,
France, and were sent to Camp Bolbec, an awful camp with
twenty thousand prisoners and no running water. Fifty men
crowded each tent, sleeping on boards and straw, huddled
against each other like spoons. At certain points during the night,
one soldier would yell the order, and they would all turn together on the floor, a momentary wave of somnambulant soldiers,
united in their dream of returning home.

That dream was finally realized for Anton a few weeks later

when he saw his name appear on a roster that read, "The follow-ing soldiers are transferred to Cage 15 . . ." That was the camp from which the soldiers were transferred back to Germany. A week later Anton was on a cattle car train with a bit of straw on the planks, gazing out the window at his now devastated, beloved Germany.

"We were hiding our heads in the straw and crying at what we saw," said Anton. "We couldn't believe what this war had done to our country, to say nothing of what we felt when we heard later about what had gone on in the concentration camps. They had tried to show us films of it in the prisoner camps in the United States, but we didn't believe them. We thought they were just propaganda films. When we learned later it was true, we were devastated."

The train arrived at a discharge station near Nuremberg, where the prisoners received their papers and were released. From there, Anton got a train back to Biebrich, where he hoped his family still awaited him. Carrying only his duffel bag and three prized cartons of American cigarettes, he ascended the steps of his old home. His mother answered the door, and fell on the floor in shock at the sight of him. Anton knelt down to her as his father came to see his son in the doorway.

"Anton, you're back," said his father, with tears in his eyes.

"Yes, Poppa. Where's Willy?"

Anton's younger brother, Willy, had also fought in the war. They hadn't seen each other for years now. Anton's mother began to cry.

"Son, Willy was killed, just a few days before the war ended, just east of Berlin," his father said. "He was hit by a grenade."

Anton held his mother on the floor as she sobbed, and his

father moved from the stairs to put his hand on his son's shoulder. Anton was home, but home was different now.

The devastation in Germany after the war was unimaginable—bombed-out buildings, closed businesses, homeless and hungry people. Anton couldn't even get ration cards for food. The government told him, "You can't live here. We can't support you. Go to the country someplace." Fearing he might get his family in trouble if he stayed, he moved in with his aunt Barbara temporarily, as she had an extra room, and he resumed the job he had before he was drafted. But the first day back he told his employer, "I won't be staying long. I'll only be here until I can find a seminary to study for the priesthood." That was the first time Anton had said the words.

Before long he did find a seminary that was still operating, in Westphalia, in northern Germany. Many of the guys there had also been in the war, and while Anton was happy to begin his studies, the economic situation there was no better than in the rest of Germany. There was little to eat.

"One day after Mass I fainted from lack of food," said Anton. "I hadn't eaten in days. You could count all of my bones. We used to have to go and beg food for the seminary from the local farmers."

After being there for one year, Anton decided to go home to help his parents who were struggling in the dismal economy where the German mark had been devalued to 10 percent of its worth. (Anton had paid for his first year in the seminary with *one* of the cartons of American cigarettes that he had brought home with him.) He missed his connecting train in Frankfurt and had to spend the night in the train station. He later referred to that missed train as "life-altering."

He slept on the sidewalk outside the train station. As the sun was rising, policemen were waking up the sleeping homeless to move them on their way. When Anton walked into the train station, a train was emptying, and he saw a familiar face.

"Major Smitty?" said Anton. "Is it you?" He moved closer to see if it could be possible.

"Anton, how good to see you," said Major Smitty, walking toward Anton and putting his arms on Anton's shoulders. "You are the first of my prisoners that I've seen here in Germany." Major Smitty, now a colonel, had been transferred to Germany from Camp Kilmer in the United States. "What are you doing now in Germany?" asked Smitty.

"I'm studying to be a priest at the seminary, but I had to leave. Things aren't good at home."

"How can I help?" asked Smitty. "You must come to see me where I live, in Lauf. We will talk about this. I'm sure Pete, my good Irish friend, can help you."

"Pete?" said Anton.

"Yes, of course. You remember him. You gave him a tour of the camp in Kilmer when he came to visit me. He was quite impressed with you. He said you showed him every part of the chapel that Helmut had furnished, with the same pride as if you had done it yourself."

Anton remembered. Peter was the man from East Rockaway, in New York, who had said he walked by the beach every day. Anton had wondered what that would be like.

"Oh, yes, I remember him," said Anton. "He was a nice man. Very religious."

"Visit me," said Smitty. "Pete will be your way back to the seminary." Smitty walked toward the train station exit, leaving

Anton to wait for his train home. Anton sat amid the din of trains and people, thinking the whole time how unusual this chance meeting was.

Anton visited Colonel Smitty at his spacious home in Lauf the following Sunday. It felt good to reconnect with this man who had always shown Anton such kindness. Over some dark German ale and homemade dumplings, they talked about the possibility of Anton studying for the priesthood in the United States. Within two weeks there was a letter from Pete in New York saying he and a friend of his would fund Anton's passage to the States and help pay the tuition for him to study for the priesthood there. It was more than an answer to prayer for Anton. It was "a miracle."

Anton's family was not as enamored of the idea. His mother was particularly opposed to it. "But we're all here now together, and you want to leave again," she said. "How can you do that to us?" And while he felt bad at disappointing his family, Anton knew that this call was something he could not avoid. He felt a sense of destiny to it. It was beyond him.

His aunt Gina, Uncle Willy's wife, had her chauffeur drive Anton through the Alps, south to Genoa, Italy. He sailed the following day for New York City, and when he arrived, Peter and his friend Ernie were at the dock to meet him. With his English-German dictionary in hand, Anton tried to express his thanks to Pete and Ernie as they drove in Pete's Ford to his home in East Rockaway. It was just before Christmas, 1949, and Anton had one more request.

"Would it be possible for me to go to Saint Patrick's Cathedral for Christmas?" asked Anton a bit hesitantly as he watched the passing buildings from the car.

"I don't see why not," said Pete. "Any particular reason?"

"I would just like to pray at the crèche there," said Anton. "I once made a prayer at another one in Italy some years ago. I need to kneel there and give my thanks."

"Well then, I'll make sure you get there," said Pete. And he did.

WE SIT IN THE CONFERENCE ROOM for the retreat, forty or so priests gathered in a circle of chairs. Anton sits with his cane between his legs, tapping his foot gently. He is still amazed that he wound up in Minnesota as a priest, all due to the fact that Pete had a friend in the priesthood who knew the bishop of the St. Cloud diocese. Pete had asked if the bishop might want a young seminarian for the diocese, and the priest said, "I think so. There are a lot of Germans there." When Anton looked at the map and saw it was farther south than the fiftieth parallel of his own hometown, he said, "Good, it will be warm." "Boy, was I wrong about that," he now says.

It is the last sharing session before the retreat ends. Many of the priests have spoken about their gratefulness for the week of rest and reflection. Others have shared their disappointment and heartache over the recent sex abuse scandal. A few have indicated doubts about their future in the priesthood. Anton has been quiet through most of the conversation—though not asleep, as in my conferences. He lifts his head to speak. He does so slowly, deliberately, his German accent emphasizing words in an unintended authoritative way.

"I, too, am grateful for the week here, and for Father Edward, though not so much for what he has said, since I missed some of that." He smiles at me, and the priests laugh heartily. "But grateful to him for what he has let me say. We've had many private conversations this week about my life, much of which I seldom talk about, perhaps because of embarrassment and shame." He stops, chokes up, as tears begin to fill his eyes. One of the priests next to him puts his hand on Anton's shoulder.

He finally continues, "But Edward took an interest this week, and as I've talked I've seen the great blessings of my life. The ways in which God has led me every step of the way. I've had a good life as a priest, ordained now almost fifty years. But there have been difficult years. Times of depression, of doubt, loneliness, and some regrets.

"When I went to visit Dachau after the war, I couldn't believe what I saw, how horrible it was, how evil." He chokes up again. "Jews, gays, nuns, priests, political opponents, all killed for nothing. My own grandfather was probably killed in the hospital simply because he was too old. And I think of all the friends in my life whom I lost, and my brother, my parents. And the soldiers I was with in the army. All of them were good men, not evil. When I think of the saints in heaven, I think of them.

"And yet, I know that forgiveness is the key. I need to be forgiven for any part of what I participated in, even though I wasn't fully aware." He stops and shakes his head. Tears fall onto his lap. "But we must be a people of forgiveness now, too. In our country, in our Church. Zero tolerance has no place in the Gospel. There must always be tolerance with true forgiveness. There can be no death penalty as in our country now, no playing God. For we were all once strangers in a foreign land. That's what the Scripture says. We must never forget that. And maybe I am here with you, a former soldier in the German Army, to help you remember that. That strangers can become friends. And friends can help us make a home."

CHAPTER THREE

Fireman's Son

"EDWARD, I NEED YOU TO GET ME A MASS CARD to send to a friend of mine who I worked with. His son Michael Boyle was killed last week at the World Trade Center."

It was my father calling me from his home in Florida the week after the September 11 attack. The name "Boyle" sounded familiar, but I had met so many firemen over the years who had worked with my father that it was hard to be sure.

"You remember Jimmy Boyle," he went on to say. "He worked with me at 217. You saw him a few years ago at Fort Tilden down at Breezy Point when we had that reunion of Engine 248. He was head of the firemen's union then. Really nice guy. I feel so bad for him."

I thought I vaguely remembered him, but again, there were so many. I told my father that I would send him a Mass card for Jimmy and that I'd be sure to keep the Boyle family in my prayers.

"How old was his son Michael?" I asked before hanging up.

"Thirty-seven," my father said. "You'd met him too."

The weeks after September 11 were numbing for many in the United States and for countless others around the world who watched the video footage of the devastation left in the wake of the terrorist attack. Those of us in New York City at the time were, of course, even more affected. Ministering in a triage-center days after the attack gave me a close-up view of the irreparable damage to so many lives. Weary rescue workers stumbling in from the ground zero site, covered in soot and debris, their faces ashen with the realization that few, if any, had survived, were a reality barometer for those of us hoping for some good news. There would be little.

At first the enormity of the loss was hard to fathom. Unless you knew someone killed at the site, the video footage of the horror, which looked like outtakes from a bad Bruce Willis movie, washed over you like a distant dream. But the call from my father confirmed that I did know someone killed in that mayhem. Although I didn't remember him, Michael Boyle was probably a kid I had played with at annual firemen's picnics when my father and Jimmy Boyle worked in the same firehouse on Engine 217 in the Bedford Stuyvesant section of Brooklyn. I had surely met Michael at one of the countless other activities each year when firemen and their families gathered to celebrate the unique camaraderie among them. But now he was gone. He had chosen to enter the arcane world that had seduced my father for so many happy years on the job, and Michael had paid the ultimate price, along with many others. It was a world I had often resented because it seemed to take the place of what I thought our family should be—connected, supportive, a "die for" love. But here was a son who had learned to love that world in the same way that his father had, something I had never learned to do. My curiosity was piqued, and my heart was moved. I set out to learn more about this fireman's son who had become a fireman himself, and whom I never got to know.

Although Michael Boyle was assigned to Engine 33 on Great Jones Street in downtown Manhattan, he still had many connections to one of his previous firehouses, Engine 40, Ladder 35, located farther uptown in the Lincoln Center area of the city. He had rotated through that firehouse with his best friend from childhood, David "Buddha" Arce, and they continued to play softball with the guys from that company. David Halberstam wrote a best-selling book called *Firehouse* about the men from this house who were lost on September 11, and he couldn't help but include stories about Michael Boyle and David Arce in the narrative, so much were they still a part of the heartbeat of that house.

Thinking I should talk to some of the men there who knew Michael, I called the firehouse to explore the possibility. Fireman Danny O'Donovan answered the phone.

"If you really want to talk to some of the guys who knew Michael, come to the softball game tomorrow in Central Park. Those are the guys he played with every week. They're dedicating a bench in the park tomorrow to the guys from the team who were lost on September 11, and everyone will be there. I think Michael's girlfriend, Rosemary, is going to be there, too."

August 13, 2002, was a brutally hot day in New York City, with the temperature peaking at ninety-eight degrees and the humidity shooting even higher. A shadeless ball field in the middle of Central Park held no allure for me, but I arrived early at Heckscher Field #5, a short walk into the park from Central Park West, and waited by the bleachers as some firemen with baseball gear began to arrive. I remembered the many games my family had gone to when my father played on his firehouse team, and how bored I had been then. These guys looked the same as my father and his firemen chums had thirty-five years before, carrying the prized coolers filled with sweating Budweisers (only back then it was Schaeffers and Rheingolds). They kidded each other with the same colorful "guy" language while the wives and girl-friends set up folding beach chairs from which to cheer their men on from the sidelines. It's a culture all its own.

I introduced myself to a young fireman wearing a blue bandana who couldn't have been more than twenty-five years old.

"Hi, I wonder if you know who I might speak to about Michael Boyle," I said.

"Hey, Father, how ya doin," he said as he rooted for bats in an oversized canvas bag. "I'd talk to Anthony Rucco if I was you. He was Michael Boyle's best friend on the team."

Anthony was playing warm-up catch with another fireman when the bandana-wrapped fireman walked over to him and told him I wanted to speak with him. Eyeing me a bit suspiciously in my Roman collar (which I had worn to give me some sort of professional entry into this protected world), Anthony took his time making his way over to me. He was short, with closely cropped blond hair. His hand was sweaty and calloused when he finally shook mine.

"Yeah, I was good friends with Mikey," he said. "We were friends for five years. We hung out together all the time." Anthony was sweating profusely, wiping his brow continuously with the back of his hand and shaking off the excess water onto the parched dirt behind the backstop. He looked straight ahead or down, rarely meeting my gaze.

"Mikey was always smiling, always ready for a good time. There aren't too many single guys to hang out with, so me, him, and Buddha (David Arce) spent a lot of time together. I really miss his being around. Sometimes I go to call him up to hang out and then I realize he's not around to hang out anymore." He looks out past center field, like he might be hoping Michael would appear laughing that it was all some kind of cruel joke.

When I ask what made Michael so special, Anthony says, "He was just always around when you needed him. He would do anything for anyone. Just the kind of guy he was. He was on the job four and a half years and never went sick. I saw him hurting sometimes, but he'd still go to work. Buddha was the same way. Mikey was also very active in the firemen's union, you know, just like his father. If heaven needs a union, they got one up there now with Mikey there."

MICHAEL WAS INDEED ACTIVE in the firefighters union, working tirelessly in the downtown Murray Street office, inheriting the legacy of his father, Jimmy, a popular two-term president of the union. Michael had gotten involved with union work even before becoming a fireman, which is when he met Paul Hurley, the owner of Hurley's Bar, a sponsor of the softball team that the firemen of Engine 40 now played on.

Hurley is an Irish immigrant with a thick brogue and an in-your-face, eye-locking intensity that makes it easy to see why he's so popular with the firemen. He had previously owned another bar on Murray Street, not far from the union offices by city hall. Jimmy Boyle was a regular at that bar and introduced his son Michael to Hurley.

"Ah, Michael was a great lad," Hurley said as he watched his team warm up from behind the backstop. "He was the mayor of Murray Street. Everyone knew Michael. He had a hard time getting on the department, you know, so he worked in the union offices first. But when he finally did get on, we had a big party for him at the bar. Everybody came. They all loved Michael.

"When I sold that bar on Murray Street," Hurley continued, "Michael got all the guys to come to the new bar I bought on Seventy-second Street. He was a great motivator, which is why he made such a good union man. He'd always round up the guys to come back to the bar after a softball game. I think he did it more for me, so that I'd have the business."

Hurley went on to tell me a story of Michael helping him exterminate the bugs at the bar of a friend of his called the Lion's Den. It was one of Hurley's many side jobs that helped keep him and his family afloat. Hurley and Michael had begun drinking at Hurley's Bar before heading out for the extermination excursion and showed up at the Lion's Den after hours, already well lubricated. They proceeded to break open some of the irresistible, colored bottles that sat temptingly on the bar and wound up drinking there alone all night. The next morning they stumbled out, never having exterminated anything save a few brain cells.

AS I WAS TALKING to Hurley under the hot sun next to the bleachers, someone tapped me on my shoulder. I turned to see an attractive woman with brown eyes and shoulder-length brown hair with blond highlights scattered throughout.

"Hello, Father, I'm Rosemary Kenny," she said. "I understand you may want to speak with me. I was Michael Boyle's girlfriend."

I had been told by some of the firemen, including Anthony Russo, that Rosemary was still having a tough time with Michael's death, especially as its one-year anniversary was approaching. They had advised me that she might not want to speak to me at all about Michael, so I was surprised when she took the initiative.

She had come to the softball game that afternoon because they were going to be dedicating the park bench to Michael and the other firemen from the team lost on September 11. Her father, Mark Kenny, had, in fact, retired from this firehouse, Engine 40, so Rosemary knew many of the guys. She had first met Michael here, though they didn't start dating until just before he moved back to the Great Jones firehouse downtown (Engine 33 had also been Michael's first assignment out of fire school some years earlier).

We were both wilting from the relentless sun, so I suggested we find a bench in the shade to talk, which seemed to make her happy. As we sat down some runners passed by, and she took them as her cue to jump right in.

"You know, Michael and I are both marathon runners. I mean, he *was* a marathon runner, and I still am. Michael's best time was 2:57, but he would have broken that time this year, had he lived." She looked off into the distance, beyond my shoulder, almost as if she was still imagining them running the track in this park. "One marathon, we ran together, and when Michael finished, he ran all the way back to find me so that he could run the last mile with me. I mean, can you imagine that? Finishing twenty-six miles and then coming back to run one more. He was just something else."

She wore a black skirt with a white tank top. A small gold cross and a half-heart medal hung around her neck on a thin gold chain.

"I'd always have some kind of system for training when I was running, like how far I was supposed to run each day, with charts and everything, and he'd say to me, 'Rosemary, just run. Run every day. Keep it simple. Don't make it so complicated.' That's so much the way he lived his life too. I'm sure it's why he jumped on that truck that morning. There was nothing for him to think about. He just did it."

Michael was technically off-duty when the call came in that a plane had flown into the North Tower of the World Trade Center. He had worked the night before and was getting ready to leave the firehouse and head to Woodside, Queens, to help his cousin, Matty Farrell, in his campaign for city council. It was Election Day and Michael was Matty's campaign manager. When the call came in, Michael jumped on the rig as it headed south to the World Trade Center, sure that for a call like this, all available personnel would be needed. His best friend, David Arce (Buddha), jumped on as well.

"We were just getting ready to move in together," Rosemary continued. "We had dated for almost four years and were finally going to get engaged. Michael had always said we needed to be engaged in order to live together. It was like his standard. He said he was only getting married once, and that this was it. That was just Michael. There was a right way to do everything. We really knew we were going to be together forever." She paused, as her eyes fill with tears. She shook her head back and forth, sensing the irony of "forever."

"I was his biggest fan," she finally said, as she blotted her eyes. "I was happiest when I was with him. It didn't matter where or what we were doing. Of course, I liked it best when we were alone, because we were always with Buddha or the firemen at the bar, or the union people, or whoever else Michael knew, which was a lot of people—all of whom I liked, by the way. But I also wanted him all to myself. I couldn't wait to be wherever he was.

"All those people think they knew Michael, but they really didn't. Most only saw one side of him. I saw all the sides. I saw

him with the firemen and his other friends, when he played softball, when he was with his family, and then when we were alone,
just him and me. He had a different kind of persona for each situation, which was fine, because we all have that. But I got to see
the whole man. And boy, did I like what I saw."

Rosemary remembers Monday, September 10, 2001, as if it
were seared into her memory. Michael had gone from the firehouse that morning to the union office to take care of some
paperwork. He called Rosemary midmorning and she conference-
called her sister, because Michael wanted to wish her a happy
birthday. Rosemary's sister asked Michael if he wanted to come
to dinner that night with Rosemary to celebrate, but Michael
told her that he had to work Monday night. He was making up
the tour for one of the firemen who had covered for him the previous month.

Rosemary took the train from Manhattan to Long Island that
evening and had dinner at the Olive Garden Restaurant with her
sister and two of her brothers. On her way back to Manhattan,
she called Michael at the firehouse and spoke to him only briefly,
because the train doors had opened and she had to board. When
she got to Penn Station, a Michael Jackson concert had just let
out and it was "a madhouse." Finally she was able to catch a cab
and got to the apartment sometime after 11 p.m. (she had begun
periodically staying over there as the engagement loomed), but
she decided not to call Michael since it was late, and went to
sleep.

"At about midnight," said Rosemary, "the phone rang and it
was Michael. He starts laughing because he had woken me up.
He said, 'I can't win. If I don't call, you get upset and when I do,
I wake you up! You're too funny, Rosemary.' I always wanted to
talk to him when he worked nights, when I couldn't be with him.

He was the last person I spoke to at night, whether he was physically with me or not. I still talk to him at night." She pauses.

"Anyway, we talked for a few minutes and then I went back to sleep. Then the next morning, September 11, at about eight-thirty, he called me again. He sounded so relaxed, which was kind of unusual because he always seemed to be in a rush to get off the phone. He said that he was getting ready to leave work to go to Woodside to help his cousin. Then he said, 'But I have to go and buy a tape measure first.' I said, 'For what?' And he said, 'To measure the apartment for our new bed. We're going to need a bigger bed when you move in.' All I keep thinking about is that we never got to sleep in that bed. But it does make me feel good to know that he was thinking about *us* that very morning."

As Rosemary spoke it was clear that the love she felt for Michael was mutual. And while they had had four years together, she felt robbed of what their future might have held had he not been killed. She now carries Michael's wallet in her pocketbook, because it was something he always had with him. She took it out to show me, and inside I saw his fireman's badge, #528, the same number as his father. Jimmy Boyle later told me that they had retired that number when he retired, but when Michael finally got on the job, Jimmy asked them to reissue the number to his son. I also noticed a large cross in the wallet, which Rosemary said she received at a memorial service for Michael at his sister's parish in Atlanta. Tucked into a side fold of the wallet is a Michael the Archangel prayer card, given to Rosemary by Michael's mother.

"You know he wasn't that religious in the churchgoing way," said Rosemary, "but he was very spiritual. I'd always say, 'Michael, I want to go to church,' and he'd say, 'I go to church.' And I'd say, 'Michael, funerals don't count.' He was so funny.

"But he lived out his faith. He didn't talk about it. He just did it. He helped anybody. He had this saying, 'Compassion makes it work.' He'd scribble it down in his notebook, as if to remind himself or something. And whenever I was being critical of someone, he'd always say, 'Rosemary, it doesn't make him a bad person.' He just refused to see the bad in anyone. He really believed in people. I try to live more that way now because of him. I feel like somehow he's always with me, helping me.

"I still wonder why I didn't feel something the moment he was killed, like I should have known at that moment or something. But then I remember that he's not really gone. The important part of him is still here. Maybe that's why I didn't feel anything."

After Michael was killed, Rosemary had a simple dream about him. He was wearing the same thing he had on the last time she saw him as he left for work—denim shorts, which she had bought him, and one of his many favorite T-shirts. She dreamed that they were walking together with her head on his shoulder, very peaceful, no words.

"It's how I remember him and it's so comforting to have that, this little gift."

She pointed to the half-heart charm around her neck and said, "I gave him the other half of this heart that I wear with my cross. He was buried with it. And I'll always wear this half. When I go, too, I'm going to be wearing this."

She also kept Michael's cell phone, which she recovered from his locker at the firehouse, with his voicemail message still on it. She took it out from her pocketbook and dialed the number so that I could hear Michael. It felt a bit eerie to hear his deep voice emerge from cell-phone space and give three contact numbers by which to reach him, knowing he couldn't be reached at any of them any longer.

"I just like hearing his voice sometimes," said Rosemary. "It took me the longest time to be able to listen to it, but now it's comforting. I've transferred it onto my voicemail at work so I can listen to it there when I want to."

The softball players and families gathered at the bench in the park for the short memorial service for Michael and the others from the team killed on September 11. Michael's family was away, so unable to attend. One of the firemen read a short tribute and gave a plaque to Paul Hurley for all he had done for the men and their families. He ended by saying, "May we never forget. May they always live in our hearts." I glanced over to see Rosemary looking at the ground, shaking her head.

I walked over to the bench as the crowd was dispersing and the softball game about to begin, and looked at the plaque fixed to the bench. It read, "In tribute to the firemen of Hurley's 2001 NYSBL Team who gave their lives on Sept. 11: Steve Mercado, Jimmy Giberson, David Arce, Mikey Boyle, Kevin Bracken."

Rosemary walked over to say good-bye to me. She had taken an extended lunch break from work, but needed to get back.

"Father, thanks for caring enough to listen to my story," she said. "Sometimes it helps just to talk about him. Makes me know that what we had together was real."

"No, thank *you*, Rosemary. I can't imagine how hard it must be for you, but please be assured of my prayers. And thanks for introducing me to Michael."

As we walked toward the exit to the park, she said, "There was a reason for Michael in my life. I just need some more time to figure it all out. People keep asking me if I've begun dating yet, but I don't want any part of it. I'm not interested. Then they say to me, 'Well, at least you didn't have any kids together,' as if that's a *good* thing. And I think they're crazy. If *only* we had had a child, I'd still have a piece of Michael with me. I talk about adopting a child now and naming him Michael and everyone thinks I'm crazy. But Michael would understand it; that's all I really care about."

I watched her walk down Central Park West toward the subway and was in awe at the depth of her love, a love beyond death. I also began thinking about the love that Michael had, not only for Rosemary, but also for thousands who were saved on September 11 because he and other rescue workers were willing to lay down their lives for them. I marveled at that kind of love and bravery and wanted to know more. If anyone might have some insight, I thought it would be Jimmy Boyle, the father of this man I was coming to know in death. How did he feel about his son being killed on a job that he had encouraged? How had his heart been reshaped by this loss?

MY FATHER GAVE ME Jimmy's phone number and I called him at his home in Westbury, Long Island, where he lives with his wife, Barbara.

Jimmy Boyle remembered me immediately. He said that he had just finished reading my book, *God Underneath*, and that it brought back great memories of my father and the old neighborhood. His New York accent was heavy, like my father's, and he sounded like so many of the New York City firemen and cops that I've known along the way. There was something warm and familiar about him. He agreed that we should meet to talk about Michael and suggested the firehouse on Great Jones Street where Michael had been stationed.

In his book *Report from Ground Zero* the famed firefighter Dennis Smith writes that "Jimmy Boyle is, without a doubt, the most beloved man within the New York Fire Department family." My father had told me that Jimmy was an extremely popular union president because he had been a firefighter before becoming president and knew the concerns of the men firsthand. When he retired as president of the union in 1994, he worked for the fire science program of the John Jay College of Criminal Justice. We met when he was finishing a stint working for the Brooklyn district attorney and was preparing to retire for good.

I arrived early at the Engine 33 firehouse on Great Jones Street for my appointment with Jimmy. I figured it would give me time to get the lay of the land and possibly talk to a few other firemen who knew and worked with Michael. The first thing I noticed was the beautiful architecture of the firehouse. A soaring, large, red arch extended to a roof framed with ornate red gilding. Black and purple bunting hung on a wrought-iron balcony that sat atop the two large red doors of the firehouse—an obvious tribute to the men lost from this firehouse.

The doors were open, indicating the trucks were in and that the men would be inside. Walking into the firehouse, I noticed that the "guardhouse" in front had a lit-up fireman's hat built into the wood of the wall, and inside the hat it read "Heroes." Tom Boaz, one of the firemen on duty, was eating his lunch, an overstuffed sandwich and green salad. I introduced myself and immediately felt his warmth.

"Hey, Father, how ya doin'," he said. "I used to do some handy work for the Franciscan priests in Staten Island." He had thick black hair and a winning grin. He told me that he had known Michael well. They both had their lockers in the basement, a prized spot that had to be won by lottery because of the extra room afforded by the coveted subterranean cubicles. "Yeah, Mikey would do anything for anybody—probably to a fault. He was a great fireman."

Just as he had started to speak about Michael, a run came in. The other firemen rushed from the kitchen in back where they were eating lunch and began stepping into their waiting boots and donning their gear. Tom began to suit up as well and called to two young boys to get in the cabin part of the truck. I must have looked surprised by the emergence of these two kids from the back because he said to me, "Those two are mine, Father. My wife's at an election board meeting, so they got to come to work with me today. Their brother's at the Yankee game, so this is their little treat. Okay, boys, let's go."

Within seconds the firemen were in position on the truck and the two young kids were staring wide-eyed from inside the cabin. The truck pulled out, its siren wailing and horn blowing, and the big doors closed behind it. I suddenly realized that I was alone in the firehouse.

The first thing I recognized was the smell—a mix of smoke, rubber, gasoline, and food. It occurred to me that I hadn't been in a firehouse since I was a kid when my brother and I got to visit the firehouse with my own father, usually when he stopped in to pick up his pay. It was a big deal when he allowed us to slide down the shiny brass poles from the dormitory on the second level to the street level where the trucks were. I can't imagine him ever letting us go on an actual run on the truck. Boaz's kids must really rate, I thought.

I took the opportunity of being alone to meander around the firehouse. After all, since September 11 this was now hallowed ground. Eleven men had died from this firehouse alone. Their pictures hang on a board framed with purple and black cloth in the front of the firehouse. Above them it reads "Lest we forget." Little else seemed changed in here from the firehouse I remember from thirty-five years earlier. Interior design was never exactly the forte or concern of firemen.

I walked to the back to that holy of holies known as the "firehouse kitchen." Everything of importance takes place there. Firemen are renowned for being good cooks, even spawning a few best-selling cookbooks. My mother's first question when my father would come home after a shift was, "So, what did you eat?" I think he played it down sometimes, so as not to get her mad, knowing that we had been feasting on Oscar Mayer hot dogs in his absence. (What many people don't know, however, is that the firemen all chip in for the food they cook. They pay to eat well. The city doesn't give a dime toward their meals.)

The kitchen dining room was as messy as I remembered. Since lunch had been interrupted, as most meals in a firehouse usually are, half-eaten sandwiches were left on plates, along with warming soda and milk-filled plastic glasses. There were papers tacked to the walls, some department notices and letters, mostly newspaper articles and pictures of their fallen comrades. Torn, heavy, clear plastic hung over the passageway from the hot kitchen to the air-conditioned, cool eating area, to keep it that way. The TV was on—a baseball game, of course. I tried to imagine Michael in this kitchen. Rosemary had told me he was a good cook. I was sure that the men had partaken of many of his meals around this table.

Off the kitchen, there was a musty-smelling "recreation room" that was so air conditioned, you could have hung meat in it. Dirty reclining chairs faced another TV, and more pictures and news articles were tacked haphazardly to the walls. The back wall had a shelf with all the trophies the firemen's sports teams had won. Michael Boyle's picture was everywhere.

While reading some of the news articles on the wall, I heard the firehouse doors opening, signaling that the engine was back from its run. (The ladder truck had been out that day covering at another house.) I walked toward the front, not wanting to give the impression that I'd been snooping or anything. As the firemen were shedding themselves of their weighty gear, Jimmy Boyle walked in behind them. I knew it was he right away, in an open tie and sports jacket, carrying a beat-up briefcase. He had come by train from the DA's office in Brooklyn.

"Eddie Beck's son," he said with a smile. "You got the same eyes as your father. Can't miss them. Hope I didn't keep you waitin' too long."

He looked to be about my father's age, mid-sixties, with a balding pate and widening girth. He, too, had blue eyes, which looked right at you through his wire-rimmed glasses. For some reason, he reminded me of an Irish monsignor.

We sat in the "meat-locker" recreation room since all the firemen were in the kitchen. He was eager to talk about Michael, as he has been ever since his death. He's committed to keeping alive Michael's memory and the memory of all those lost.

Jimmy was in his office at the Brooklyn DA's office early the morning of September 11. He looked out the window of his office, which faced the World Trade Center, and saw smoke coming out of one of the towers. He had had an 8:35 a.m. phone message from Michael, saying that he'd be leaving the firehouse to go to Queens to help his cousin, Matty Farrell, who was running for city council. It was Election Day.

"So I'm watching out my window," said Jimmy, "and suddenly I see the second plane go into the other tower, and I knew that something was terribly wrong. Just then I got a call from a friend of mine, saying that there was a big job at the World Trade Center. So I knew I had to get down there."

Jimmy walked across the Brooklyn Bridge into Manhattan, turning down offers from a few fire rigs to drive him in. He knew they had a job to do, and he had a stop to make first anyway. He had remembered that the first time the World Trade Center was bombed, police transcripts said that those responsible had gone to J&R Music World so they could watch from the big windows that faced the World Trade Center. Jimmy was intent on seeing if anyone suspicious was lurking at J&R this time.

"But it was mayhem," he said. "I couldn't get near the place. So, I'm walking toward 250 Broadway, near City Hall Park, when I hear the roar of the South Tower falling. I ducked into the lobby, where there were other people gathered. When the cloud of dust lifted a little, I started walking again to the corner of Barclay and West Streets, when suddenly I hear another roar and the North Tower comes down, knocking me off my feet, blowing me toward the intersection of West and Murray Streets. I was lying on the ground and couldn't see a thing, covered with all kinds of crap."

He felt his way east along a building, knowing that District Council 37 had an office there. He met some firemen inside who had run for cover and cleaned himself off so that he could at least see again.

"When I finally came out, I turned back toward West Street. As soon as I saw the scene, I knew that everyone was dead. There were about a hundred cars on fire in the parking lot, and buried fire trucks. There was this eerie silence, like a war zone. I had a gut feeling at that moment that Michael was dead. I knew that if there was any way he could have made the rig, he was on it. So I started searching for his engine, hoping against hope."

He saw Chief Hayden standing on a truck directing fire-fighters, and he said to Jimmy, "They're all dead." But he didn't say anything about Michael. Jimmy walked on to the command center, asking for Engine 33, when suddenly he saw the rig, covered in soot. He looked on the riding list that he found in the cabin of the truck, but Michael's name wasn't on it.

"I had this glimmer of hope. Maybe he missed the rig and made it to Queens. I prayed so hard that he had."

Jimmy walked farther and met the company driver. "John, what about Michael?" said Jimmy, not wanting to hear the answer.

"I'm sorry, Jimmy, but he jumped on the rig at the last minute. They were about thirty seconds away from making it out when the tower collapsed."

"It felt like I had just been knocked down again," said Jimmy. "I couldn't believe he was actually telling me that my son was dead. It was one thing to feel it might be true, but to hear it . . ." Jimmy shook his head.

"I have to tell you though," he finally said, "that I don't have anger about his death, so much as trying to come to terms with the fact that he's gone. I find myself thinking, 'Where is he?' and 'What is heaven?' It's tested all the beliefs that I simply took for granted. I find myself listening closely to sermons now, wanting to find some answers, wanting to see if anyone seems to know more about this stuff than me."

Jimmy had lobbied to get Michael assigned to a Manhattan house, since that was where Michael lived. But Jimmy now battles the inevitable questions: What if Michael had been assigned somewhere else, to another borough? Would he still be around today? Jimmy would have loved for Michael to follow him in the job as an elected union official, and is sure that he would have. "I think I'll miss that the most."

Jimmy says there was a spiritual side to Michael that few got to see. It came through most in his desire to help other people. "I've gotten so many letters from people that he helped, letters that made me cry, saying what a great son I had. It meant a lot to me that people saw that, because Michael could have a hard edge to him, but underneath there was a real soft side.

"There's a story that Dennis Smith tells about Michael finding a hungry person on the street and bringing him into the firehouse for something to eat. I'm sure all the guys just loved that," Jimmy said with a smile. "Or the time he gave a cashmere sweater to Father Mychal Judge, because he thought somebody might be able to use it, and Judge gave it to a homeless person on Thirty-fourth Street the next day. It's just how Michael was."

Perhaps that spiritual side was never more visible than at the November 5 memorial Mass at Saint Patrick's Cathedral in Manhattan for Michael Boyle and his best friend, David "Buddha" Arce. A pumper truck pulled up to the cathedral with two large floral arrangements on the back, each with a fire helmet centered on it. Although Barbara Boyle had wanted a low-key ceremony for her son, she realized there were too many people who were touched by Michael's life, and she had agreed to the Saint Patrick's ceremony. She and Jimmy took their place behind the firefighters, who were carrying their helmets in somber reverence. Rosemary Kenny was with them, as was the family of David Arce. The crowd of firefighters, dignitaries, and well-wishers stretched for blocks up Fifth Avenue.

Father Delanick, the Fire Department chaplain, said the Mass and preached to the overflowing crowd. The mayor and the fire commissioner spoke. Some firemen said that when the commissioner mentioned the name of Jimmy Boyle and said that nobody knew how to treat firefighters in need the way Jimmy did, a thunderous applause shook the cathedral and everyone leapt to their feet, giving Jimmy a sustained standing ovation. Cardinal Egan spoke as well, saying, "The firefighters climbed the hill of Calvary, like Christ, to their deaths. And, like Christ, they cared for others more than they cared for themselves."

"It was a beautiful ceremony," said Jimmy, as he sat with me in the Great Jones firehouse. "A real tribute to Michael and David. But it really tests your faith, trying to figure out the next life. How can billions of people be reunited? It's beyond our comprehension, but there had to be a Creator to all of this. I believe that I will see Michael again in the next life, and that belief gets me through to another day."

Former New York governor Hugh Carey spoke for Governor Pataki at the ceremony. Carey had just lost a son for the third time. He ended his speech by saying, "Death is not an ending, but a continuation of the spirit."

"Well man, if he can still say that after losing three sons, then so can I," said Jimmy.

I realized that it was time for me to go, that I'd taken up enough of Jimmy's time. He still had more meetings to attend about the upcoming anniversary of September 11 before he could go home to Long Island. But I had one final request, to see Michael's locker downstairs, the prized possession that Tom Boaz had spoken of earlier.

We walked downstairs to a musty and dimly lit basement that had secondhand chairs and a couch parked in front of another TV. Along the walls were large wooden lockers, some of them like little cabanas. On the right side of the basement was a big wooden locker with the name "Michael Boyle" written over the door. We walked over to it and Jimmy opened the door, something that was obviously hard for him to do.

"You know, I really have to get down here and clean this out so that some other guy can get in here, but I just haven't been able to bring myself to do it yet."

Michael's clothes and various personal items were hanging inside. An overnight bag hung on a hook and had printed on it "A Proud Profession, A Bold Union, A Brighter Future." There were shelves with all kinds of union and department forms and medical and benefit information.

Jimmy stood in front of the door, holding on to it, as if he needed the support to stay standing. He said, "You know, I got closer to Michael later in life, because when he was younger, I was working all the time. Sometimes I feel guilty about that. Probably like your dad, and a thousand other firemen."

Yes, I thought, that's probably true. But my father can call me up and talk about it. We still have the chance to try to get it right.

"Jimmy, would you do me a favor?" I finally said, after standing there in some moments of silence.

"Sure, what is it?" he asked.

"Say hello to my dad. I'm going to call him up right now on my cell phone so that you can say hi."

"Sure, I'd love to speak to Eddie. It's been years."

I dialed my parents' home in Florida as we stood by Jimmy's dead son's locker. My father answered.

"Hi, Dad, it's me. I have someone here who wants to say hello."

I passed the phone to Jimmy and watched him as the two fireman fathers spoke. I could hear my father's voice, more animated than usual, through the receiver pressed to Jimmy's ear. I thought about the paths our lives take. Why was I standing there with Jimmy, and why wasn't his son? I couldn't help but think that Jimmy was wondering the same thing.

I called my father later that night.

"How did Jimmy seem to you?" my father asked.

"Okay," I said, "but obviously still hurting."

"Yeah, that's really tough," my father said. "I'm not sure you ever get over the loss of a child. A spouse you can heal from maybe, but not a child."

"Dad," I said, somewhat hesitantly, "were you disappointed that Chris and I decided to do something else with our lives? I mean, would you have wanted us to be firemen?"

He paused.

"Look, Edward," he finally said. "I'm very proud of you and your brother and what you've done with your lives, just as I'm sure Jimmy is proud of Michael. I loved the fire department, and I always will. Next to my family, it was the most important thing in my life. I became a fireman because it was a great job with great benefits for someone who never went to college, and I got to make a difference every day.

"You and your brother were able to do something else with your lives, and you have. And I thank God for that. But we also need people like Michael who are willing to risk their lives every day for other people. You save people in another way, but it's different, that's all."

It was more than my father usually said, but I was aware that he never did really answer my question.

CHAPTER FOUR

Lost and Found

I WAS FEELING INSECURE AS I SLUNK into a chair in a school building on the Upper East Side that was used in the evenings for Continuing Education classes. It was the beginning of my sabbatical year, and I was still trying to figure out what to do with the largesse of time that I'd been given. A writing class seemed liked profitable filler.

After noticing the peeling paint on the azure ceiling and the decorative bars on the large windows, I turned my attention to more pressing concerns—like sizing up my classmates. What had brought them here? I wondered. What were they writing; *could* they write; were they more advanced than me? A bald guy with black-rimmed glasses and a red-and-white sweater with a large hole on the left shoulder mumbled to himself as he pored over a manuscript. I began to worry. *He's already written something before the first class? Maybe I'm in the wrong level.*

Although no teacher was in sight, the chairs were positioned in a semicircle, an obvious nod to a collaborative pedagogy. A woman two seats away nodded and smiled at me. She was pretty, around fifty years old, with blond hair, perhaps lightened with some help. Next to her sat another blond-haired woman, slightly younger, with protruding eyes and a hot-pink Lycra top. I wondered if they knew each other because they seemed to be talking comfortably and comparing shoes. Then again, women can do that sort of thing. Men take longer to share even superficial pleasantries.

"So, what brings you to the class?" the slightly older one said, as I paged through my glaringly empty notebook.

Startled, I looked over my shoulder, not sure to whom she was speaking.

"Me?" I said, pointing at my chest.

"Yeah. If you don't mind my asking." She smiled and leaned forward. I hesitated. *What do I say? I'm not really sure why I'm here. Don't want to appear too green.*

"Just thought it'd be fun to take a class like this. Maybe brush up on my writing skills. It's been a while."

"Are you working on something in particular?" she asked.

"Oh, not really. Just playing around a little. But who knows, maybe I will, now that I have some time."

"Oh, you've been laid off?"

Gee. This is a lot of questions for a first go round. Where's the teacher anyway?

"Laid off? Oh, no. I'm on sabbatical."

"Oh, you're a teacher?"

Boy, this one doesn't quit.

"Well, not exactly," I managed to say. Just then a girl, who looked like the youngest in the room, hurried to the desk in the center of the semicircle of other desks. *Saved by the teenager.*

"This is the teacher?" the blonde mouthed to me in a half whisper, as she covered her mouth.

I shrugged.

"She looks like she could be my daughter," she said. "I hope she can teach."

Unfortunately, she couldn't. It turned out to be an awful class and none of us learned much about writing. But it had its value. I had met Judy there. With uncommon openness, she revealed the intimacies of her life to me, and our friendship grew quickly. Beneath her machine-gun-paced questions, I was to discover a woman of deep compassion and pulsating life. But at the time we met that life was wan and tired.

"WOW. SO YOU'RE WORKING on a real book?" I said, as the two of us sat in a French bistro on East Seventy-fifth Street a few weeks after we had met. We had agreed to meet for dinner before class to compare notes on the ineptitude of our teenage-like, poet-instructor.

"Well, I say *book*, but I don't know if it will ever get published," she said. "I don't think I'm that good of a writer. But I've been told that it's an interesting story. And it's kind of helped me to put it all down, you know? Somewhat like therapy, I guess. Get it all out."

She wore a high, white turtleneck with gold earrings that hung just beneath the extended collar. Her pretty hazel eyes were awash in sadness.

"So it's *your* story?" I asked.

"Yes," she said. "But not only mine. It's about my father, his difficult wife, my lost sister, my distant husband. You know, the whole nine yards."

I laughed. "That's quite a loaded sentence. Sure you didn't leave anybody out?"

She hesitated, her eyes narrowing, her lips pursed.

"Judy, I'm kidding. I'm kidding."

"Oh," she said. "I can't always tell. I'm gullible that way. *Very* gullible."

FOUR YEARS AFTER WE HAD MET came the phone call that I knew would be the defining moment of a long saga.

"Edward, my father just died." Her voice was muffled, distorted by the cell phone static we pay such high rates to endure.

"Judy, I'm so sorry," I said. This was the moment she had been dreading since I'd met her. Now it was here. "It seems so fast," I continued awkwardly. "He was fine last week, right?"

"I know," she choked out, her voice almost a whisper. "He just stopped eating. Look, I'll talk to you later. I just wanted you to know. Say a prayer for me. The services are on Wednesday. I hope you can come."

JUDY'S FATHER, BENJAMIN MOSS, had been one of the most respected Reform rabbis in the country. He had been the spiritual leader at a prominent temple in Connecticut for over thirty-five years. From their reserved pew, Judy and her family had beamed with pride at her father's eloquent sermons.

"I was five years old when my mother first took me to the Sabbath services on Friday nights," said Judy. "It was a mystical experience because it was like watching and listening to someone totally removed from me. He had an aura about him."

Rabbi Moss would stand in front of the ark, its light shining on the velvet-covered Torahs. The glow of the dome of the temple, highlighted by the stained-glass windows, provided a celestial canopy as the rabbi waxed eloquent about such social issues as civil rights and Vietnam and the congregants' responsibilities before God and neighbor.

"When I was older, I was still awestruck at the effect he had on people," said Judy. "After services I would stand in the receiving line and people would come up to me and rave about him. How brilliant he was, how kind, how articulate. And while I was impressed by what they said, I also saw all the other aspects of him. He was my dad, and not always perfect. But he was a great man, and he made a difference in people's lives. It's so hard for me to now see what's happened to him."

I NOW SAT IN THAT SAME TEMPLE that Benjamin Moss had helped design and build. He lay in a coffin beneath the large brass doors that housed the Torah. An eternal gas flame flickered above the doors while below, robed cantors, rabbis, and rabbis' assistants filed into the sanctuary. Benjamin's family sat in the first row of pews on both sides of his coffin: Cynthia, his second wife, sat on one side with her children and grandchildren, and Judy and her family sat on the other. Their separation seemed symbolic of the rift that had characterized the previous ten years.

Rabbi Moss had remarried when he was sixty-eight, the first rabbi in the history of the temple to be married in his own sanctuary. Judy's mother had died of metastasized breast cancer four years before. She and Rabbi Moss had been friends with Cynthia and her husband, Charles, and when Charles died, the Rabbi and Cynthia consoled each other in their mutual grief and, before long, they married.

Judy had sat in the pew she had sat in her whole life and watched her beloved father take vows to a woman she would eventually come to mistrust and dislike. As Benjamin Moss stomped on the glass that Rabbi Epstein had placed by his foot, the noise shattered the quiet of the sanctuary. (A rabbi told me that, originally, this custom symbolized the breaking of the hymen of the virginal bride, but that political correctness had led to its now being said to symbolize the destruction of the second temple in Jerusalem and to be a reminder that there is always bitter with the sweet.)

At the funeral I looked at Cynthia seated in the first row, erect posture and lifted chin. Wearing the pearl necklace and earrings of which Judy had so often spoken, and a perfectly tailored gray suit with a black velvet collar, Cynthia was smaller and slighter than I had imagined her. She smiled proudly as her son eulogized his stepfather, Benjamin, and she cried when the cantor chanted a soulful lament. She didn't look like the powerful matriarch whom Judy said had been so destructive to her life. But I've learned that looks rarely tell it all.

THINGS SEEMED FINE AT FIRST. Although Judy had feared a diminishment of her family when her father remarried, his words on the night before his wedding brought her comfort. That night he led his daughters to an upstairs bedroom while relatives and friends downstairs toasted the soon-to-be-remarried rabbi. He closed the bedroom door and put his long arms around Judy and her sister, Jeannie.

"My darling girls. You mean more to me than you will ever know."

Judy felt sheltered and safe, encircled in warmth, as family pictures of their lives together hung on every visible wall and seemed to envelop the three of them.

"Even though I am getting married tomorrow, both of you

must know that we are still a family, the three of us. No one and nothing can ever change that."

The words eased their way into Judy's heart like a soothing balm.

"I want to explain something else to you," he continued. "I've had a prenuptial agreement drawn up with Cynthia, so that there will be no confusion with regard to finances. Her money will remain hers, and ours is ours. We are agreed to this. And if there comes a time when I am unable to tend to my financial affairs for any reason, you girls will jointly handle everything. Is that understood?"

Not knowing what else to do or say, Judy and her sister nodded in agreement. Money had never been discussed. It felt strange to even hear their father speak of it.

"We will always have each other," he said, and took each of their faces between his hands and kissed them. To Judy, it felt like a covenant sealed with a kiss.

JUDY'S SISTER, JEANNIE, sat in the front pew, ten feet from the coffin of her father, and about just as many feet from Judy, who sat at the end of the pew next to her husband, Alan. Jeannie's hair was wild and red, held back by a headband that seemed thrown on as an afterthought. I was surprised to see her here. She had taken her seat with her children without the other family members, who had gone in together. This absent daughter hadn't seen her father in eight years. *Why show up for the funeral?* I wondered.

JUDY HAD NEVER been close to Jeannie, but after their father's remarriage, their relationship grew even more fragile as Jeannie's own marriage crumbled. She seemed constantly on edge, her anger flaring at every turn, irrational in her accusations and suspicions about almost everything.

Years before her father's death, Judy had agreed to meet her at Le Train Bleu, the restaurant at Bloomingdale's. It was the first time they had seen each other in months. Judy approached the table with trepidation, wondering what kind of mood Jeannie was going to be in. Judy always worried about having conversations with her in public places because Jeannie often grew loud, unleashing her rage with no notice. Judy had sat but a moment before the tirade began.

"You *must* talk to Daddy about the way he treats me—or doesn't treat me," said Jeannie.

"Jeannie, what are you talking about?"

"I get no support from him whatsoever. He has *never* supported me." Her voice began to escalate. "He knows the trouble I am having with Harold, but he refuses to even talk to me about it. Why does he always ignore what's important to me? He's done it for years."

"Jeannie, if you are going to scream in this restaurant, then I'm going to leave. I'm warning you."

"Don't warn me about anything," Jeannie spat back. "I don't care who hears me. I'm tired of being dismissed. You just don't get it, do you, Judy? You never have."

The women at the neighboring tables began to stare. A waitress offered more coffee, perhaps as a buffer to the meltdown she perceived coming.

"Jeannie, I *do* get it, but you have to calm down."

"That's easy for you to say. You're not in a miserable marriage where no one is helping you."

This struck Judy as ironic since her marriage was suffering, too, only Judy wasn't telling anyone.

"Jeannie, maybe you just need to see somebody to get some help."

Judy's profession as a family therapist had never impressed Jeannie. She saw only a younger sister who had always had it easier.

"I don't need that kind of help. My husband is the one who needs to talk to someone, but he won't go. He doesn't want to work on this. And all Daddy cares about is our staying together for the sake of the kids. All anyone cares about is the children. I've had it. Why doesn't he care about *me*? He helps everyone else, but he doesn't care about my needs."

Jeannie had begun spending more time at the beach house while Harold and the children remained at home in New Jersey. Her estranged son, Sammy, left for his first year of college without speaking to his mother, while her daughter, Dara, slept in Judy and Alan's guest room for much of her senior year in high school. Before long, Jeannie filed for divorce and seemingly divorced everyone else in the family as well.

I thought about how sad it was that Benjamin was now gone and that Jeannie would never have the chance to reclaim those lost years. I wondered what she was feeling as people rose to the pulpit to eulogize her father. She sat expressionless. She was hardly mentioned. Did she hurt? Did she care? What had died inside of her?

WHILE IT SADDENED JUDY when her sister virtually disappeared, in some ways it was easier for Judy. She became the full-time daughter to her father, since he never heard from Jeannie anymore either. Judy took Benjamin to lunch at least once a week and enjoyed listening to his wisdom and insights. He always wore a jacket and tie, held his head high, kept his posture erect. People noticed Benjamin Moss.

"Daddy, you seem disturbed today. Is anything wrong?" said Judy, at Joey's, one of their favorite restaurants. Judy had begun to notice that her father was forgetting things and repeating himself, and she wondered if it was normal for one his age.

"It's that wife of mine. She's constantly bossing me around. I'm going to explode if she doesn't leave me be."

"Daddy, what is she doing?"

"Oh, it's everything. She's working on this damned country house in Massachusetts, and you'd think it was the most important thing in the world. She spends hours deliberating over the most insignificant things. The woman is insufferable."

Judy tended to agree, but was startled to hear her father speak with such discontent. Cynthia had begun to annoy Judy long ago, but she didn't think her father had minded Cynthia's eccentricities. The one that bothered Judy most was the slow and belabored way that Cynthia spoke every sentence, as if weighing the fate of the universe. *Spit it out already*, Judy thought more than once.

"Daddy, it's hard when you try to make a life with someone at this age. You're both very set in your ways. Cynthia is used to her life before you, and she doesn't seem willing to make accommodations now. You're going to have to get used to that. You knew what she was like before you married her."

"No, I really didn't. You don't know somebody like this until you live with them. How could I have known that her social calendar would be the most important thing in her life? I feel trapped in it. But I suppose you're right. I've made my bed. Now I must lie in it."

Soon Cynthia began to complain, too, saying that life with Benjamin was wearing her down. She would call Judy, ranting about his sleeplessness, and thus hers too, as well as his forgetfulness.

"Juuudy, you must speak with him," she said slowly one day on the phone. "You are the *only* one he will listen to . . . I'm worried about my health."

"I'll speak to him, Cynthia. But he's getting older and more forgetful. You're going to have to make allowances for him. He's not doing it on purpose. You're a much younger woman, and you knew that when you married him. There's only so much I can do."

"He's also drinking, which is making it worse. I will not have him embarrass me in front of my children and my friends. I'm not used to this kind of behavior in my house, Judy. Do you understand me?"

"Yes, Cynthia. But you have to understand that my father has limitations that are only going to get worse as he gets older."

"Well, then we are going to have to deal with that at the time."

When it became apparent that Benjamin's mental capacity was waning, Judy and Robert decided to meet with him to discuss his finances. Although he was in control of his faculties, Benjamin's memory loss was allowing bills to go unpaid and others to be paid two and three times. Benjamin, who had corresponded with Albert Einstein in the 1940s about the complexities of nuclear physics, was now unable to balance a checkbook. He had begun entering sweepstakes that he thought required him to buy subscriptions to magazines. Hundreds of magazines began piling up throughout the house that he still maintained as an office on the other side of town, separate from Cynthia's home, where he slept.

"Ben, you understand that you have appointed me power of attorney?" said Alan. "I want to explain the steps that are necessary to protect what you have worked for. Okay?"

"Yes, of course, Alan. You are my attorney and my son-in-law. And you do well at both. It makes sense that you should be the one."

"Are you sure you don't want Cynthia to do this, Daddy?" said Judy.

"My wife?" Benjamin answered, obviously surprised. "No, that wouldn't make any sense. She's not a lawyer. What does she know about the law? Our money is separate."

"And what about making decisions about your medical care, should someone ever need to do that?" asked Judy.

"Well, you're my daughter. You know my wishes in that regard. You should be the one to make those decisions."

Alan agreed to draw up a living will as well as the document appointing him power-of-attorney. It all seemed settled until months later when Cynthia called and asked for a lunch meeting at a French café not far from where she lived.

ALAN HUGGED HIS SON, Andrew, who had just finished eulogizing his grandfather, and stepped into the pulpit himself. He pulled at his shirt collar nervously. I was surprised to see him with his arm around Judy in the pew, since they had separated seven months before. As he began to talk about his deceased father-in-law, his affection and love for him were obvious. "I was like a son to Ben," said Alan. I wondered if he still regretted what had happened.

* * *

"BENJAMIN, ALAN IS STEALING your money. You must know this."

Cynthia's words felt like a punch in the stomach to Judy. Alan blanched, seemingly not able to believe the turn this seemingly innocuous lunch had taken. In response to Cynthia's request, they had met in a French café on the Upper East Side of Manhattan. Judy and Alan hadn't expected an ambush.

"Cynthia, is this why you have asked us to lunch?" Alan managed to blurt out. "To perpetuate this ridiculous lie to a man who cannot even comprehend what you are saying?"

"Benjamin, take out the paper in your breast pocket," said Cynthia, ignoring Alan.

"What paper?" said Benjamin. "I have no idea what you are talking about."

Cynthia reached across the table, knocking over the salt and pepper shakers with the sleeve of her pink Chanel jacket, and tapped the breast pocket of his jacket. "In here, we put it in here," she said, frustrated.

"I don't know what you're talking about," said Benjamin. "What money did Alan steal? Judy, do you know what she's talking about?"

"*Benjamin*," Cynthia practically screamed, "I know I put the paper in your breast pocket. Now take it out and show them."

Benjamin patted his chest and finally produced a piece of yellow, legal-sized paper.

"Is this what you're talking about?" he asked.

It was a paper that showed Benjamin's bank account numbers and the assets he possessed. He and Alan had gone to the safe deposit box together and had listed all the stock certificates, annuity certificates, securities, and bonds in Benjamin's possession. They had written down the value of each of the accounts and had found that Benjamin had more money than he knew. With Benjamin's permission, Alan had reduced the assets to avoid undue tax consequences.

"Benjamin, don't you see? Alan has stolen your money. All of these accounts have gone down, and he's given the money to his children and his family without ever consulting you or me." She glared at Alan. "I am his wife and I had a right to know what you were doing. You're a thief."

"Cynthia, you have no idea what you are saying . . ." protested Alan.

Judy gripped her stomach, no longer able to listen to the surreal conversation taking place. *Alan stole money? What was she talking about?* Unable to speak, Judy looked at her father, wondering if he believed any of what Cynthia was saying. The confusion on his face registered that he was clueless. Judy stood up and fled to the ladies room to the sound of Cynthia's slow drone, as she once again repeated for Alan her determined accusation.

"I LOVED HIM LIKE A FATHER," said Alan from the pulpit. "And he loved me like a son. I learned more from this man than any other human being. His loss in my life is a tremendous one."

He sat down in the pew next to Judy and squeezed her shoulder with his left hand. She rested her head on his shoulder. They didn't look like a separated couple. But Judy said that was always the problem. They did fine in public, but in private any intimate connection seemed to disappear.

* * *

Although Alan had tried to explain that, as specified in Benjamin's will, Alan had given the allowable distributions of money to Benjamin's daughters and grandchildren to prevent the money from being consumed by taxes after his death, Cynthia persisted in her accusations. She had secretly convinced Benjamin to sign over power of attorney to her and away from Alan. By then, Benjamin had been diagnosed with Alzheimer's and couldn't really grasp the significance of his actions. Judy blamed Alan for allowing it to happen, for not fighting hard enough for her. To Judy, it was one more failure on Alan's part to be there when she needed him.

It became difficult for Judy to even get out of bed. Nothing seemed to matter anymore. Cynthia had convinced her that Benjamin needed to be in a nursing home because she could no longer care for him at home. It was the hardest thing Judy had ever done. The morning they brought her father to the Hebrew Place nursing home, he looked like a lost, betrayed, and wounded man. *How could she have allowed this to happen to him?* Images of her mother, her sister, Alan, and now her unhappy father haunted Judy's dreams. Fears consumed her. Scheduled dinners with friends produced panic and dread. Grocery shopping was overwhelming. The thought of having to see clients and deal with their problems incapacitated her. Bed became her only sanctuary. And Alan seemed to notice none of it.

One evening, after a disastrous attempt to celebrate their wedding anniversary, Alan and Judy returned home. Judy had cried through most of the dinner, not really knowing why. It seemed crazy to her to be celebrating an anniversary of a marriage that contained little about which to rejoice. One more loss was staring her in the face.

"Let's get you into bed," said Alan. "You look tired. You'll feel better tomorrow."

The words seemed kind, something rare and bright. For Judy, perhaps a fleeting sign of hope. She went upstairs and changed her clothes and brushed her teeth. Trembling from the cold, she put on a heavy flannel nightgown and gray woolen socks and crawled into bed. Alan came in to check on her.

"Could you just lie down next to me?" asked Judy. "I need you to hold me. I'm such a mess."

"I really can't tonight," said Alan. "I have to prepare for a deposition tomorrow. I'll be downstairs."

"Can't you just lie down and hold me for just ten minutes?" pleaded Judy. "Just ten minutes?"

"I can't, Judy. I have to get this work done."

He moved toward her awkwardly, quickly kissed her forehead, and turned out the lights. She heard his footsteps going down the stairs as her tears soaked through her down pillow.

A few nights later, Judy was in bed when Alan came home from work. Rising, she put on a robe and walked slowly down the stairs. She asked him to take her to the hospital because she couldn't go on the way she was.

"There's no reason for you to go to a hospital," he said. "There's nothing wrong with you. Just go to bed and get some rest."

"Alan, that's all I've been doing is going to bed. Haven't you noticed that? I can't do this anymore. I need help. Please take me to the hospital. I can't drive myself."

"Judy, you just need some sun. Maybe a trip to Florida. That would make you feel better."

"*Fly* to Florida, when I can barely *walk* to the kitchen? Please help me," she begged.

Alan sat on the couch, silent, and looked at the floor. Judy managed to pull herself slowly up the stairs and crawled back into bed. When Alan came up later that night, she asked him to sleep in another room.

BY THE TIME OF BENJAMIN'S FUNERAL, Alan was sleeping in his own apartment while Judy still lived in the house that they had shared together. Alan had agreed to support her financially until she could figure out what came next. As I watched them sit together at Judy's father's funeral, her head upon Alan's shoulder, they looked more like friends than spouses. That was what Judy had always said, too. I wondered what she was feeling in that moment. So many losses: her husband and her father, just months apart; her mother and sister, some years earlier; her kids now on their own; even her spiritual dwelling, this temple, no longer a home, the spirituality her father had worked so hard to cultivate seemingly gone as well as the family pew in which she had sat her whole life, now occupied by Cynthia and her family. *What about Judy?* I wondered. What was there for her now?

"I'M TAKING A TALMUD CLASS," said Judy a few years before her father's death. "There's only a few women in the class with mostly men."

"Gee, you're a regular Yentl," I kidded.

It was obvious that she was searching, wanting more than her life was offering.

"Except I'm not studying to be a rabbi," she said. "We already have one in the family. I just want to learn more about my tradition. I'm enjoying connecting with my Jewish heritage. I'm thinking of taking a Hebrew class, too. Funny, it's all become so important to me this late in life."

"Yeah, but you grew up with it. Your father is this learned rabbi who wrote books about philosophy, theology, science. You lived in a house of learning your whole life."

"Yes, but it never really filtered down to me. I didn't get it then. I'm only starting to appreciate it now."

"Do you know why?" I asked.

"I think I'm finally realizing there has to be more to life than I've gotten up to this point. So much has been stripped away in the past few years. I need to know what's there for me now. Maybe I'm finally getting to the core. To God, perhaps, even though I don't know what that means."

Some months after he had been placed in a nursing home, Judy was cleaning out her father's house, attempting to sort through possessions her father and mother had accumulated for years. There was a small storage room in the basement that smelled of mildew. When she turned on the light, she noticed some boxes and files stacked on two shelves. She carted them upstairs and sat in the empty living room with the papers surrounding her. They were her father's writings, some from his stint in the Army, others written during his time as assistant rabbi in Richmond, still others composed when he was senior rabbi in Dubuque, Iowa. Articles he had written for professional journals and copies of play manuscripts that he had attempted were strewn at her feet. She began reading.

"I was overwhelmed by what was there," she said. "It was as if I was holding his whole life in my hands, everything that mattered to him. His sermons in the late nineteen forties and fifties about science and religion, humankind's origin, evolution, his strong anti–Vietnam positions in the sixties, his pleading for civil rights. His essence was really there in those writings, his goodness, what everyone saw in him.

"I realized that I'd spent years trying to hold on to the vision of my father under the golden dome of the temple, preaching, teaching, getting back what had been taken from him. Yet even though he was now ill and his mind was gone, the essence of the man was still there. He was connected to God, deeply connected, always talking about his trust in the 'Almighty.' And that's what I'll miss most when he's gone, his warmth, his deep commitment to his faith, and his love of life."

Judy began to organize the newspaper and magazine articles about her father into scrapbooks, documenting his career. But as she lovingly bound the books together, a deep awareness took hold: it was over.

"As I sat on that floor I knew what I had to do. I had to finally let go—of him, and everything else. Even though he hadn't died yet, it was time to look at the reality of what *was*, not what I wanted it to be, not what I hoped for. So much of my life had been built on this perfect image: the rabbi's daughter, the good mother, the faithful wife. But that had all been shattered. It was gone. But I was still here. Maybe it was finally time to come home to me."

After getting word of her father's death, the realization took hold even more profoundly.

"My father was dead. My marriage was over. My kids have their own lives. My sister is gone again. But I'm not. I don't know what's ahead, but I'm going to lean into it. I have so much life still in me. I want love and connectedness, and to be held again. I've never really had it. I need some joy."

AT THE END of Benjamin's funeral service, it was finally Judy's turn to take the pulpit. She was the last to speak. The rabbi's daughter. She seemed shaky on her feet as she stepped into the imposing wooden pulpit from which her father had preached for over thirty-five years. Avoiding looking out, she put on her glasses and, with a slight tremor in her hand, began to read from her prepared notes. I watched her family watching her. Cynthia straightened her skirt. Alan tilted his head to the right and locked his eyes on her. Jeannie, the sister, crossed her legs and looked at the floor, listening, but not wanting to appear to be. Judy's children, Andrew and Rebecca, sat next to their father, slight smiles, wet eyes. Oblivious to it all, Judy spoke softly, deliberately, finally her turn . . .

". . . As I watched my father struggle with his pain and disappointments, it was the conviction of his spirit, his steel strength of faith that anchored him. He believed that his Almighty God would gently lead him when and where he was supposed to go.

"It was simply luck that I had the privilege of being his daughter. I loved him very much. Many years ago, he ignited a spark in me, the gift of his ebullient spirit. That spark has since developed into an ember, and the ember has served as a light to guide me home. He leaves me now, but I'm stronger, imbued with his spirit, sowing the seeds of faith that he planted deep in my heart. He was truly my greatest gift."

IN THE PAST YEAR, two years since the death of her father, Judy has suffered more than she could have ever imagined possible. She didn't think it could get worse than the death of her father, but it did. After attacks of acute colitis, which the doctors claimed were stress-related, her colon was removed in emergency surgery that left her debilitated for months. She has suffered the indignity of a reversible colostomy, the breakup of a loving relationship that had, for a time, given her some hope again, and the emotional setback of the realization that she is ultimately alone in the world—despite the well-meaning intentions of her children and friends. While she is now on the road to recovery, sometimes the road just seems too long.

"I miss so much," she says. "Even though Alan and my children stood by me in the illness, it was different because everything has changed. We're all changed now, and I have to accept that. There's no going back to before. When I was sick, I wanted my father there to comfort me, to tell me everything would be all right, just as he always had, but he's no longer here. No one is here in quite the same way. Not their fault, just the way it is.

"But a part of me will never give up hope that there's a place for me again. I think some of it has to do with being a Jew. We've been through so much as a people, but we've survived. Even when we were almost snuffed out, a flame flickered and grew again. That's me. That spark in me that I said my father gave me, I guess. Flickering, but not going out. And even though I do feel a bit lost these days, I know I'm going to be found. Someone is going to find me."

✕✕✕ CHAPTER FIVE ✕✕✕

Jailhouse to Jesus

EVERY ONCE IN A WHILE I feel I'm in a place where I don't belong. Like the time I got lost driving in a rough area of Harlem at 1 a.m. on a street where police were raiding a crack house. Or when I stumbled into a post–Emmy Award party in Los Angeles and found myself chowing down with the cast of *Friends*. The State Correctional Institution at Graterford had that kind of feel to it— foreign turf. Built in 1929, thirty-one miles west of Philadelphia, it is Pennsylvania's largest maximum-security prison.

As I drove down the long entranceway, I could have been entering the sanctuary of a blueblood's mansion nestled in the hills of suburban Pennsylvania. Newly planted trees tethered to support sticks with red rubber rings lined the serpentine road through the lush green acres, striking me as a forced symbol that shouted "new life up ahead." But a mile or so down the road loomed a large concrete wall with watchtowers that housed armed guards, putting the kibosh on any Easter-themed reverie.

After parking my car in the farthest lot, designated "Visitor's Parking," I walked slowly toward the intimidating monolith while buses pulled up to the entrance and dispensed mostly women, the majority of them black, with children in tow. I followed them through the front door and was bombarded with a cacophony of noise as security personnel shouted instructions and chatting visitors sprawled out on wooden benches like bored high school students.

Edward W. Schenck III (aka EM 3674—his prison ID number) had written to me after reading my book *God Underneath*, and his letter, well written and highly articulate, had touched and intrigued me. His story had struck me as an apt contribution to this book, and so, after enduring a Byzantine process of clearance, I was approved to come to the prison to interview him.

Having been warned to come early, I got lost on some back roads and arrived just as visiting hours were beginning. I had no idea of the dizzying procedure for visiting an inmate. The few times I had been in a jail before were to visit parishioners who were being held temporarily in county jails on minor charges. But this was the Big House, and I was unprepared.

With people staring at me as if I'd wandered into the wrong movie, I took a seat on the benches with the other visitors. Although Saturday was considered a busy visiting day, I was surprised that there were less than one hundred visitors for a jail that houses over four thousand inmates. The woman next to me was fingering a metal square that looked like a dog tag with a number impressed on it. I noticed the woman across from me had one, too.

"Do I need one of those?" I asked, somewhat hesitantly, nodding at the metal square while fingering my priestly Roman collar that had begun to choke me.

"You sure do, Reverend," said the woman seated next to me. She was a large African-American woman with a sleeveless, orange blouse and matching headband that encircled her braided magenta hair. "Unless of course you want to sit on this bench all afternoon." She smiled at the woman seated across from her who had a small boy straddled between her legs. There was no hiding that this was my first time.

I walked to the guard manning the check-in desk. "Excuse me, I need a tag," I said.

"A what?" he said, without looking up at me from the paper he was writing on.

"A visitor's tag," I said. "A number."

He pointed to tags piled on a long stick, like horseshoes. I took one, number forty-four, just as he called out number one. The lucky woman showed him an approved ID (driver's license) and then had her hand stamped with yellow goo that was invisible on the skin. She then got in another line to "sign in" and wait for her visitor's pass to be approved and her inmate located. And so it went. By the time a bored-looking guard called out, "Edward Schenck" and handed me a pass, I had waited an hour and fifteen minutes, time well spent because I had to run my wallet and briefcase back to the car after being told that no money or personal effects were permitted inside, and then wait in another line to get change from "Charlie the Change Man" to purchase tokens for food and drink available once inside the visiting room. When I finally walked through the security door, it was like being admitted to an exclusive club where clipboard-armed, Nazi-like bouncers decide who gets in. I missed the velvet rope and spotlights.

"What's that?" a rotund female guard said to me, as she pointed to the stack of blank white paper in my hand. (I had been instructed to not bring a spiral notebook, since prisoners could unravel the spiral wire and use it as a weapon to hurt themselves or somebody else. Were pointy pens less effective? I had wondered. I also learned later that metal baseball bats are available in the exercise yard and that razors are sold in the prison commissary. So much for any reasonable logic.)

"Just paper," I said, as innocuously as I could.

"For what?" she said, in seemingly the nastiest voice *she* could.

"To write on. I'm going to be doing an interview, and I need to write."

"Can't bring it in," she said, shaking her head horizontally with more fervor than necessary.

"But I have to," I said. "It's my whole purpose for coming here. I can't do an interview without taking notes." I felt like adding, "Duh."

Putting one hand on her hip, she walked to the phone and said, "Charlie, the Reverend here wants to bring papers and pens in, but I don't see any clearance on the sheet for that . . . Uh-huh. All right."

She came back to me and said, "A few sheets and one pen."

"But, I'll need more than that. I'm going to be in there the whole day."

"Sorry, you'll have to make do," she said, crossing her linebacker arms.

"Twenty sheets," I bargained. "I'll write on both sides, though I hadn't planned to do that."

"Fifteen," she said, "Though *I* hadn't planned to *allow* that. Write small." Then turning to another female guard, she said, "Lonetta, check through these papers and make sure they're clear. Have a good one, Rev. Next."

I deposited the other paper and the extra pens that I had conscientiously brought along in a holding bin and walked through a metal detector that, thankfully, remained silent. Then

I put my hand under an infrared light that transformed the invisible yellow goo into a glowing purple lesion. Finally receiving clearance from the silent nod of a guard buffing her nails, I walked tentatively down a staircase to the visiting room.

When I opened the door, the scene was chaotic. Inmates in brown jumpsuits were everywhere, interspersed with mostly female visitors, some kids carting toys, and crying babies. The sound was almost deafening. A few couples were holding each other on the long padded couches that looked like the ones in airport terminals. One couple was kissing rather passionately, seemingly ignoring the "no lewd behavior" signs posted around the room, and another was crying into each other's sleeves. Scanning the room, I hoped to connect with someone who looked like he was expecting me. Three guards surveying the crowd like judges on a monitoring bench sat in a wooden pen that was raised two feet off the floor. Other guards were milling through the fluid crowd of reunited relations. Then I saw a young man coming toward me.

"Father Edward?" he said, a bit hesitantly.

"Yes, Ed, how are you?" We shook hands. He was about five feet eight inches tall, maybe a hundred forty pounds, and wore glasses. He seemed a bit nervous, not looking me directly in the eyes.

"I've arranged for us to be able to use one of those rooms back there," he said, pointing to three glassed-in cubicles in the rear of the visiting room. "They're usually used to meet with attorneys, but I got clearance for us to use one for our interview."

"That's great," I said, relieved, not being able to imagine conversing in the reverberating din.

We walked into the room and closed the door. It was like entering another reality—sudden quiet in the midst of the frenetic activity swirling around us, like a movie abruptly losing its soundtrack. It was to be our haven for the next six hours.

We sat in wooden chairs at a desk in the five-by-eight-foot room. A female guard sat on a tall barstool chair outside the door, occasionally turning around suspiciously to make sure we weren't snorting lines or changing clothes, I guess.

"So, we finally meet in person," I said. "Thanks for agreeing to this."

"No, thank *you*, Father Edward. I appreciate the opportunity to be helpful. Maybe someone else can learn from or even be inspired by my story. That's what it's all about, right? Some good has to come from this horror show."

He was wiry and not quite at ease, like he had imbibed too much coffee at breakfast (though I learned later that green tea and Vioxx taken for back pain were the morning stimulants). His short-cropped brown hair was gelled and pushed forward. I noticed that one of his eyes turned slightly, making it difficult to tell if he was looking at me straight on. But as he began to speak, the superficialities faded, for I soon realized that he was one of the brightest, most articulate persons I had ever met.

EDWARD SCHENCK WAS BORN in Allentown, Pennsylvania, in 1978, but grew up in Nazareth, Pennsylvania, which is right next to Bethlehem. "Yeah, I guess the Jesus thing was in the genes from the start," he says, smiling. He is the only child of Barbara and Edward Jr., wherein lies its own mini-opera.

"I was always a mama's boy," he says. "She was at home all the time and took care of the books for my father's fire protection company. She was ironfisted and overprotective, but I loved her fiercely."

Ed's father ran the business from the family's well-appointed three-story farmhouse, in which everyone had an office, even young Ed.

"I was really big into computers as a child," he says. "I was always on them. So, I'd be working in my office at eleven years old, and my father would be in his. When it was time to eat, my mother would buzz the intercom in my office and say, 'E.J., dinner is ready.' I was extension twelve. I'd close up my desk and go to dinner."

When Ed was thirteen, his mother, Barbara, got sick with lymphoma, a tragic blow to the son who had always depended on her to buffer the shaky relationship he had with his father. A resolute health food enthusiast, she refused to go to a doctor for treatment and instead began treating herself with herbs. But by the time she was finally admitted to the hospital, the disease was well advanced, and Ed remembers a painful three-month ordeal of watching her die. On that fateful day he began feeling uneasy in Spanish class.

"I went to the school nurse and told her I didn't feel well," he says. "My father came and took me to the hospital. My mother's skin felt like rubber, and she looked gray. I started bawling. I remember our veterinarian was there, trying to distract me by asking me how our five horses were doing, but I couldn't have cared less at that moment.

"I went home and started a wood fire in the stove in my mother's favorite room, even though it was June second. Guess I needed her warmth. When a nurse called a few hours later to say that she had died, for some reason I didn't cry. I realized that now I was left totally alone with my father, and that I had to stay strong or it was gonna be bad. When people started coming to the house to offer condolences, I went downstairs and installed a new sound card I'd just gotten for my computer."

When the tensions and conflicts between Ed and his father became insurmountable, Ed was convinced he needed to "get the hell out of there."

Ed's aunt, Sue, who became secretary for the business and began running the household, made things tolerable for a bit longer.

"At first, Aunt Sue and I clashed," says Ed, "because I viewed her as a threat, someone trying to be my mom. But we eventually became close friends, and she *was* like another mother to me. But even that wasn't enough. I still needed to move out."

At sixteen, Ed went to live with a family friend; one year later, even though he was in honors classes and had been classified as "mentally gifted," he dropped out of school. A job at Circuit City selling "advanced consumer electronics" had nurtured a gift for helping people solve their electronic problems, a challenge that engaged him more than the puerile world of high school. A job at Xedex Communications in Staten Island followed, with Ed making the daily hour-and-fifteen-minute commute each way from Allentown. Known as "the beeper hospital," the office was an ideal environment for Ed to revel in his fascination with electronics and to learn how lucrative computer transactions could be. It was here that his criminal activity took flight.

He began laser-printing fraudulent checks with highly sophisticated computer software, depositing the checks in fake accounts, opened via the Internet, and then removing the cash through electronic transfers. It was good while it lasted, but the state police showed up one day with search warrants and confiscated Ed's computers. He fled in a Mustang that he had purchased by falsifying the application to approve the lease. Slidell, Louisiana, the home of his grandfather, seemed as good a destination as any.

Ed pulled up to the large house with its lush, tropical gardens after having used cash and fraudulent checks to pay for stays in Virginia and Georgia. His Macy's credit card had also provided him with "a new wardrobe and enough cologne and hair products to last for a few months." His grandfather greeted him in the driveway.

"Look, I know you're in trouble, E.J.," his grandfather said. "Just don't tell me what kind of trouble. Better I don't know. You can stay here for as long as you want, for as long as you can. But, please, I don't want any trouble down here."

Two weeks later, trouble is just what he got. Ed was tooling down a country road in his freshly detailed Mustang not far from his grandfather's house. He sped through a stoplight, smoking the tires, and saw police lights flashing in his rearview mirror. He pulled over. A burly sheriff sidled up to the driver's window.

"License and registration," said the sheriff.

Ed hesitated. The police had confiscated his driver's license in Pennsylvania during his apartment search before he fled.

"Um . . . I don't have it with me, officer," said Ed. "I've left it at home."

"What's your name, son?"

"Edward."

"Edward *what*?" said the sheriff impatiently.

Ed hesitated again. If he told him, the sheriff could run a search on the name and see that Ed was wanted. By now the charges had been upped to grand larceny and bank robbery.

"Schenck," said Ed, hoping the sheriff would ask him to spell it so he could give an incorrect spelling, perhaps thwarting the search.

"Schenck? Hey, don't I know your grandfather?" the sheriff said, seemingly distracted. "Doesn't he live over on Bradley Drive?"

"Yes," said Ed, relieved.

"Let's go over there," said the sheriff. "We'll see what your grandfather has to say."

His grandfather covered for Ed, asking the sheriff to give him a break, but by the time the sheriff left, it was clear that Ed had to leave, too.

"E.J., you're going to have to go," his grandfather said. "They'll be back once they run a search. If you stay here, they'll get you."

"I know," said Ed. "I just don't know where to go."

"I'll take you over the border to Alabama," said his grandfather. "Mobile's a nice town. You can stay there for a while. I think you'll be safe."

Although Ed checked into one of the finest hotels in Mobile, he was soon bored there, missing connections with anyone familiar. He remembered that a high school friend, Tim, had a brother, Frank, a marine who lived in Pensacola, a short drive from Mobile. The only problem was that Frank loathed Ed because he thought that Ed had been a bad influence on Tim in high school. But while Frank may have despised him, Ed remembered that Frank did have one passion—Mustangs. And Ed had the crème de la crème, a black Motorsport Limited Edition, which he had freshly detailed before heading to Pensacola.

Ed called Frank on his trendy black Startac cell phone once he arrived in Pensacola.

"Frank, how are you? E.J. here. I'm in town."

"E.J.? What the hell are you calling me for? Look, you little runt, do not call here. I have nothing to say to you." Frank hung up the phone. Ed called back.

"Now, c'mon, Frank. It's time to bury the hatchet. Let me come over and say hi."

"E.J., if you come over here, I will bury *you*. Do you hear me? *I will kill you*. I'm warning you. Stay away from here."

By this time, E.J. was pulling into Frank's condo complex.

"Frank, c'mon. Look, just ten minutes. For old times' sake. I have something I want to show you."

"E.J., I'm warning you."

Ed was now in the parking lot, a few hundred feet from Frank, who stood on the porch of his condo on his cordless phone. The Mustang gleamed like buffed onyx under the hot Florida sun.

Ed heard Frank mutter, "Sweet car," into the phone, though Frank didn't yet realize that Ed was the driver.

"Isn't it?" Ed shot back, as he beeped the horn at the marine, who now stood only twenty feet away.

"Why, you little shit," said Frank, clicking off the phone and bolting for the car.

He pushed Ed out of the driver's seat and got behind the wheel, excited as a kid on Christmas morning. Driving the car down the streets of Pensacola, Frank seemed less concerned with the past and more interested in the turbo-engine horsepower. The hatchet had been buried without any blood being shed.

Ed convinced Frank that New Orleans at Mardi Gras time would be a great idea. His grandfather had spoken about how much fun it was and, coincidentally, the festival had just gotten under way. Frank invited some Marine and Navy buddies to join them, and they all checked in to two rooms at the Chateau Lemoyne, one of the swankiest hotels in the French Quarter, costing Ed, who paid for everyone, three thousand dollars for five nights.

"I really enjoyed Mardi Gras," says Ed. "I met a lot of neat people. I remember we were in TGI Friday's one night drinking Bourbon Street Iced Teas, and I don't hold my liquor too well. There was a big black woman there, Jackie, and I began talking to her, kind of pouring my heart out to her. She said I had a 'little-boy-lost look' about me. It occurred to me that night that she was right. I was somehow lost, but I didn't know how to get found."

When the Mardi Gras revelers returned to Pensacola, Ed thought it wise to lay low for a while, so he rented a two-bedroom townhouse not far from Frank's condo complex. Unbeknownst to Ed, when he applied for the townhouse rental, the office ran a credit check and an inquiry was launched. Ed and Frank were lounging around on a hot summer's day watching *The Jerry Springer Show* when four sheriffs appeared, two at the front door and two at the back, with guns drawn. They arrested Ed and charged him with twelve counts of forgery and fraud. He was held for two months in jail in Florida before being transferred to Lehigh County Prison back in Allentown, Pennsylvania, where he began serving a nine to twenty-three-month sentence.

While in Lehigh County Prison, Ed met three people who made an impact: Leo, also known as "Leona," a six-foot-four black transvestite; Mike, a Health Bureau worker whom Ed describes as "my gay dad"; and Ellen, a lesbian guard who took a special liking to Ed. This triumvirate was key to Ed finally "coming out" and admitting that he, too, was gay.

"I had long ago admitted it to myself," he says, "but I hadn't been comfortable enough with it to be out to my family and friends. I saw that these three people had somehow made peace with who they were, and it made me think that maybe I could, too."

One late-night conversation with Leona, whom Ed described as "Aunt Jemima on steroids," was the defining push Ed needed. He was visiting Leona in her cell, which she had made as comfortable as is permitted in jail, even taping colored construction paper on the light fixtures to filter the harsh, unflattering fluorescent light. Softening colored pencils with hot water, she used them as lipstick and eyeliner. Think *Kiss of the Spider Woman*.

"Sugar, you are just going to have to get over yourself," said Leona, tousling her contraband hair extensions and sipping a cup of green tea. "It's time for you to come out into the light, child. Stop hiding in those long shadows."

"But, Leona, I don't know if I can," said Ed. "I've heard what they do to young men in prison. If they know I'm gay, I could be in even more trouble."

"Oh, and you think they don't know, sweetie pie? We had you pegged as a sister soon as you wiggled your little white boy ass in here. It's not *Oz* in here, you know. Don't believe everything you see on the TV. It's not *us* you have to worry about. It's living the lie. I'll protect you on the block, don't you worry none about that. You be my little sister. But I don't want no little sister who don't know who she is. So you find out, sugarplum."

"It was kinda like *Will and Grace* meets *Jailhouse Rock*," says Ed, smiling. "And so I came out, and then *got* out, of prison, that is. It was February, 1998, and Aunt Sue had come down with breast cancer. She had kept in touch with me through visits, letters, and phone calls, and when I was released, she was in Mexico undergoing some radical cancer treatment. When she got off the plane after coming home, I couldn't believe it was the same woman who used to let her hair fly loose as we raced down the highway in my Mustang screaming, 'I feel young again!' Now she was in a wheelchair looking so thin and jaundiced.

"I moved in with her, and we began homeopathic hospice care. I wasn't too keen on the natural approach, after seeing what'd happened to my mother, but it made Aunt Sue happy. We spent a lot of time just talking, and I realized that she wasn't afraid to die, which really surprised me. She had this indescribable inner peace. She talked of 'mustard seeds and mountains,' which, to someone as irreligious as me, meant very little. I thought mustard seeds were part of her therapy or something.

"When Aunt Sue died, I fell apart. Any inkling of faith I had in a loving God was gone. All I could think was, 'What kind of a cruel God makes a kid go through this twice?' I became bitter and angry at the world. It didn't take long before I landed back in jail."

Ed was rearrested on fugitive charges from New Jersey. Apparently, a bad check he had passed before going to prison the first time caught up with him. While speeding on Route 22 in Pennsylvania, he was stopped by a state trooper. When the trooper ran Ed's info, the warrant popped up, and he was locked up for another year.

When he finally got out of prison again, out of necessity he moved in with his father and his father's new wife, Bonnie. But his real family became Diane, who had been his Aunt Sue's best friend, and her two daughters, Sarah and Shaina, sixteen-year-old twins who became like Ed's sisters.

"It was almost as if Sue left me another family," Ed says. "I had such fun with my new sisters. I remember going with Sarah to IKEA and looking for these obscenely named Swedish home furnishings. I've never laughed so hard. We walked out of there with *Dick* boxes, *Seks* lamps, and *Volva* chairs. You can't make this stuff up.

"Oh, and I finally began dating some guys through online hookups. But it wasn't pretty. I started hanging out with the wrong kinds of people again, people into money and material things. I began wanting what they had in order to gain their acceptance. It wasn't long before I was working my computer magic again. I'd done a lot of thinking in jail about where I'd gone wrong, meaning why I'd gotten caught. I thought I was smart enough to not let that happen again."

So in addition to making money doing freelance photography, capitalizing on a talent he had cultivated in high school, Ed also began to play with money on computers again, making fraudulent intrastate transfers of funds. For example, he purchased ten Gateway computers and had them sent to a Mail Boxes Etc. station in Minnesota. Then he called the postal service office and asked them to hold the computers until his "business" had relocated there in a few weeks. A few days later, he called back and had the computers sent by overnight FedEx to another Mail Boxes Etc. station in another state. He did that two more times, until the computers were virtually untraceable; then he collected them and sold them at a profit on eBay.

By this time he had graduated from Mustangs to Jettas. "Is there anything more cool than a well-made German car?" he says. In August of 1999, while driving down the highway in his midnight-blue Jetta, he hit a mammoth rain-grate hole in the highway that had been left open by a grossly negligent construction worker. The jolt catapulted him into the steering wheel and windshield as the car crashed into a concrete barrier. He was rushed to Saint Luke's Hospital, the same hospital in which his mother had died, where he was admitted to the trauma ward with a damaged spleen and liver. On regaining consciousness in the ICU, he realized that not only was it the same hospital, but the same *room* in which his mother had died. Despite being given ten milligrams of Valium, he was restless, thrashing in the bed, asking the nurses to get him out of there. A familiar face appeared at his bedside, one of the nurses who had cared for his mother. She recognized him immediately and realized why he was so agitated.

"Oh my God," she said, "move him out of here, now!"

In addition to recuperating from the spinal damage he had suffered, Ed's hospital stay also became a time to reassess his life, which had almost been taken from him. He decided he had to begin living differently. He vowed that, once he got out of the hospital, he'd stop committing crimes and hopefully make his deceased mother and aunt proud of him.

Ed did stop committing crimes after his release, but the damage had been done. One rainy day, only a month after he had been released from the hospital, two policemen showed up at the front door with a warrant for his arrest. Ed's pecuniary computer shenanigans had once again landed him in handcuffs. But this time it was more serious, because federal charges were also pending in his defrauding of two companies and UPS.

"I was sitting in the dayroom in jail one evening feeling pretty depressed," says Ed. "I couldn't believe I was back inside again. I noticed a group at a table on the side and saw a guy I'd become friendly with in the group. When he told me they were conducting a Bible study, I rolled my eyes and wanted to back away, but I couldn't for some strange reason. Instead, I sat down and listened. I was hooked immediately and started attending Bible study regularly. I drank it in like a sponge.

"Then, during one of the sessions Reverend Archer mentioned the faith of a mustard seed being able to move mountains. I couldn't believe it. A lightbulb came on, and I remembered Aunt Sue's words and the quote on her gravestone about mustard seeds and mountains. I was so excited. It was as if Aunt Sue and I had this secret language or inside joke. I suddenly knew what she was trying to tell me. But still, I didn't know what direction to go in."

There was a Catholic chaplain, Father Mike, who used to come on Saturday nights to talk with the inmates. He was a big Irish guy but spoke Spanish, and he became a favorite of many of the Latino prisoners. Ed asked to see him.

"So, Father, tell me," said Ed, as he leaned forward in his chair, "how come you guys think I'm going to burn in hell for being gay?" Ed was testing the waters, almost wanting the priest to react badly so that Ed could scratch Catholicism from his investigative list. He awaited the "hellfire and brimstone" speech, but it never came.

"I *don't* think you're going to hell," the priest said simply. "Love the sinner, hate the sin. God loves you just as you are."

Ed was nonplussed by the response. He had expected stones and got roses instead.

"Where is your church, Father?" he asked.

"In Hazleton," said Father Mike.

"You don't by any chance know the Mancuso family, do you?" said Ed. He had met a guy online, Peter Mancuso, who had mentioned that his mom was a devout Catholic, and that he had found solace in the Church despite his homosexuality. Ed remembered that Peter had said he went to a Catholic church in Hazelton.

"I sure do know the family," said the priest.

"That's so weird," said Ed. "Do they have a son, Peter?"

"Yeah, he's about your age."

"I can't believe this," said Ed. "I met Peter online, but what's even stranger is that as we're chatting, I find out that he was a guard in a prison I was in. He was actually *in* my cell once. And now you tell me that you know him. I mean, what are the chances of that?"

Ed saw it as a sign and began his studies to become a Catholic. Father Mike answered Ed's questions, taught him about Jesus, gave him books to read, like *The Complete Idiot's Guide to Understanding Catholicism*, and comforted him when he felt he couldn't get through another day of prison life. And Father Mike told Ed something he never forgot: "Ed, I don't know why you are on this unique path. But God has a reason for it. I believe that." It was the first time Ed had ever considered the possibility that there could be some "divine plan" to his dodgy, circuitous path.

When he was finally sentenced to the State Correctional Institution at Camp Hill, Pennsylvania, Ed pasted a Scripture quote on the inside of the Bible that he brought along: "Amen, I say to you. If you have faith the size of a mustard seed, you will say to this mountain, 'Move from here to there,' and it will move. Nothing will be impossible for you" (Matthew 17:20).

Although Camp Hill was supposed to be only a "holding prison" for Ed until he was medically and psychologically tested and classified, he wound up staying and attended his first Catholic Mass there. When he entered the chapel, Father Allen was saying the Mass and preaching on the gospel of the Wedding Feast at Cana, from John. The elderly priest was eloquent and funny.

"What kind of a man turns perfectly good water into wine?" the priest asked rhetorically. "But not just wine, the best Chianti in Galilee. I'll tell you what kind of man, a man who knows how to party. That's who we are. A people who know how to party."

Ed became even more convinced that this was the religion for him.

"I somehow ended up getting a pass to attend RCIA [Rite of Christian Initiation for Adults] classes, though I don't ever remember requesting it. It struck me that my being a captive audience probably wasn't just a coincidence. God knew I'd never commit to these courses on the outside, but in here was a different story.

"So I went through the RCIA, and on April 14, 2001, I was confirmed and took 'Basil' as my confirmation name. I didn't know what name to pick, so I got this book on saints and looked up what saint's feast day was on my birthday. And for March 22, it said 'Saint Basil.' After taking his name I learned that there was a Saint Basil of Russia who allegedly threw rocks at the merchants who defrauded the people. As soon as I read that, I knew I'd chosen the right name.

"My Easter Vigil confirmation was such a beautiful service. By the time we got to the Litany of the Saints, I was bawling my eyes out. I knew I was finally home."

What Ed didn't realize was that "home" isn't necessarily always a hospitable place. During his RCIA classes he had met Michael, a handsome inmate who assisted Deacon Lorry in the instructions and chapel duties. Michael was a Jewish convert to Catholicism, whom Ed befriended and eventually told that he was gay. Michael was supportive, almost like an older brother, and influential in getting Ed kept at Camp Hill after his medical exams and classifications. Michael had taught Ed much of the RCIA material and had counseled him on how to stay out of trouble while in prison. As their friendship grew, so did Ed's love of his newfound faith. He read the Bible assiduously, marveling at the new world he was discovering. The bump in the road ahead couldn't have been more unanticipated.

It was June, and Ed was alone with Michael in the chapel. Michael was acting a bit strange, more playful than usual. "Touchy and lewd," is the way Ed described the behavior. Michael pulled Ed to the side and opened his pants, exposing himself to Ed.

"This is what you want," said Michael in a tone of voice that Ed had never heard him use before. "It's what you've wanted since we met."

"Michael, cut it out," said Ed, suddenly nervous. "Put it away. We're going to get in trouble. Let's go."

But Michael had other ideas. He pushed Ed's head down to his crotch and held him there, forcing him to perform oral sex. Ed was shaking the whole time, feeling as though he was going to throw up, sure that someone was going to walk in and find them. When Michael finally released him, Ed ran and took a shower and popped some muscle relaxers that had been approved medication as a result of his car accident. He slept fitfully that night, knowing that everything had changed. He could never be comfortable in that chapel again, especially if Michael was there.

Their friendship deteriorated rapidly. Ed couldn't look at Michael the same way, even though Michael tried to pretend that nothing had happened. Michael started to resent Ed's aloofness and began making threats, especially during yard time. Ed decided he had to go to Deacon Lorry, Michael's supervisor, and tell him what had happened. It was the only way to stop what appeared to be a dangerously escalating situation.

"Lorry, Michael sexually assaulted me in the chapel," Ed said hesitantly, not being able to bring himself to look at Lorry.

"You're lying," said Lorry. "You can't even look at me when you say that. Michael is a good kid. He'd never do anything like that. You've had the hots for him since you got here. What happened, did he rebuff your advances?"

Ed couldn't believe that he wasn't even getting a hearing. He left dismayed, wondering what kind of test this was to his new-found faith. He went to Mass that Sunday, after prearranging with Father Forrey, one of his favorite priests, to speak to him afterward. Perhaps the priest would have some suggestion on how to handle the situation. As Ed walked to the confessional after Mass, Deacon Lorry stood in his way.

"Where are you going?" said Lorry.

"I'm going to confession," said Ed.

"No, you're not," said Lorry. "Leave now, or I'll have you thrown out."

"Deacon, are you denying me the sacrament of reconciliation that is my right as a Catholic?" said Ed.

"You don't want to go to confession. You just want to keep spreading your vicious lies and cause trouble. Now, get out of here, I said."

Ed left the chapel and never went back. It was the last Mass he attended at Camp Hill. He began praying his "own Mass" in the solitude of his cell, using the Bible, *The Word Among Us*, and his *Magnificat Prayer Guide* as his resources. Fall had arrived and the Ordinary Time readings brought him peace not found anywhere else.

On September 11, 2001, Ed remembers waking to the news reports on the radio about the World Trade Center attack. "I couldn't believe what I was hearing. But that night, something else happened that I couldn't believe. U.S. Marshals unexpectedly came to retrieve me for a federal investigation and took me to the Federal Detention Center in Philadelphia. I began wondering if my faith was in vain and if my beliefs were just a crock. I mean, here I was supposed to be going home, and now they're bringing this new case. I became so angry with God."

While in Philadelphia at the Federal Detention Center, Ed met yet another priest, Father Daniel Barry, a funny and lighthearted Jesuit chaplain. Once again Ed found himself "spilling [his] guts to a priest in hopes of an answer." But Father Barry was in no mood for Ed's self-pity.

"Look, son," said the priest. "The World Trade Center just blew up and you're worried about your little problems. How can you possibly lose your faith over the small stuff? What about those people killed and their families? That's the stuff of a faith crisis. Pull yourself together. You'll get through this. It'll be okay."

"I don't know why," says Ed, "but I knew he was right. I think my little trip to Club Fed was a way for God to get me away from my problems at Camp Hill and give me time to contemplate what really mattered. I realized that I was making Michael more important than Jesus. I was so distraught over losing Michael as a friend, but what if I lost Jesus? I reevaluated my priorities. Instead of trusting the world, I decided to trust God. I left that place with my faith back on track."

There would be other tests along the way, however. When Ed was sent back to Camp Hill, the situation with Michael hadn't changed. One night an intelligence team officer came to Ed's cell and asked him to tell him what had happened with Michael. Rumor of the incident had apparently made the rounds. Ed gave him a full statement after being told that Deacon Lorry had never even reported the incident, something he was required to do by prison policy. A few days later Ed was called to see his parole agent.

"You're going home next week," said the agent.

"What?" said Ed. "You're kidding. But what about the Feds?"

"Who knows? Maybe they're not charging you. Sign these papers. You'll probably be out next week."

Ed was ecstatic. He returned to his cell and read psalms of praise, believing that God could indeed fling open jailhouse cells, just as He had done for Saint Paul in the Scriptures.

Later that day, however, four guards and a lieutenant came to Ed's cell and handcuffed him.

"Back out of the cell!" one of them ordered. "And no sudden movements."

"What's happening?" Ed asked.

"You're going to the hole," the guard responded.

"For what?" said Ed.

"While your *allegations* are being investigated."

They kept Ed in the restricted housing unit for three days before releasing him to be questioned again and to make a statement on tape. Then they asked if he'd be willing to take a polygraph test.

"But why should *I* be the one to have to take it?" said Ed. "Why not the deacon, why not Michael? Those tests aren't always reliable anyway."

"Look, if you want to clear yourself, this is the best way," the security captain said. "Until then, your parole is on hold."

Ed reluctantly agreed to the polygraph exam, during which he was asked four relevant questions and six irrelevant ones. They were asked in ambiguous ways, almost suggesting there could be two ways of answering. In addition, due to the stress, Ed's asthma kicked up during the exam, and he took his inhalation medicine while taking the polygraph, something he didn't know could seriously compromise the test results because of the erratic increase in his blood pressure. He failed the polygraph and was sent back to the hole for sixty days for "lying to staff."

"In retrospect," Ed says, "it was the most spiritual experience I had, because everything had been stripped away this time, but I didn't lose faith. I read the Scriptures and prayed the Psalms, whatever ones fit my mood. I had to put up with the Chihuahua-sized roaches and mice in the hole, and the guards calling me a faggot as they threw the awful food in the door at me, but it didn't break me. Something had shifted. God was in that hole with me."

On his third appeal to the authorities at the Department of Corrections in Harrisburg to have the polygraph results thrown out, Ed received a letter from the secretary of corrections, a most unusual occurrence.

"It would be like you getting a letter from the pope," he says.

The secretary wrote that, as a result of reviewing the case, he was throwing out the polygraph results, determining that "the misconduct charge is rescinded without prejudice." It was an amazing turnaround.

Ed was transferred to the state penitentiary in Dallas, Pennsylvania, but despite his being exonerated of the misconduct charge in August of 2002, they refused to grant his parole back. The board interview he finally got in March of 2003 was grueling, due in part to the examiner's penchant for demeaning inmates, not an uncommon practice in the system. Ed got berated with questions like, "Why did a scumbag like you commit such crimes? Why are you now using religion as a crutch? How could a homo like you be sexually assaulted anyway?" The last question betrayed the belief that "no" doesn't really mean "no" when the victim is gay. Ed had had enough.

"Look," he said, "do you give this much hassle to child rapists and murderers? I had already been paroled, and a staff member lied about my misconduct. I won my case and was exonerated. Case closed."

This perspicacious and bold response seemed to impress the examiner. He began asking about Ed's various accomplishments while in prison: his tutoring, his editing of the *The N-Side Voice*, the prisoners' newsmagazine, and his Catholic ministries of lectoring, catechesis, and evangelization. By this time Ed had also become involved in the Secular Franciscan Order and spoke of his newfound vocation with heartfelt fervor.

"I'd been told that I could never have a religious vocation because I was a criminal. Told that by a prison chaplain, no less. But the Franciscans have received me like a brother and have supported me. Their charism is to respect all people and creatures, and they live by that charism. I'm testimony to that. I only hope that I get the chance to use my talents for good under the guidance of the Spirit through my order."

The examiner was silent for a few moments. Then he finally said, "You should be good to go. I think it's great what you've done, and you have a fine support of religious people around you."

Three weeks later the green-sheet parole plan/decision arrived. Ed was paroled, based on acceptance of responsibility, excellent adjustment and conduct, and the recommendations of the staff at Dallas. But his saga was still not over, because the lackadaisical Feds had waited to bring their charges, and their case still wasn't settled. When I met Ed at the prison at Graterford, he was still awaiting his court date in the Federal Circuit Court in Philadelphia after having been to court twice before, trying to get the Feds to allow his time served to count in the new federal indictment.

"I pray that God pushes the time-served deal through for me," he says as we sit in the visitor-room cubicle. "The judge can still do whatever he wants and change his mind. But I don't believe God has brought me this far on this unique path to drop me on my face.

"I often think of the parable of the talents. I know I've been given many gifts. I've been told I'm intelligent, articulate, and compassionate. I've tried to cultivate those gifts in prison and to use them to help others. All the talents I used to use to defraud people I now use for good. My agoraphobia totally disappears when I stand up to lector and read the word of God at liturgy. And I got my certification to be a literacy instructor and took a job tutoring and teaching guys trying to get their GEDs.

"And I've even learned something about being gay here in prison. I have a great devotion to the third Sorrowful Mystery, Jesus Crowned With Thorns. Jesus did nothing but be who he was born to be. And they mocked him, hurled insults at him, slapped him, beat him, and spit on him. All simply because of who He was. I can relate to that. The 'thorn in the flesh' that Saint Paul talks about in Corinthians is really painful at times. Gay hurts. And no matter how hard one might pray to change, you don't. You *can* become more chaste, though. I know that because I have. But even though I no longer act on my urges, I'm still gay. And what does God say? My grace is enough for you. My power is made greater in weakness. I now know that His grace *really* is enough for me."

Lots of movement began to occur outside of the glass cubicle in which we were seated. I noticed people hugging and crying as guards walked around, seemingly announcing that visiting time was over.

"It looks like they're making us leave," I said, gazing over Ed's shoulder at the activity in the visiting room. He turned around and looked.

"Yeah, it's time," he said sadly.

I began collecting my notes from the table.

"You think you'll be able to come back?" he asked.

"Gee, I don't know, Ed. Let's hope that you'll be out before I have to. I'm going to pray that the Feds simply sentence you to time served and hand you your walking papers."

"I'm praying that, too, but I have to find a place to stay first. My father said he won't take me in, and unless I have a housing plan, they won't release me."

"There's nowhere else you can go?"

"Not right now," he said, "but I'm working on a few things. Not everyone's rushing to have a repeat offender, ex-con move in, you know?"

I wanted to say, "Well, then you can move in with us." After all, we're a religious community whose mission is supposed to involve giving shelter to those who have no place else to go.

But instead, I said, "Oh, yeah," realizing that I'd have to convince the priests and brothers with whom I live and who hadn't met this bright, articulate, and holy man, that he'd be worth the risk.

"Well, Ed," I said lamely, "I'll keep my ears open. I'm sure something's bound to turn up."

"I know it will," he said. "Like I said, God hasn't brought me this far to drop me now."

He opened the door and the noise flooded in. We walked toward the door leading to the staircase I had come down. Women around us were stalling for every last moment with their men as guards were motioning them toward the door. I turned to Ed.

"I'm going to try to tell your story. And I know it's going to have a happy ending." I hugged him good-bye.

"Thanks, Father Edward," he said, suddenly looking like a little boy being left behind. "Thanks for coming, and for listening. There's a lot more I would've liked to tell you, but maybe there'll be other opportunities for that."

"There will be, Ed. I promise."

I opened the door to leave the visiting room and looked back to see Ed become part of a formation of brown jumpsuits, prison numbers waiting to be checked for contraband, human beings herded into a line that seemed to rob them of any dignity the visit with loved ones may have bestowed. I walked up the stairs, collected my extra paper and pens, nodded at the linebacker guard who actually smiled back, and walked slowly to my car.

As I drove down the winding exit, past the fledgling trees lining the road, I prayed, "Yes, new life. Please, new life."

NB: As of this writing, Ed still remains in prison because of the rejection of his proposed housing plans. He is finally scheduled for release in June 2004.

CHAPTER SIX

Pietà

DEBBIE WAS HAVING TROUBLE SLEEPING, just like she always did when her son wasn't home yet. The few times she would nod off, she would dream of him in a car accident or passed out somewhere. When she finally heard the squeak of the front door, she decided to go into the living room to make sure he had locked the door behind him. When she walked in, he was standing there with a hateful look on his face.

"Cary, why are you so late again?" said Debbie. "You know I have to work tomorrow, and you have to go to school. I'm so tired of this."

"Yeah, well, I'm fucking tired of you, too. Why don't you just leave me alone, you stupid bitch." He had obviously been drinking.

When he slurred those hateful words to her, something snapped inside of her. *How could this be the same son who used to be eager to serve 6:30 a.m. Mass as an altar boy? How could this be the son who used to bring home cards from kindergarten with huge red hearts surrounding the word "Mom"? How could this be the angelic-faced son who had tenderly nursed at her breast?* She raised her hand to smack his face, and he grabbed her arm and pushed her toward the couch. She fell onto the coffee table behind her, hit her head, and screamed. The cry awakened her husband, David, who had been sleeping in the bedroom after working a double shift at the local college where he maintained all of the boilers. Waking him was the last thing Debbie wanted, because she knew that now this would escalate into something she couldn't handle. David came into the dark living room and switched on the light. He saw his wife lying on the coffee table holding her head, and Cary standing there with a stupid drunk grin on his face. David went wild. He leapt across the room at Cary, and his hands were around Cary's throat before Debbie could even get up from the coffee table.

DEBBIE STOPPED SPEAKING, unable to go on. She sat in a blue chair and stared out of the church office window, unable to meet my gaze. Tears trickled down her ashen cheeks as she fingered the zipper on her gray, hooded sweatshirt. I waited. She had come to speak to me about problems she was having in her home. "Problems" seemed like an understatement.

To the outside world, they had appeared to be a typical Bay Ridge, Brooklyn, family. Debbie had tried to create a home similar to the one she grew up in, minus some of the pathological and neurotic behavior that had taken up residence there. Her own mother had cleaned obsessively and pretended not to know that her husband visited Debbie's and her sisters' bedrooms late at night. It started when Debbie was about eleven years old and continued through her teenage years, though she never talked about it with her mother. She and her sisters began to broach the subject with each other only when they were married adults. Debbie vowed to be aware of what was happening in *her* home.

She took a deep breath and sighed. "I knew from the time he was a little boy that Cary was different," she finally said. "He had certain phobias, unusual tics, odd kinds of obsessive-compulsive things. Everyone told me he'd outgrow them. But instead, they got worse as he grew older. And he became angry and more distant."

Debbie had met her husband, David, during her sophomore year at Fort Hamilton High School. He was an avid softball player and worked in a butcher's market after school, saving his paychecks for a future that he hoped would be brighter than his past, one laden with disturbing memories of an alcoholic father and an ineffectual mother who seemed overwhelmed by everything, especially by her four sons.

David struggled with his own obsessive-compulsive behavior. He washed continually and checked locked doors two and three times. Although his neurotic patterns concerned Debbie, he was caring and made her laugh. It was enough to help her overlook some of his quirks that drove her crazy. When he would ask her the same question five different ways, to be sure her answers were consistent, she'd finally say, "David, shut up, already. You can be *so* annoying."

"What do you mean by annoying?" he'd say. "Annoying in a good sense or a bad sense? Would you say it's a personality flaw?"

While dating they would spend hours together in David's bedroom listening to the Rolling Stones and drinking Budweiser. Debbie thought he drank excessively, but she didn't worry too much about it then. She preferred that he drink beer rather than snort cocaine or smoke marijuana, which many of his friends did.

Once they were married, David still drank, but he rarely got drunk; and when he did, he was repentant and abstemious for months afterward.

"The first year or two was okay," said Debbie. "He didn't drink all that much in the beginning. He was good to me and played a lot with the kids. I have some wonderful memories of that time. But it didn't last long enough. After we were married about three years, he began drinking a lot again. Once it started full steam, no matter what I said to him didn't make a difference. We started fighting all the time. Suddenly, I realized I had these young kids and a husband who was hardly around. And when he was around, he was drunk or useless."

Debbie was convinced that David had inherited his father's alcoholic genes. "He used to complain to me about what a son of a bitch his father was when he drank, and now he was turning into him. It was so ironic, but he couldn't see it."

The kids learned to steer clear of David when he walked in the house late and drunk. The belligerent and foul-mouthed man, who wound up sleeping on the couch those nights, seemed like a different man than their patient father who, when sober, helped them do homework and took them to the mall on weekends.

Debbie first began to notice changes in Cary's behavior when he was in the second grade, while David was still drinking. It was then that some of the tics began. He was able to control them in public, but once home in the house, he'd let loose like a prisoner finally free.

"I could see all this stress on the face of my beautiful son, and I didn't know what to do about it," said Debbie. "He'd come home from school and he'd be so agitated and unsettled, moving his head abruptly to one side, stuttering and blinking. It was awful. And when I took him to be tested, they all said, 'Wait a bit.

He'll probably grow out of it.' But he didn't. It only got worse. And by then, it was too late. Even medication didn't help. Our home became the place where he did and said everything he couldn't in the real world. It was as if everything overwhelmed him out there, so he'd come home and overwhelm us."

Debbie resented picking up the slack during David's emotional and physical hiatus from her and the kids. Attending the school meetings and baseball games alone was embarrassing for her. "They all wanted to know where David was. And I couldn't tell them." Later, she would call this period "the lost years."

Finally responding to countless ultimatums in which Debbie said she was going to leave him, David stopped drinking and went to his first AA meeting. They had been married ten years. While Debbie was relieved, she could see the damage that had already been done to her family. She was convinced that Cary's problems had been exacerbated by her husband's erratic behavior. By the time David cleaned up and went on the wagon, Cary was eight years old, and memories of his father's alcoholic rages would be hard to expunge. Debbie knew those memories contributed to Cary's emotional instability.

"There's no way you're going to tell me," she said, "that all that fighting and yelling don't affect a child. I know David isn't totally to blame because my other two kids are basically fine. But I think Cary was just more susceptible to all the negative crap that flew around our house. He was *always* more sensitive. I just don't think he could handle it. So he dealt with it the way he could and grew angry. Now we're all feeling the brunt of that anger."

When Debbie came to speak to me, things at home had begun to spin out of control. Their seemingly typical Brooklyn home had been turned upside down by a son whose anger and destructive behavior seemed to know no bounds. Cary was now the one drinking excessively—and doing far worse than that. Debbie recounted stories of his rampages and verbal and physical abuse toward her and David over the previous year. It was sometimes hard for me to listen because of the severity of the ill-treatment.

Cary had been arrested that month for having open beer and liquor bottles in his car after a traffic accident. He and his friends had been driving home from a night spent in a motel room with their girlfriends when his red Mustang collided with another car after Cary ran a stop sign. Debbie was shocked to learn later that some of the other parents knew their children had spent the night drinking and having sex in a motel room.

"The parents said that at least they knew where their kids were, and that they weren't out driving," Debbie said with amazement. "I mean, is this what it's come to? We have to settle for this kind of behavior because we just can't control these kids anymore? There are just no words . . ."

Cary, a handsome eighteen-year-old boy with light brown hair and freckles that took a long time to begin fading, had been arrested two other times in the previous year—once for stealing clothing from a department store and once for disorderly conduct when he trespassed on private property while drunk. Both sentences were suspended after Debbie and David paid hefty fines and Cary had agreed to community service.

He is tall and gangly and fond of wearing hip-hop pants that hang off his hips and form a caboose of material that drags on the floor. (When he showed up for a court date with his shirt hanging out of the oversized pants and his tie askew, the lawyer told him that the judge would throw him out of the court if he walked in looking that way.) A thick gold chain wraps around his neck; a diamond stud and gold ring pierce his left ear. He wears a tattoo of a dolphin on his upper left shoulder like a badge of honor.

"I wish you could have seen him when he was an altar boy in grammar school," says Debbie. "You wouldn't believe this could be the same kid. He used to be up before I was, getting ready to serve the 6:30 a.m. Mass. I'd come out of the shower, still in my bathrobe, and walk into his and his brother's room, and he'd be sitting on the edge of his bed, fully dressed, waiting to go. He never wanted to be late. He used to drive me crazy. I just don't know what happened to the son I once had."

As Debbie sat in my office, trying to understand that for which there seemed to be no rational explanation, it was apparent that the situation had reached a crisis point. Cary was destroying the family Debbie and David had tried so hard to nurture. Their other two children—one, a year older than Cary and the other, five years younger—were resenting Cary's destructive behavior and the way it seemed to dominate every family moment. Everything seemed to be about Cary and his "problem." They were feeling lost in the daily scuffles. And Cary was well on his way to being lost as well.

Debbie was being crushed by Cary's disrespect and lack of concern for her and David. She couldn't understand how Cary could act this way after all they had done for him. She marveled at her husband's attempts to continually reestablish a relationship with Cary, despite Cary's constant rebuffs.

"I think maybe David feels guilty because he wasn't really there when they were younger. So he tries to make up for it now, but it doesn't work. He tries to buy their affection, but it's no longer for sale. They've moved on. And Cary's really moved on. I just don't know to where."

Debbie recounted one of David's attempts to connect with

Cary. She said that Cary is a big Backstreet Boys fan, surprising since the band usually appeals to younger kids. He has all of their CDs and sings their songs by heart, despite his friends' razzing that they are "a girl's group." David noticed in the paper that the Backstreet Boys were going to be performing at a local arena, and decided to buy tickets for Cary and his girlfriend. (I was amazed to hear Debbie say this since nothing about Cary's behavior seemed to warrant this kind of largesse. Why would David spend over one hundred dollars on tickets to surprise a son who acted like he couldn't stand being in the same room with him? I didn't get it.)

"So David bought the tickets," said Debbie. "But he didn't say anything to Cary. Cary hadn't even mentioned anything about this concert. I'm in the kitchen one afternoon about a week later, and David's in the living room reading the paper. Cary walks in with another newspaper in his hand, moaning about the fact that he just read that the Backstreet Boys are going to be in concert and that he doesn't have tickets. He said that, even if he had the money to buy them, they'd probably be sold out by now. He was genuinely upset.

"David, without looking up from his paper in the living room, says, 'Well, gee, I have my tickets. Too bad you didn't get yours.' Well, I thought Cary was going to go crazy. 'What do you mean *you* have tickets,' he screamed. 'How'd you get tickets? You're shittin' me. You don't have tickets.' So David reaches into his back pocket and pulls the tickets from his wallet and waves them at Cary. I thought Cary was going to jump across the coffee table. David smiles and hands Cary the tickets, his face glowing, so pleased with himself that he'd been able to do this for Cary. Do you know that Cary ripped those tickets out of David's hands and walked out without so much as a thank you? I couldn't believe it.

David slumped in the couch like he'd just been punched in the stomach. I knew at that moment that something else had to take over here, because we were failing—not only our son, but each other."

It was hard for me to understand why David would buy those tickets. Didn't he realize that Cary was already spoiled and that such actions would only worsen the situation? Why did he keep setting himself up to be knocked down by a son who didn't care about anyone or anything but himself? Was this love or stupidity? In any event, David's course of action didn't seem to be producing results, so why not abandon it for a "tough love" approach? What was he thinking? Perhaps he was thinking that he was responsible for some of Cary's problems. Rather than seeing Cary as a spoiled brat, maybe David saw him as his lost son, one he wanted desperately to find again.

The night that David had his hands around Cary's throat as he pinned him to the coffee table was both a breaking and turning point. Cary had been out with his friends, and although he had a curfew of 1 a.m. on the weekends, he rarely staggered in before three or four. Debbie and David had tried every kind of disciplinary action, from denying certain privileges to double-bolting the front door after 1 a.m. Nothing worked. Cary ignored what they said. Once when they had bolted the front door, he broke the window in the back door and let himself in—after cutting his hand on the broken glass and bleeding all over the beige carpeting. But he didn't care. He had gotten in and once again had won. Cary treated his parents like ciphers, ignoring their rules, mocking their attempts at restoring order. In Debbie's words, "He'd become a monster."

* * *

AS DAVID LAY on top of his son, choking him, Debbie started screaming, "David, let him go! You're going to kill him!" But David was like a man possessed. Debbie jumped on his back to try to get him to stop, but he wouldn't let go. As she was trying to pull his hands from around Cary's throat, Cary kicked David in the groin and David doubled over in pain as he and Debbie fell to the floor.

Cary ran into the kitchen, got a broom that was next to the refrigerator, and came back into the living room, swinging like a madman. Debbie got up, but David was still on the floor, bent over in pain. She screamed at Cary to put the broom down, but instead he walked over to David with it and pinned him down to the floor with the handle of the broom on David's neck. He started to push down on it. Unable to breathe, David started to turn red. Debbie started pounding on Cary's back and tied to pull him off, but couldn't. She thought of calling 911, but knew it would be too late. Just then, her son Daniel ran up the stairs from the basement, saw what was happening, and punched Cary in the side of the head. He fell off of David, who had nearly passed out by this point. Cary started sobbing as David lay there, trying to catch his breath. Debbie got a cool rag and some water.

But the trauma didn't end there. David began to have an anxiety attack, feeling as though he couldn't breathe again. Debbie was finally forced to call 911—not for the police for her son, but for an ambulance for her husband. He was rushed to the hospital while Cary went to his bedroom to sleep. Cary didn't go to the emergency room and never asked afterward about how his father was.

I sat stunned by the story. Although I'm aware such chaotic violence does occur in upper-middle-class families with caring parents, it surprised me anyway, seeming to shatter so many of the stereotypes. Temporarily muted by her painful accounting, I finally asked Debbie why she didn't have Cary arrested. Didn't she realize that her other children could only be negatively affected by such disruption in the house? Besides, Cary was eighteen. Throw the bum out. They should at least press charges with this kind of abusive behavior. Why didn't they?

Debbie slightly smiled at me as if to say, "Poor, naïve Father, you just don't get it."

"First of all," she said, "the rights of the child are always protected, even over the rights of the parents. All Cary would have had to say to the police was that his father was choking him, and they would have taken David away in handcuffs, no questions asked. There's zero tolerance for any kind of physical abuse by parents right now.

"Second, we've thought of having Cary arrested and letting him spend a few nights in jail, but do you know what they do with boys in jail? Do you think we could live with ourselves if our son was harmed in any way in jail, after we'd him put there? There's just no way. And it's the same with trying to have him committed in some institution. If they decide he's a danger to himself or to other people, they can keep him in there indefinitely. He's not *that* bad or that sick. He can go weeks being fine. We just couldn't do it. We keep convincing ourselves that we're going to have some breakthrough with him, and that's the hope we hold on to. It's what keeps us going."

I realized that because I didn't have a child, I couldn't really know what she was feeling. I couldn't understand why she put up with it. While I could give her all kinds of rational, objective advice, I couldn't know what it was like to be her. So hard as it was, I could only keep listening. But I still wasn't sure why Debbie had come to see *me*. Given the severity of the situation, it seemed more appropriate that she should be speaking to a family therapist rather than to a priest. While it is not uncommon for people to seek me out with all sorts of problems, I eventually try to get to the spiritual side of the matter and leave the therapy to the professionals. I wasn't seeing a spiritual side to any of this—only a dark, seemingly evil pall that had overshadowed a family as a result of a wayward son's horrific descent.

When I asked Debbie to help me understand what had brought her to see me, nothing could have prepared me for what she said. She said that she hadn't come to me for advice—not that I had any to give her. She had come instead to tell me what she had discovered about God in this ordeal. It was a turn I hadn't expected.

"I've told you all of this for a reason," she said. "Although I know how horrendous it all sounds and that it obviously still upsets me, something in me has begun to change. And I can't talk to just anyone about this part. I think that I've finally begun to see God in some of it, and I want to make sure that I'm on the right track."

For so long, God had felt absent to Debbie. She had started praying when Cary was younger, when she first began seeing signs that something was wrong, but her prayers seemed to go unanswered. He just got worse. She couldn't understand why God wasn't helping her.

"It says in the Bible, 'Ask, and you shall receive. Seek, and you shall find. Knock, and the door will be opened to you,'" said Debbie. "Well, I was asking and seeking and knocking all over the place and nothing was happening. And nothing had really happened to change the situation.

"Even now, Cary may be a bit better, but who knows for how long and what kind of a future he has? He may never be able to function like everyone else in the real world. But I've recently begun to think that maybe I've been asking for the wrong things. Perhaps I've been missing the answers to some prayers. Because, believe it or not, some good has come out of all of this. And maybe God has been in that."

It is difficult, at times, to know what to pray for in horrendous circumstances. Most often, we just want relief. "God, make it end. Get me through it." While we are in the midst of turmoil, we can see little else. We feel alone and abandoned, as if no one understands what we are going through. When it seems as though not even God understands, we can feel truly alone.

But sometimes, distance from the pain gives us another perspective. We look back on a dreadful experience, and we see layers of meaning that we could not have seen in the tempest. Perhaps there was a kind word here, or a helping hand there. Or there was a day of unspeakable beauty that gave us a peek at unseen possibilities that began to be the way out, a way home. We have a glimmer of companionship on the journey. And while it may not be the totality of an answer to prayer, it is the beginning of a nod of recognition and a felt presence assuring us that we are not alone.

Debbie began to realize that her and David's marriage had never been stronger. "Never. Not even in the good times in the beginning. We didn't know what it meant to be bonded together then. Now we do."

Cary, in a strange way, has become the cement of their marriage, because they've had to be united to get through it and to help him get through it. They talk more now than they ever have before, and escape for dinners alone to keep their sanity.

"We're finally truly partners," said Debbie. "And it's more than just having this common enemy that's easier to battle together. It's about being so appreciative that we have each other to walk this rough road with. I don't know what I'd do without him. And I've come to see that this is real love. David now comes before everything else, including Cary. I couldn't have always said that."

Debbie spoke about previously taking Cary's side in an argument against David, forming an unholy alliance with a son who had learned to play her against her husband. David felt betrayed and hurt; Cary walked away as the self-satisfied instigator of further conflict. Disintegration can occur in a marriage when children get in the way of a couple's tending to one another, and resentment builds as the spouse feels as though he or she has become a second-class citizen in the land where children rule. Debbie came to see that she and David needed to present a united front, even if some of the difficulties of that union needed to be worked out in private. "And the two shall become one," became a mantra of their marriage. They came to realize that the sacrament of their union was the strength that led to "real love" coming to full fruition.

And then there was more. Debbie began to go to therapy to cope with the problems with Cary and found she was talking about herself and her life before she was even married.

"I opened up for the first time about my own abuse by my father when I was a child. It got me in touch with stuff I'd denied or repressed for years. None of that would've happened if I hadn't been forced by the situation with Cary to get some help. But soon I wasn't talking about Cary at all in those sessions. I began to see how my own life struggles were affecting how I was dealing with him and with the problems we have in our family. It was this major revelation. And I'm so much better because of it. Tremendous healing has taken place over stuff that I've carried my whole life. So maybe God's been in that, too. Not exactly an answer to my specific prayer, but an answer to prayer that I hadn't yet even begun to formulate because I didn't know how."

An old adage says, "God writes straight with crooked lines," implying that good can come from that which, at first, is perceived as only bad. God works with us in spite of ourselves. Paths we would never choose become illuminating and instructive. Dark woods contain mysterious secrets that are unearthed only when we venture into them.

Debbie found succor in being forced to confront issues she never would have tackled if left to her own predilections. Her pain about Cary led her to a deeper pain about herself, but ultimately it was a path to begin healing. While this may connote a sequence we'd rather avoid, Debbie's experience suggests that painful experience can produce enlightenment not attainable otherwise. Debbie says it was a piece of an answer to prayer she couldn't have articulated if not prompted to by Cary's problem. Smooth sailing would have disguised the tempest brewing beneath that would have eventually overcome her. She needed to confront the issues that stemmed back to her own childhood and the early years of her marriage. Unwittingly, her volatile son encouraged her to do just that.

"AND FINALLY, I have to tell you that, in the strangest way, my family and my other kids are stronger because of this. Even though I know they've suffered negative repercussions from it, they have a sensitivity and compassion they would've never had if we hadn't gone through this hell with Cary. Do you know that when my son Steven sees a kid who looks troubled, or who has a tic or stammers or something, he feels like he wants to do something for that kid because he says he reminds him of his brother Cary. I mean, how great is that? I couldn't have taught him that in a million years. Maybe that's what they mean by the school of hard knocks. I can tell you that my children have been wonderful students in that school, and there's a part of that I wouldn't trade for anything."

It was good to hear Debbie make these spiritual connections, especially since she was still in the midst of her problems with Cary. I am sometimes skeptical when people overly spiritualize bad experiences, because it can lead to denial or avoidance of the real issues. But Debbie didn't seem to be doing that. (Although I was concerned that she risked putting her other sons in harm's way by not protecting them more from Cary's dangerous excesses.) She was aware that spiritual lessons are learned in life experiences, even bad experiences. She was astute enough to perceive the depth of meaning to be culled from events not of our choosing, but ones that have the capacity to hold wisdom for us if we are attentive to the signs. Her experience had made her a judicious sign reader, a holy wayfarer.

I was surprised to realize, as she reached for her coat, that she was finished with me. She seemed to be concluding our meeting before I had offered her any words of advice or counsel. In fact, I had hardly said anything. She had been the sage instructor in this get-together and I the novice student. I made one last effort to tie up the loose ends that seemed so bountiful and troublesome—at least to me. We hadn't even approached any resolution about what she should do about Cary. She was going to be returning home to the same situation she had brought to me—a son whom, she said, she hardly knew anymore.

"What are you going to do now?" I asked her. I will never forget her response.

"Father, a few months ago I was in Saint Patrick's Cathedral in New York. I had brought my youngest son, Steven, into the city, and we stopped into the church to make a visit. It was in the midst of a horrendous episode with Cary just two days before, and I was at a loss as to what to do. I'd been crying for two days. I took Steven around the church, showed him the side altars and the beautiful stained-glass windows. When we went behind the main altar, the Blessed Sacrament was exposed for benediction and prayer. We knelt there for a while, and of course I prayed about Cary. I asked God to help him and to get us through this. I wanted a miracle, and I think I even said so. But I didn't feel much of anything as I was praying. I usually don't.

"Steven and I got up to leave, and we turned left to go down the other side of the church. Suddenly there was this enormous statue of the Pietà in front of us. It's a reproduction of the Michelangelo statue that's in Saint Peter's Basilica in Rome. I'm sure you've seen it. I couldn't move. It immediately spoke to me. Mary was holding the broken body of her son. Jesus seemed so lifeless, so mangled, and while Mary looked sad, she seemed serene in some strange way. She wasn't crying or anything, just kind of peaceful as she held the body of her son.

"I had this image of me holding the body of Cary. He wasn't dead, but totally worn out, asleep, tired of fighting for a place in this world. And I was just stroking his hair gently, absorbing his pain in some way, knowing that it was part of my mission as his mother to simply hold him, to be there for him when everyone else had abandoned him. It was such a moment of grace. I'll never forget it. And I've often returned to that place in my heart. I see myself still standing there. And no matter what else happens, he is my wounded son, and I will be the mother who holds him in that woundedness."

She stood up, reached out her hand to me, said nothing else, and walked out the door.

ONCE SHE LEFT I realized that I had learned one more spiritual lesson that she had not articulated. My struggle during our time together had been to understand the kind of love that allowed her and David to remain faithful to Cary, even in the midst of his despicable behavior. It seemed unwarranted, foolish, and maybe even detrimental. But perhaps the word for which I struggle is "unconditional." Not surprisingly, it's the same word some use to describe the way God loves us—unconditionally, no prerequisite, no payback necessary. Free gift. It's a hard concept for us score-keeping types. But Debbie and David seem to have mastered it. And in their acumen they reveal something to us about the love of God who proclaims in the Book of Isaiah, "Even should a mother forget you, I will never forget you." But this mother didn't forget. So Debbie prompts me to ask, How much more wondrous is God's mindfulness of me, even in the midst of my transgressions?

While excommunication is a venerable option we have long exercised in our supposedly forgiving Church, a more ancient choice is faithfulness, even in the midst of sinfulness. Debbie and David choose the latter. In the Scriptures conversion never happens as a result of abandonment, but rather by the steadfastness of people (and God) who stand with the sinner even in destructive life choices. People turn their lives around because others believe in them enough to walk with them until they find their way home again. Debbie and David still walk beside Cary. I have to believe that someday their fidelity will be his salvation.

Zero Tolerance and Hundredfold Forgiveness

PATRICK REMEMBERS THAT NIGHT being very dark. Even in their beds, he and the other twelve- and thirteen-year-old campers were swaddled in sleeping bags to keep warm from the chill of the night mountain air. The director of the camp was in the room by the beds of the other campers. Massages were one his ways of getting the boys settled down at bedtime in the small wooden cabins that each housed eight campers. At the time, Patrick didn't know if they were getting the same kind of massage as the one he received that night.

I HAD FIRST MET PATRICK at a National Youth Conference in Cincinnati in 1986. He was twenty-one years old and working with the CYO (Catholic Youth Organization) in Seattle. I was a newly ordained twenty-seven-year-old priest in my first assignment at a parish in Union City, New Jersey. Patrick and I had been paired up in a faith-sharing exercise the first day, and we palled around with each other for the remainder of the conference.

I could tell from the start that he was a remarkable young man. Tall and large-framed, with green eyes and shiny black hair that covered the collar of his button-down shirt, he made an immediate impression. No stranger to the outdoors, he was a skilled camper who wore the requisite hiking boots and Levi jeans. While he looked as though he'd be comfortable logging in the Great Northwest, his soft demeanor and heightened sensitivity cut an unusual contrast.

Patrick's faith-sharing that weekend was candid and passionate, especially for someone so young. We sat in a large meeting room with five hundred other participants. "You know, I'm thinking about being a priest, too," he said during a break in the workshops.

"Really?" I said. "That's great." Since I was always on the lookout for young, talented men who might be interested in joining my own religious community, he piqued my interest.

"I'd love to talk to you about it, if we have the chance," said Patrick.

"That would be wonderful," I said, and figured I'd wait for him to bring it up again.

I had retired to my hotel room early the last night of the conference, spent after three days of networking and schmoozing with young adults and youth ministry leaders. While the speakers had been top-notch and the participants full of zeal, my limited extroverted skills had been exhausted. I drifted off to sleep early in the plush feather bed, so much more comfortable than my lumpy, nonfeathered bed at the rectory back home.

I'd been asleep about two hours when someone knocked softly on the door. The neon numbers on the alarm clock glowed

10:15 p.m. *Who in the world . . . ?* I wondered, as I felt my way to the door like a blindfolded partyer playing pin the tail on the donkey.

"Who is it?" I asked.

"Hey, Edward. It's Patrick."

When I opened the door, he was grinning sheepishly, his windbreaker wet from a nighttime rainstorm. He had just returned from dinner with a group from Seattle, charged with a few double espressos and ready to chitchat about the conference.

He plopped in a chair by the desk, wet jacket and all, and talked effusively about friends and family members whom I'd never met. (With nine siblings and a lot more friends, he had much ground to cover.) But even in the midst of chatting about his sister Nora or his friend Paul, Patrick kept veering back to speaking about his faith and his call to service.

"I've always felt connected to the Church and my faith," he said. "One of the nuns I had in grammar school, Sister Julia, used to ask me if I ever thought about being a priest. I remember that, even in first grade, we had this gift table that we could pick anything we wanted from, and I picked the statue of Saint Don Bosco, a nineteenth-century Salesian saint committed to working with youth. Well, I guess I don't have to tell you who he is."

"Are you pursuing the priesthood now?" I asked.

"Not formally. I still have some things to work through about that, but the thought has never really left me. I'm talking to some people in the archdiocese. We'll see what happens."

"Well, if you don't get any satisfaction there," I said, "consider a religious community. We're always looking for good men like yourself."

"Thanks, I'll keep it in mind. By the way," he said, seemingly wanting to change the subject, "I didn't wake you or anything, did I?"

"Oh, no," I said assuringly, "I was just doing some reading" (even though there wasn't a book in sight).

After trading stories for about another hour, we both started to fade. Time to call it a night, he got up from the chair and walked toward the door, but before reaching it, he turned and said, "You know, it's really been important for me to meet you this weekend." His hands were in his jeans pockets while his over-sized, tattered, gray sweater hung beneath his windbreaker. "It was good for me to meet a young priest like you. Kinda' gives me hope. I'm not sure I'll ever do what you do, but it's more tangible having met you. Thanks for that." He paused and looked down. The warm glow of the dim, overhead light cast amber shadows on his face.

"And sometime," he said finally, "if and when we meet again, I'd like to share something else with you. I'm not ready to talk about it yet, but someday . . ." We embraced and he left. It would be six years before that conversation would take place.

WE WERE HAVING DINNER at Bardolino, a seedy Greenwich Village restaurant named after a sailboat. Although we had seen each other just a few times since Cincinnati, Patrick and I had talked periodically by phone and had penned occasional letters. Patrick hadn't mentioned what he'd hinted at that last night of the conference, though, and I hadn't inquired. Perhaps distance had stifled our relationship a bit, and further disclosure didn't seem appropriate for our sporadic communications. But undeniably, in some way we felt linked, and after two glasses of California merlot, Patrick finally talked about the summer he had just turned thirteen.

"I was at Camp Don Bosco," he said, looking at the votive candle on the table. "It was my fifth summer. I started going there when I was eight years old. Same camp I'm the director of today."

Reverend David Jaeger, a priest from the archdiocese of Seattle, was the director of the camp that summer of 1978. Patrick's parents had sent him to Camp Don Bosco, a magnificent spot in the Cascade foothills east of Seattle, just as they had sent many of their other nine children through the years.

"I was thrilled the first time I met Father Jaeger, because he seemed like a great guy," said Patrick. "It was as if I could see myself someday doing what he was doing. I mean, here was a guy who was a priest *and* worked with CYO. It seemed perfect."

Thirty-five at the time, Jaeger had been a priest for nine years. Patrick and seven other boys were preparing for sleep when Jaeger entered the cabin to quiet the boys down for the night.

"I remember lying on my stomach and feeling his hands on my back," said Patrick. "He didn't say anything. My heart was beating fast. I was nervous and excited at the same time. A part of me liked having him so close because I had always admired him. He was rubbing my legs and back, which was fine I guess, though in retrospect I can't see why he was even doing that. It was definitely inappropriate for a priest with a thirteen-year-old boy.

"But then it took a turn. He put his hands under the leg bands of my underwear and touched me. I started to get very nervous and afraid. I couldn't understand why he was doing this. I wondered, was this what he did to the other campers?

"I didn't know what to do. I just lay there, not moving. Then he stopped. I don't really remember how long it went on, but it felt like forever. He whispered, 'Good night,' and then he was gone."

Patrick said he didn't know how "massages" became part of Jaeger's nocturnal duties, but by the time he had finished telling me about the night of abuse, he had tears in his eyes and could hardly speak.

"Patrick, I'm so sorry," I said. "How awful that you had to go through that."

"Yeah," he finally said, "and I wasn't the only one. But I sure felt like it at the time."

"What do you mean?" I asked.

"Well, no one talked about it, but I knew he'd done *something* to them too. I just didn't know what. So I felt like I was the only bad one, like maybe I was the only pervert who'd let him do more."

The abuse came at a time when Patrick was questioning his sexuality anyway, and it further exacerbated his confusion. Even at thirteen, he knew that the Church taught that homosexuality was wrong. But here was a *priest* doing this to him. It was more than he could handle.

"I didn't tell anyone for ten years," he said. "It was pretty awful carrying that around all that time. Amazing how much it had affected me. I had so looked up to him, and then it was all shattered."

"Didn't anyone suspect anything?" I asked.

"Yeah, my mother did. She noticed I was quieter, more withdrawn when I returned from camp, but she didn't know what to make of it. So, who does she go and speak about it to? A local priest. Geez. He told her it was probably just adolescent stuff, not to worry about it."

As I sat listening to Patrick, I started to feel a little uncomfortable. After all, *I* was a priest. I couldn't help but think that perhaps Patrick linked me with Jaeger, if only subconsciously.

"Patrick," I said, attempting to mollify my discomfort, "this must have really changed your opinion of the Church and priests. You'd had such a great experience up to this point and then this guy comes along and ruins it all. And now you're telling this to me, *a priest*. Isn't it a bit confusing?"

Patrick looked at me, seemingly unsure of what I was driving at. "Well, it's very strange, Edward, because, at the time, my love of the Church wasn't affected by what happened with him, if that's what you mean. In an odd sort of way, I think it actually drew me closer. It's like when someone tries to take something from you that you love and value, and then you want it all the more. My faith was so important to me that I didn't want to let him damage it. I was going to fight it. *And* fight *him*."

That "fight" would take a circuitous route. Three years after the abuse at camp, Patrick saw Jaeger unexpectedly when he came to the camp to open the season with a Mass. Sixteen years old by then, Patrick had been hired as a staff member at CYO and was working as assistant cook at one of the camps.

"When I saw him, my stomach dropped," said Patrick. "He just came out of the blue."

Jaeger walked up to Patrick as if nothing had happened.

"Patrick D'Amelio, how are you? Nice to see you."

Patrick was stunned that Jaeger had remembered his name.

"I mean, there was no reason for him to remember me," said Patrick. "I was just one of hundreds of campers. It's funny though . . . I wasn't really afraid, more relieved that he didn't seem to remember what had happened. But I was still feeling guilty and ashamed, like I was the pervert kid or something." He skipped the Mass and avoided Jaeger for the rest of the day.

After that Patrick didn't see Jaeger for another three years, until Patrick, then nineteen, was in his second semester at Catholic University in Washington, DC. It wasn't a happy time. Overcome by depression, a first for him, Patrick knew something was wrong but couldn't pinpoint what. Working as a peer campus minister at the university by then, he was still struggling with issues of sexuality and priesthood. It was his first real crisis of faith.

"The shit hit the fan that year," he said. "I felt so over-whelmed, but didn't know why. I was having these bizarre dreams—really nightmares, I guess—about sexuality and the priesthood, all linked together. It felt like God was telling me to make up my mind about the priesthood, but I just couldn't because I was so confused. It was crazy. I knew I was screwed up, but didn't know what to do about it."

Patrick was walking through the quadrangle on the campus of Catholic University when he spotted Jaeger coming toward him. He braced himself, looking for a way to avoid the priest, but it was too late. Jaeger had seen him. "He walked up to me," said Patrick, "as nonchalant and friendly as three years before, and asked me how things were going."

While nervous about seeing Jaeger, Patrick wondered if these chance meetings might be an answer to prayer. By then Jaeger had been appointed vocations director and director of seminari-ans and was visiting candidates for the archdiocese of Seattle who were studying in Washington.

"I wondered if God was trying to tell me something," said Patrick. "I mean, Jaeger *was* the director of seminarians, so maybe God was saying I should be a priest. I know it sounds wild, but I was pretty messed up." Patrick didn't mention the priesthood to Jaeger at the time. They simply traded awkward pleasantries and Jaeger went on his way.

Soon after that encounter, Patrick began a downward spiral, sleeping late most days and skipping many of his classes. Not being able to focus, he wondered if his religious calling was the key to his distraction. He decided to return home to Seattle and make an appointment to see Father Jaeger.

"It was so hard for me to make that phone call," said Patrick. "But I knew that, if I wanted to pursue the priesthood seriously, I couldn't do it without meeting with Jaeger and getting his okay." As soon as he walked into Jaeger's office, Patrick felt uncomfortable. "I panicked, actually," said Patrick.

Jaeger sat at his desk across from Patrick. "It was as if I was watching the whole thing from outside myself," said Patrick. "I kept feeling like I was playing with fire, that I shouldn't be there. I knew that day that I'd have to finally start dealing with all this shit."

Jaeger asked some questions about what Patrick had been doing and why he felt called to priesthood. Patrick gave perfunctory answers, all the time wanting to get out of there. "In retrospect," he said, "I probably went to see him because it was my unconscious way of reaching out to him, hoping he might bring up what'd happened. I was saying, 'Help me with this. You're the cause of it, after all.' " But Jaeger never did bring it up. Patrick left frustrated, still unsure of what to do.

A few months later Patrick had an emergency appendectomy. While coming out of the anesthesia, he started calling out Jaeger's name. His mother thought Patrick wanted to speak to the priest for prayers of healing, so in a chilling turn, she picked up the phone and called Jaeger. She put the receiver to Patrick's ear while the priest said prayers over the telephone. Patrick lay more confused than ever in an anesthesia-induced stupor.

The following summer, Patrick, then twenty-two, accepted a job as the camp director at Camp Don Bosco, the same camp at which he had been abused nine years earlier. He and the other camp staffers were in Thunderbird Lodge, listening to a lecture by a therapist on "appropriate contact with children." This had become a hot topic for anyone working with kids, and the staffers were being educated on pertinent issues when supervising young children. The therapist said that, in any group of adolescents, you could be sure that one or more had been abused in some way. She then asked the staff members to "draw a picture of an experience when you were touched as a child and it felt good." Patrick drew a picture of his mother hugging him. It was the following directive that opened the floodgates: "Now draw a picture of a time when you were touched and it felt uncomfortable."

Patrick couldn't draw anything. He sat frozen, tears welling up in his eyes. He left the room without speaking. Later, Shaughn, a woman on staff who was director of outdoor ministries, came out to see him.

"Patrick, what is it?" she asked, as they sat on the grass not far from the lodge.

"I was one of those kids," he said. He then told her about Jaeger.

"Patrick, I'm so sorry," she said. "Is there anything I can do?"

"No, I don't think so. Just finally telling someone is a relief. Thanks for being here and for listening."

Sometime later, Shaughn asked to speak to Patrick again. "Patrick, I've been thinking about what you've told me," she said tentatively, "and I have to report this to the bishop."

"No, you can't do that," Patrick protested. "I don't want him to know it's me."

"Patrick, this has gone on for too long. I *have* to report it."

Patrick finally agreed, but secretly wished that none of it was necessary. He longed to return to "before"—before the abuse, before the nightmares, before the shame. But he knew that there was no turning back now.

After claiming that Jaeger had denied the charges, the archbishop offered to pay for counseling for Patrick. While it angered Patrick that the archbishop seemed to believe Jaeger's denial, Patrick agreed to counseling. At least it was a start.

A few months later, in a surprising turn, the archdiocese sent one of their therapists to Washington to "assess" Patrick. He told Patrick that Jaeger had, in fact, finally accepted responsibility for what he had done. No explanation was given for the turnaround.

"But it was so good to hear those words," said Patrick. "Somehow, it meant that I wasn't crazy. That I hadn't imagined it all. From the very beginning, my goal was always that Dave Jaeger and I would come out of this reconciled to the Church, and hopefully to each other. That's what I *always* wanted most. I felt like maybe now we had a chance at that."

It was now time for another revelation. Patrick had yet to tell his parents what had happened. With his home diocese now becoming involved, Patrick thought that his parents had a right to know. In July of 1989 he flew home to Seattle to inform them of that summer night eleven years before.

"It was hard for me to do," he said, "because I knew they'd be wondering why I hadn't said something before. But when I told them, they couldn't have been more loving and supportive."

The three of them sat in the living room in which they had shared so much as a family of twelve. Fighting back tears,

Patrick's mother spoke first. "Patrick, I knew something was wrong when you came home from camp that summer. I'm so sorry. I wish I could have done something for you then. We love you very much and we want to help."

"Mom, there's no way you could have done anything. You didn't know. I didn't even really know."

"But we all know now," said Patrick's father. "And we *can* do something."

"Yes, Patrick, we really should," said his mother. "After all, this guy is still out there. Who knows what he's still doing? I think we should go speak to Randy."

The three of them went to see Randy, the family attorney, the following day. As they sat in his office, Patrick spoke first.

"Randy, I don't want this to be primarily about money," he said. "It needs to be about him agreeing to get help and making sure he doesn't do this to anyone else. I'm not looking to punish him. I'm looking for some peace and healing and to finally put this behind me."

Randy understood immediately what Patrick was asking for. Being of the same mind, he suggested that, together, they develop a model to present to the archdiocese for how it might deal with the issue—not only in Patrick's case, but also for any other victims. Satisfied after a few meetings that they had come up with a cogent proposal, Randy presented it to the archdiocesan lawyers.

The archdiocese offered a settlement and guaranteed that Jaeger would receive treatment and never again be placed in a position where he could endanger a minor. The archdiocesan officials also agreed to establish guidelines for dealing with abuse based on what Randy and Patrick had requested. Content that he had done what he could, Patrick continued his own therapy, assuming that his career in Church ministry was finished for good.

But that assumption saddened Patrick. Although he hadn't yet completed college, he had still harbored a childhood dream of someday working for CYO in Seattle again, possibly as a priest. When we left Bardolino restaurant that day, I wondered how he could realize that dream in light of what had happened. I also wondered what made Patrick want to keep going back there.

In 1994, Patrick left Washington and returned to Seattle. Since it was obvious that Patrick was still drawn to working with CYO, a friend urged him to follow his heart and see if jobs were available. Figuring he had nothing to lose, Patrick applied for the position of director of the CYO program. To his surprise, the archdiocese hired him and gave him an office on the third floor of the Seattle archdiocese's chancery building. While it appeared his dream was finally coming true, there was one caveat: Jaeger, now director of AIDS ministry for the archdiocese, had his office one floor below. How ironic that Patrick now held the former position of the priest who had molested him and who now worked in the same building.

By this time, Jaeger had completed a sex-offenders treatment program. Psychological evaluations had said that he was safe to return to ministry, provided he continue therapy and not be alone with minors. Convinced that Jaeger was no longer a threat, the archdiocese assigned him to the chancery position.

When Patrick was given an office in the same building, Church officials, aware of the unfortunate history, offered to move Jaeger if it would make Patrick feel less awkward. Patrick declined, deciding it was time to meet with Jaeger once more, to put this behind him for good. They agreed to meet at a coffee shop near the chancery building.

"It was so weird for me," said Patrick. "I was having mixed feelings about it all. I was nervous waiting for him to get there. But I was so ready to finally move on."

As usual, Jaeger was friendly and solicitous when he walked into the coffee shop. He slid into the booth by the window and started making small talk about CYO and his own ministry. Patrick politely feigned interest, but knew they were there to speak about something else.

"I remember being aware of people walking by and the other people in the restaurant, wondering what they'd think if they knew what we were there to discuss. It was awkward at first. I ordered coffee and a scone, although eating was the last thing on my mind."

After the initial innocuous chatting, Patrick told Jaeger why he'd asked for the meeting. "Dave, you have to know how hard this has all been for me. How confusing. *I* was the one who felt guilty, but *I* didn't do anything. I'm not here to make you feel worse, but you need to know how wrong what you did was, and how your actions affected me. I'd looked up to you. I even thought I wanted to be a priest, but somehow it's all too confusing now. I can't separate it out from what happened. But I do need to try to move on. We're going to be working in the same building, for the same Church. I want to feel okay with that."

Jaeger told Patrick that his coming forward had been the hardest thing in Jaeger's life. He said that he was grateful though for Patrick's courage, because it had forced Jaeger to deal with his own sexuality. Although he had never meant to "cross a boundary," he could see that he had. Unwisely, he had convinced himself that touching a child was a safe outlet for years of repressed sexual impulses. His own adolescence had been completely asexual, so lacking any frame of reference, he had believed that the massages were harmless. He said that, if he did anything more than massage Patrick that night, it was not deliberate and that he had no memory of it. Apologizing, he said he was sorry for whatever pain and confusion he had caused Patrick.

"I told him that I had long since forgiven him," said Patrick. "I just needed to say my piece and to hear his response. It was time to move on."

They shook hands and left the coffee shop. Continuing to work one floor apart, they passed each other occasionally in the hallway, always courteous, never more. Patrick thought he had "moved on," until the infamous priest sexual-abuse scandal of 2001–2002 erupted. Suddenly, it was on the front page of all the newspapers, and before long, so was Patrick.

Newspapers were calling it the most serious crisis of the Catholic Church in its modern history. Once the *Boston Globe* began its investigation of some pedophile priests from the Boston archdiocese in the spring of 2002, there was no turning back the tide of accusations and media attention. It soon became apparent that the ranks of the priesthood were sullied by some incredibly sick men who had caused irreparable harm to innocent children and their families. It was as if smoky incense had lifted to reveal a cluster of lechers behind what was believed to have been a veil to the holy; or as if, in the *Wizard of Oz*, a curtain had been pulled back, exposing ecclesiastical shamans who had manipulated the controls for too long.

The mishandling and cover-up of the number of cases that surfaced stunned Patrick. The zero-tolerance policy of the American bishops had caused all old abuse cases to be reevaluated in light of the new guidelines. Father Jaeger, on administrative leave and facing ouster under the new policy, went on the defensive in an attempt to salvage his priesthood and reputation. On the evening news and in morning newspapers, Jaeger said that he had never molested anyone. He admitted only to having acted "inappropriately."

On September 1, 2002, the *Seattle Times* quoted Jaeger as saying that he touched the boys under their underwear only if they seemed okay with it. "A massage feels better direct than through material—that's what I was thinking . . . If I brushed against genitals, it was not deliberate, and I don't remember it. That would have been crossing the line I had set."

Patrick was at Camp Don Bosco in June when the news about Jaeger broke and was disheartened, to say the least. *How could Jaeger have denied sexual intent or contact?* Even more disturbing was the support Jaeger seemed to be receiving from the archdiocese and the people to whom he ministered. Patrick felt forgotten and began to grow angry again. Old feelings that had lain dormant began to reemerge with an intensity that surprised even him. Now *he* was being made to look like the liar. After all, according to Jaeger, Patrick must have "seemed okay with the massage."

"There's an undertone to what Jaeger said, that, 'What I did wasn't that bad,'" said Patrick. "What I'm saying is that it *was* that bad."

Patrick felt that, by Jaeger's publicly minimizing what he had done, he had disrespected the process of reconciliation that had taken place. It seemed like one more betrayal. The apology from Jaeger had obviously meant nothing. Patrick couldn't sit back and let this charade unfold without saying something. If the bishops said that zero tolerance is the policy, then they had better enforce it. Patrick was convinced that bishops, priests, and victims "have kept dangerous secrets for too long, and at too great a cost."

"We're comfortable denying priesthood to women, married

people, openly gay people," he said. "Now we're suddenly going to be up in arms because we are going to deny priesthood to people who have molested children? It doesn't make any sense to me."

The hypocrisy finally pushed Patrick to call the *Seattle Times* to tell his side of the story. It was the front page of a Sunday issue a few weeks later, adding yet one more account to the growing canon of abuse accusations.

ALL OF THE NEWSPAPER ACCOUNTS of abuse paled in comparison with hearing Patrick's firsthand account and witnessing the aftermath. The emotional trauma to him was as bad, if not worse, than the physical. Patrick had trusted this priest, had looked up to him, emulated him—wanted *to be* him. And yet the priest dishonored that trust, taking advantage of a vulnerable child, with no consideration of the effect his actions might have. Disillusionment can indeed be traumatic, especially when caused by hero figures who fall mightily, but who refuse to acknowledge, or even be aware of, their plummet. It seems similar to the disillusionment of faithful Catholics who had revered Church leaders as upright and holy men, only to discover that they were accomplices in the perpetuation and cover-up of the sexual abuse of minors. Sacred worldviews are shattered, and the damage may be irreparable.

While it may not surprise many people that the priesthood has its share of pedophiles (the statistics of the number of pedophile priests remain roughly consistent with the number of pedophiles in the general population), the egregious actions of the Church hierarchy more than surprise—they shock, anger, and disgust many who had thought Church leaders above such blatant wrongdoing. It appears as if the hierarchy has committed the far greater sin of covering it all up. The faithful's recovery from that abuse of power will be a long and painful one.

As this process continues to unfold, I am amazed that Patrick has not lost faith. (The same cannot be said of others who, perhaps, have begun to look elsewhere for spiritual solace.) Patrick has continued to speak his truth, his dignity intact. Although his respect for and trust in Church leadership has been damaged, his faith has increased and matured. He still shows up in church on Sunday, a "voice of the faithful," praying to a God he knows is bigger than human frailty and failure.

"It took me a long time to realize that it was God's hands who formed me, and not Dave Jaeger's." That realization refuses to allow Patrick to relinquish his Church because of errant and duplicitous leadership. He knows that this chapter in the Church's history will end, and he stands by ready to help author a new page.

I can't help but think that Patrick's persistent vocational stirring to be a leader in the Church has reached its fruition, almost in spite of the Church. While not "officially ordained" by the laying on of hands of a bishop, Patrick lives a ministry of *priestly* service—championing the voice of the oppressed, offering solace to the brokenhearted, instilling in young people a hope of what is possible when we love instead of hate. It is a priesthood to which I and many others still aspire.

CHAPTER EIGHT

Then There Were Seven

I'LL NEVER FORGET MY FIRST IMAGE OF THEM—lined up in the first pew of the church like the von Trapp family—five golden-haired girls and a stocky, smiling son who loomed over them like a bodyguard. The girls all wore the same dress, white with stenciled blue flowers, and the boy's tie matched the girls' dresses. Undoubtedly, one creative *or* obsessive-compulsive mother was behind this fashion coup. Then I noticed the maternal Diana Vreeland standing next to the youngest girl, stroking her hair gently. The mother was blond herself, petite, and luminous, easily passing for the oldest daughter from where I stood at the altar, except that her ensemble didn't match the rest. Instead, she wore a white, sleeveless dress that paled further against her richly tanned skin. The father stood at the other end of the six kids, a dead-ringer for the actor Robert Morse in his heyday, only more preppy. He wore a blue blazer, button-down shirt, khaki pants, and later, when he came forward to receive communion, I noticed Bass Weejuns without socks. Though appearing youthful, he was obviously the senior in this line of blond princesses and his son, who stood next to him looking politely bored.

After Mass I greeted the exiting churchgoers on the sidewalk. It was my first retreat on Martha's Vineyard, and an interesting mix of the summer crowd was out in full force on this July Sunday. Moneyed people and those who cleaned their houses came to shake my hand, many saying that they were looking forward to the retreat.

"Great homily, Father," someone shouted from across the street.

I turned to see the father of the brood from the first row waving at me, standing with his wife and six kids, all of them eating ice cream from Mad Martha's—the kids with dripping cones and he and his wife with spooned cups. I crossed the street, still in my church vestments, no doubt a dissonant sight on Main Street in Waspy Edgartown.

"Hi, how're you all doing?" I said. "You make quite an impression in the front row."

The younger girls giggled and held their hands to their mouths. The son looked like he couldn't wait to take off his necktie.

"We're just great," said the mother. "How could we not be on this gorgeous day?" She was right about that. The sun shone brightly in a cloudless blue sky, a definite beach day.

"What are your plans for the rest of the day, Father?" asked the husband.

"Well, I may take a run on the beach and then I'm going to work a bit on the talk for tonight. Are you coming back for the retreat?"

"Oh yeah, we'll be there," he said. "Just don't make it too

long, though, huh? I got six kids to put to bed when I get home, and it's quite a production."

The wife rolled her blue eyes a bit and smiled, revealing unusually white teeth that rivaled the dress she was wearing.

"Pay no attention to him, Father," she said. "I do all the work anyway."

"Yeah, sure you do," he said. "In your dreams."

The youngest girl tugged at her mother's dress. "Mom, can we go to the beach now?"

"Yes, Meghan. We're going. Father, take care. We'll see you tonight. Have a great day. Say good-bye, girls."

Almost in unison they chimed good-bye, then the family of eight turned and walked down the street, one shy of a "league of their own" baseball team.

THE NEXT TIME I SAW THEM was the following January, in Winter Park, Florida. I was standing in the back of the church waiting for the beginning of Mass, and there they were again, like a gaggle of geese, this time in the last row. As I walked past them, I did a double take, to make sure it was the same family, but there was no mistaking this clan. Two of the girls pointed at me and smiled, as if I'd been the patsy in a conspiratorial joke.

Once again the whole family waited outside of church for me. "Boy, father," said Ed, the husband, "you've got this retreat thing down pat. Martha's Vineyard in the summer, Florida in the winter. Not bad."

"Right back at you, Ed," I said. "After all, you *live* in both those places. I only get to visit for a week or so."

"Yeah, but I didn't take a vow of poverty," he said, and smiled. "Though sometimes it feels like I did with this crew."

"Oh yeah, you have it so tough," said Karen, the wife. "Give me a break." She then turned her attention to me. "It's so good to see you again, Father. How funny is this—you giving a retreat in *both* our parishes. When I saw your name in the bulletin, I couldn't believe it. Hope this retreat's as good as the one on Martha's Vineyard."

"Well, you'll have to be the judge of that," I said.

"We'd love to have you come over to dinner this week, if you can."

"That'd be great. Name the night, and I'll be there."

When they walked away from me once more, I couldn't have known how significant our inchoate bond would become; how much they would teach me about living and dying; how much they would expand my heart.

KAREN AND ED FIRST MET in an evening real estate law class that Ed was teaching at George Washington University in Washington, DC. Karen was his student, and smitten from the start with Ed's boyish good looks and obvious intelligence. She was disheartened, however, by his constant reference to "we" when giving personal examples in real estate cases, *and* by the fact that he drove a station wagon. Both made Karen assume that he was married with a litter of kids. She was relieved to find out later that the "we" referred to him and his business partner, David.

Ever the professional, Ed says he hardly gave her the time of day, though he surely noticed her. It was hard not to, since she stalked him at his house one evening, wanting to find out where he lived and if he was, in fact, unattached.

"That is so not true," she said halfheartedly, as we sat around their dining room table.

I had gotten to know them well through periodic visits to Florida and their occasional trips to New York City. They had somehow made the rare leap from parishioners to whom I ministered to friends in whom I confided.

"It is *so* true," said Ed. "You and your stepmother were spying in my window. What are you talking about, not true?"

"We couldn't even see anything. It was dark," admitted Karen with a smile.

"Lucky for me," said Ed.

The class had ended and the students had to send their exams to Ed at his home. Karen held on to the address when she noticed that Ed lived only a few blocks from her. After the failed stalking excursion, she asked her father to call Ed and invite him for dinner. Bob Casey was a well-known, influential Washington lawyer who had many connections on the Hill. During the class, Ed had asked Karen, "Why are you in this paralegal class when your dad could get you a job anywhere?" That comment told Karen that a dinner invite from Bob would surely entice Ed.

They ate at a famous steak house in DC, but Karen hardly said a word the whole evening. Bob and Ed talked about lawyers and politics, while Karen sat impressed by Ed's matching of her father's political acumen.

"I was always shy anyway," said Karen, "but even more so with Ed in the beginning. He was so bright that I think I was afraid to say anything wrong."

Toward the end of the meal, Bob and his wife excused themselves to go to a piano bar, leaving a nervous Karen alone with Ed. Out of necessity, he continued to do most of the talking.

"I knew she was smart and attractive," said Ed, reflecting on that first date. "But she was so quiet. I figured I could always send her to finishing school if we stayed together," he said, kidding.

"You were the one who needed finishing," Karen shot back. "God, you're from Syracuse. Look at your dad and brothers, not exactly top-shelf."

"Yeah, but you're not married to them, my dear. You're married to me."

A WEEK AFTER THE MEAL at the DC steak house, Karen was home baking when the phone rang.

"Hi, Karen. It's Ed. Ed O'Neill. I was wondering if you might want to come for dinner on Friday night."

"You mean to your house?" asked Karen.

"Yeah, I thought I'd cook something here, if that's okay. We'd be able to relax a bit more, talk without the noise and rush of a restaurant."

Wow, he cooks too, Karen thought.

"Sure, I'd love to," she said. "Can I bring something?"

"Nah, just your pretty self. See you about seven."

He made stuffed Cornish game hens with mashed potatoes, cranberry sauce, broccoli, and homemade gravy. The dessert was a store-bought apple pie. (Ed says that he didn't want to spoil her too much.)

"I think I realized that night what a catch this guy would be," said Karen. "Bright, cute, a lawyer, *and* a cook, too." She paused. "Oh yeah, and I guess I was also attracted to him."

"You're damned right you were," said Ed with a boyish grin.

After the dinner they didn't do much of anything but watch some TV and talk intermittently, which was fine with Karen.

"I was afraid he might ask too many questions right off the bat, and God knows I didn't want to scare him away. After all, I hadn't exactly come from the most stable of backgrounds. The longer he thought that my father walked on water, the better."

It is easy to understand Karen's initial hesitancy at revealing too much about her family life. *Leave It To Beaver*, it wasn't.

"I KNEW MY FATHER WAS CHEATING on my mother when I was in the fifth grade," said Karen. "They started sleeping in separate bedrooms around that time."

Karen's mother suffered from severe mental illness for most of her life. She was thin and petite, with dark hair and sad blue eyes. Her bipolar disorder produced severe highs and lows, making it difficult for Karen and her four siblings to anticipate the tenor of each day. Her mother would sometimes lock herself in her room for weeks at a time.

"I would come home from school and never know what to expect," said Karen. "We had a nanny, Elaine, who took care of us until I was about twelve years old, and then we basically took care of each other. I was cooking meals and cleaning the house when I was in the sixth grade. I don't think I realized that it was so strange, because it's all I ever knew."

Most of the time, Bob Casey lived in denial of his wife's illness. He retreated into his many affairs, which seemed to push his wife even further to the brink of despair. He acted as though her illness justified his affairs, giving him carte blanche to do as he pleased. He seemed to reason that, with a sick wife, he had to look for solace somewhere. One night Dan, Karen's younger brother, heard their parents arguing in the bedroom.

"I want a divorce," said Bob. "I'm sick and tired of living with you like this. I won't do it anymore. This is no life. You're crazy and you're making me and everyone else crazy. I want out."

"You've been *out*," said Patricia. "But I'll never divorce you. I won't make it that easy for you. You've made your beds—lots of them, now sleep in them all. But you're not *going* anywhere."

A few days later, it was Father's Day. Things seemed to have settled down, though Patricia hadn't been out of bed for days. Karen, then sixteen, went into her mother's bedroom with some gifts.

"Mom, I have some Father's Day presents for you to give to Dad," she said. One was a tie that had the word "Dad" spelled horizontally and vertically, producing a design of many small crosses.

Karen's father entered the bedroom. "I'm going to go to Mass with the kids. Rest a little and then get dressed, and when we come home, we can all go out to brunch."

Patricia nodded halfheartedly, without speaking. Bob kissed her on the forehead and then left for church with three of his children: Martha, the oldest girl, who was married by then and home visiting, Dan, the youngest, fourteen at the time, and Karen. (Ellen, the middle girl, was off the radar screen, having succumbed to mental illness herself, and living in a hippie commune in Massachusetts. Jerry, the older brother, had been discharged from the service and was living in Boston.)

During Mass Dan felt ill, as though he couldn't breathe. Bob Casey, an usher in church, escorted his son outside.

"What's the matter with you?" asked Bob.

"I don't know, Dad. I just felt really bad all of a sudden. Kinda weird."

After a few minutes Dan felt better and they returned to the church for the rest of the Mass. After Mass, they pulled into the driveway at home. Karen and Martha noticed that the disabled boy who lived across the street was sitting outside his house. The Casey children went to say hello to the boy while Bob went into the house to get his wife for brunch, an unusual overture since he usually waited in the car while the kids did the retrieving. A few moments later he ran breathless out the back door, his face flushed, screaming for Dan, who hurried into the house with his father, down to the basement. When they got there, Dan saw his mother hanging from the ceiling with a necktie wrapped around her neck. Bob made Dan hold his mother while Bob cut Patricia down from the ceiling. Dan wept as he held the lifeless body of his mother, a scene one family member would later refer to as a "reversed Pietà."

By the time Karen and Martha walked into the kitchen, Bob and Dan were carrying Patricia up the basement stairs. "Your mother's not breathing," Bob shouted. "Call Dr. Pelinka."

But Karen sensed it was too late for Dr. Pelinka. The necktie with little crosses spelling "Dad" was still wrapped around her mother's neck. Happy Father's Day.

Karen's relationship with her father was understandably strained after the death of her mother. She and her siblings attributed her mother's suicide partly to his philandering, and he seemed to show little remorse, entertaining a girlfriend in a spare Washington apartment within months of his wife's death. It was hard for Karen to understand how such a bright and respected man in his profession—a lawyer, a "good Catholic," and a Knight of Malta, to boot—could be so dumb and callous in ordinary life.

"And you cannot imagine the bimbo he hooked up with," said Karen. "This woman had absolutely no class, no taste, no sense of style. She was all boobs and beehive hairdo. It just amazed all of us. Powerful and influential Bob Casey could have had practically any woman in Washington that he wanted, and he hooks up with the likes of her. Boggles the mind."

ALTHOUGH THAT HAD ALL happened years before Karen and Ed met, Karen initially wondered how Ed would react to her unfortunate history. Treading slowly, they began dating regularly after the home-cooked dinner with which he had charmed her. They went to movies, ate dinner in reasonably priced restaurants, and took long walks while talking about the dreams each of them had—Karen's to be a better mother than her mother was, Ed's to be successful and to have a family for whom he could provide. But the idealism of those dreams was tempered on Valentine's Day that year.

Karen, somewhat of a romantic, had always made a big deal out of the lovers' holiday. Ed wasn't quite on the same page of that romance novel. Soon it was more like pulp fiction.

"He did absolutely nothing for me on Valentine's Day, and I was livid," said Karen. "Here I am at work and all these women are getting flowers and cards and candy, and I'm sitting there like an old maid spinster. I went nuts."

Ed had been traveling frequently, sometimes being away for weeks at a time, giving tax seminars for doctors and lawyers. It seems that something as "insignificant" as Valentine's Day had simply slipped his mind.

"No, you had *lost* your mind," said Karen, "if you thought I wasn't going to react to you not doing *anything*."

"I just didn't think it was a big deal," said Ed. "I mean, you knew I cared about you. I cooked you dinner for God's sake."

"God, one Cornish game hen and he thinks he's done for

life," said Karen. "Well, I showed you just what a big deal it was, didn't I?"

A guy at work had been asking Karen out for some time. She kept telling him she was seeing someone, but after the St. Valentine's Day Massacre, she felt no obligation to feed him that line anymore.

"I know you've been asking me out for some time now," she said to him at work the next day. "Well, I'm saying yes. I'd be happy to go out with you."

Ed reacted in a big way. Since he had forgotten flowers and cards on Valentine's Day, now every day became an attempted makeup. Karen's office and bedroom soon looked like a funeral parlor.

"And he kept calling me," she said. " 'Just have dinner with me,' he would say. 'Just one dinner. I was wrong. I'm sorry. I want to marry you.' "

Karen didn't know if she was ready for marriage, even though she did believe that Ed loved her. Watching her parents all those years had made her skittish about the "fidelity and forever" thing. She couldn't bear the possibility of winding up in a marriage like her parents. So in a preemptive strike, she and Ed started seeing a marriage counselor.

"I needed to convince her that I wasn't like her father," said Ed.

The marriage counselor was duly impressed. "I must admit that I've never had a couple come to me *before* the marriage," he said. "I think he's serious," the counselor said to Karen. "You're going to have to trust him. You don't have a choice if this is going to work."

Karen did trust him, but battled feelings of low self-worth and inadequacy. The love she craved from both her mother and father had never been available. She had to make sure that Ed's love was.

"So I tried to put up another roadblock," said Karen. "I told him that I'd marry him, but he'd have to change jobs. I wasn't going to be with someone who was traveling all the time and never home. I wanted to have children and he needed to be there. Amazingly, he agreed."

"Yeah, I agreed," said Ed. "I said that I would go to Hilton Head and get involved in this real estate development thing, but that if I did that, she had to say yes to getting engaged, or we were finished."

"So I said yes," said Karen.

They were married eight months later.

Unfortunately, the Hilton Head deal went bust, but Karen didn't mind because she disliked living there anyway.

"It wasn't like it is today," she said. "There was nothing there. So when this opportunity came up for Ed to get involved in another condo deal in Jacksonville, we took it. I thought, it couldn't be much worse. Shows you how much I knew."

WHILE LIVING IN JACKSONVILLE, Karen and Ed joined the Florida Yacht Club, one of the oldest private clubs in Florida. Ed became friends with some other lawyer members who decided to propose an African-American dentist for membership in the all-white enclave. The "redneck crackers," as Ed called them, didn't take kindly to the Northern boys' attempts at integration. They blackballed the candidate, and as one member put it, "He really *was* 'blackballed.' "

When the dentist wasn't approved for membership, Ed and his compatriots decided to go public with the overt discrimination perpetrated by the club. The story made the morning papers. This wasn't the first time Ed had been quoted by the "hack reporters of the *Jacksonville Daily Record*," as Ed called them. When the city had inexplicably purchased a restaurant that Ed thought a ludicrous business deal, and it eventually flopped, Ed was quoted in the papers as saying, "Frank Nero [the mastermind behind the ill-fated plan] and the termites are the only ones having a good meal at the Ale House."

When Ed opposed an elevated rail system that the city was attempting to get more funding for by inflating the number of passengers who actually rode it, Ed called a press conference to decry the dishonest tactics. He referred to it as "Tilly's Trolley," a swipe at Tilly Fowler, the congresswoman who had lied to the Department of Transportation about the number of riders. Ed was quoted as saying, "The only ones riding the thing are my kids and their schoolmates on school outings."

But it was the country club controversy that catapulted Ed to the status of local celebrity. The paper called and asked Ed why he belonged to a club that obviously discriminated against racial minorities. Ed's response was that he was trying to change that. But the quote that got the good old boys twitching in their boots was when Ed said, "They don't mind blacks running up and down Florida football fields or between the hedges at Athens, but they don't want them running up and down Yacht Club road." It was the headline in that Sunday's paper.

Unfazed, Ed left for Atlanta the next day on a business trip, leaving behind Karen and the five children they had at the time. A neighbor who had been out walking his dog that evening called Karen. "Karen, you're not going to believe this, but there's white paint all over your car in your driveway." Karen phoned Ed, who returned the following morning from Atlanta.

The phone rang the next day, and an ominous voice on the other end said, "The Yacht Club hates nigger-lovers. I'd watch those five kids of yours very carefully, if I were you." The line then went dead. Karen and Ed called the police, who, because a hate crime had been committed, contacted the FBI.

"It was such an awful time in our lives," said Karen. "Friends just stopped talking to us. Certain parents wouldn't let my children play with theirs anymore. I'd go to the pool and people would tell me that Ed was crazy. They'd say, 'Why can't blacks just find their own country club?' I felt as though I was living in Birmingham, Alabama, in the 1960s. I wouldn't let Ed leave town anymore because I was so frightened."

Karen and Ed took the kids to Martha's Vineyard for vacation that summer, but as the time drew near to return to Jacksonville for the beginning of the school year, Karen grew more apprehensive, knowing she could never feel comfortable living there again.

"Of course, I couldn't have us all living like that," said Ed. "So without telling Karen, I went to Orlando, enrolled the kids at Lake Highland School, and came home and showed her a Polaroid picture of a rental house I had seen."

They left for Orlando two weeks later.

DURING THE WEEK of one of my Florida spring retreats, Karen and I were walking around Lake Eola in Orlando a few years after we had met. She and Ed were living in a beautiful Georgian brick house that they had designed and had built on another lake in Winter Park. I had been to their house many times and had watched the children slowly mature. By that time, Ed and his business partner, David, owned forty-five oil change stations throughout the state of Florida. With law and teaching behind him, Ed had become a full-time dad and husband, working in his office above the garage in the mornings, and then taking Karen for lunch most days at Dexters or Subway. Although he had to visit the various stations periodically, he was home a lot and took the six kids to school each morning. He was happy he had decided to enroll them in a school that went from pre-kindergarten through high school, necessitating only one drop-off and pickup.

Karen and I stopped walking and sat on a bench, gazing at the swans floating by on the unusually blue lake. She seemed a bit preoccupied, not her usual cheerful, effervescent self.

"Anything wrong?" I asked.

"No, I'm okay. Just a little concerned about Jerry."

Karen's older brother, Jerry, had been diagnosed with throat and mouth cancer a few weeks earlier and things were not looking good.

"Have you spoken to him?" I asked.

"No, he doesn't even want me to know. I'm finding out everything secondhand, which makes it even worse. I'd love to talk to him about it, or even visit him, but he won't have it. It's so weird. I'm sure this is related to all the crap he was exposed to in Vietnam."

It struck me how much loss Karen had endured up to this point—her mother, her best friend (who had recently died of non-Hodgkins lymphoma), and now a brother who was dying. Yet she never seemed to lose her ebullience and resiliency. I wondered what her secret was.

"Karen, how do you do it?" I asked.

"Do what?" she said.

"Keep going, keep smiling, keep putting yourself out for others. I mean, you've been through such awful stuff, but it hasn't seemed to do you in. So many people, including myself, would have probably just given up by now, wallowing in our self-pity. But you don't seem to do any of that."

She looked out at the lake, her clear blue eyes filling up slightly. Finally, she said, "I don't know. I guess I've always had to just keep going. There was always some goal, something to get me to the next point. And then, with six kids, you really can't just fall apart at everything because they depend on Ed and me. I may be having a crappy day, but they still have to be dressed and fed and taken to school. They kind of get me out of myself. I look at them, and how wonderful they are, and I know they're my greatest gift. I'm not saying they cancel out all of the bad stuff, but they give me a real reason to celebrate life, too. It's just not all bad."

That night Ed was going to meet us at a restaurant not far from the lake in Thornton Park. Unbeknownst to Karen and Ed, I had arranged for their pastor, a kindly gent from Ireland, to join us for dinner. They always spoke of him in glowing terms, and I had gotten to know him a bit while giving the retreat in their parish. I knew they'd welcome his presence at dinner.

"SO, KAREN AND ED, how are those sweet children of yours?" asked Dick Walsh, the pastor, with his Irish lilt, once we had settled into our chairs in the dimly lit, very hip restaurant.

"Oh, they're fine, Father," said Ed. "Pizza and movie night for them. I'm pretty sure I have all the bases covered." A vigilant dad, Ed would do a bed check each night, never ceasing to be amazed at the rotating sleeping patterns of his kids. He and Karen would set their alarm for 5:30 a.m., so they'd have a half hour in the morning to talk before rousing the troops at six. Ed would conclude the morning tête-à-tête by asking, "So now, what's the game plan for today?" Karen would fill him in on who was going where.

"By the looks of this menu, we're going to be eating a lot better than them tonight," said Karen. "Do you feel guilty, honey?"

"Not in the least," said Ed. "Besides, I'm only getting a salad. It's you who should feel guilty."

"A salad?" said Karen. "What's the matter?" A devoted carnivore, it was rare for Ed to pass up a steak if it appeared on a menu.

"I'm not too hungry. I have a headache."

"Still?" said Karen. "You've had this cold for weeks. You better see somebody."

"It's been going around," said Father Walsh. "I've had it myself."

A FEW DAYS LATER IN THE BRONX, my phone rang. It was Karen. She was crying.

"It's Ed," she said. "He collapsed on the golf course this afternoon with some kind of seizure. We're in the emergency room, but they think he has a brain tumor." The words hit me like an unexpected blow. My mother had recovered from a benign brain tumor years earlier, so I knew the possible complications.

"What kind of tumor?" I asked, hoping Karen would say "benign."

"They don't know," she said. "They're going to operate tonight and biopsy it. I don't think it looks good." She began crying more profusely.

I flew back to Florida two days later. Ed's head was bandaged and his eyes were closed, but he was conscious and making jokes with the nurses.

"Are conjugal visits by my bride permitted?" he said to one buxom, Jamaican nurse.

She put her hand on her hip and said, "They are when you get up out of that bed and start walking for me."

"Nah, she's not *that* pretty," said Ed.

"Well, you really do have your eyes closed now, don't you," said the nurse. Karen shook her head and rolled her eyes. Ed could talk a cat away from a bowl of milk.

"How's he doing?" I asked Karen once we were in the hall together.

"Great," she said in her chipper, reflexive response. But I knew it wasn't great. It was the worst kind of cancerous tumor Ed could have. They gave him six to eight months to live.

After seeing a *60 Minutes* segment on an experimental treatment program for brain cancer patients at Duke University, Karen called Dr. Friedman, who headed the program. He was known as a risk-taker. After all, what did his patients have to lose? They admitted Ed to the experimental program, and for a while things seemed to improve, but it didn't last long. Before long, Ed's memory was vague and his gait unsteady. The inevitable was staring Karen in the face.

"I've always kind of had these goals," she said to me on the phone one day. "I plan stuff to get me to the next thing. But I can't plan anymore. We're all just living in limbo. I don't even know if Ed is going to be around for Patrick's graduation or Meghan's First Communion. Used to be I'd think about him walking the girls down the aisle for their wedding. Now that's all gone."

"I can't imagine what it must be like for you to see your whole life and future disintegrate before your eyes," I said. "How do you keep going?"

"I told you. I just have to. I don't have a choice."

"And you're not mad at God?" I said—maybe, because I was.

"No, I'm really not. I know God doesn't have anything to do with all this, though I do sometimes pray that He would just make it all go away. He can do that, can't He?"

"Well, I guess God can do anything," I said. "I mean, that's what it is to be God, right?"

"You're asking me?" said Karen. "Geez, you're the priest."

"But what if God doesn't make it go away?" I asked. "How does that make you feel?"

"Shitty. But it doesn't stop me from asking for a healing. But I guess everybody's got something."

"Yeah, but you've had more than your share."

"I know . . . Hey, where's this resurrection, new-life part you priests are always talking about? Can I have a little piece of that, please?"

"Karen, I wish I could give it to you."

LAKE HIGHLAND SCHOOL offered to have an early graduation ceremony so that Ed could attend, albeit in a wheelchair. Father Dick Walsh also agreed to let Meghan make her First Communion early, at the same ceremony. We gathered with about one hundred friends and family members in the chapel at Saint Margaret Mary Church one Friday evening to celebrate these new signs of life while Ed sat mostly unconscious in his wheelchair next to Karen and the rest of the children.

When Dick Walsh and I walked out to begin the Mass, I knew I wasn't going to get through it without breaking down. I started thinking of all the previous times I had seen this family lined up in a church pew, and how different this configuration was, how unfair, almost grotesque. Ed, always the stalwart father, now could hardly keep his head up. Karen sat there knowing she'd soon be alone with the children. The kids seemed remarkably poised and calm, almost immune to the sadness and emotion that shrouded the chapel like a premature funereal pall.

I AM STANDING BESIDE ED as he lies in a hospital bed brought into the home by the local hospice. It is three months after the graduation–First Communion Mass. Ed is bald, with wisps of fine brown hair holding on, until I stroke his head and they, too, fall gently to the white Cloroxed pillowcase. An oxygen tube is in his nose, as he breathes laboredly, in gasps, the sound of his mucous-filled lungs filling the room like a precursor death rattle. His extremities have turned slightly blue, cool to the touch. I bless him with a pewter cross that I bought in New Mexico a week before, as Karen and the home-care nurse stand by reverently, somberly. Tears stream down Karen's face. Her brother, Dan, walks in and out of the room, as if not able to bear it all for too long. I lean over the bed until my mouth is against Ed's ear.

"Ed, it's Father Edward. It's okay. Don't fight it anymore. It's time to go home." I stroke his head and rub his chest. "Karen and the kids are going to be fine. You've done a good job, Ed. You can go. Be at peace. Let go, Ed. God's waiting for you. Don't be afraid. Go home, Ed." I think, that if Ed could, he'd tell me to mind my own business.

His breathing settles a bit. His eyes never open. It occurs to me that the *real* Ed is already gone. The rest of him just has to catch up, to be liberated from a body no longer functioning, released from this left-behind shell from which his spirit will, I trust, rise like a warrior Phoenix. It is the final waiting.

THE NEXT MORNING I walk into the bedroom and Karen is atop the bed, sitting on Ed, holding him. Her tears wet the sheets in which he is wrapped. He breathes even more laboredly; his eyes bulge with a glazed stare. It's not clear whether he can see or hear us, though Karen thinks he can. She has her mouth nuzzled to his ear. I sit on the bed and put my arms on her shoulder and back.

"Ed, it's okay," she says. "You have to go. We'll be fine. I promise. Close your eyes. Be at peace, my darling. I love you so much."

She cries in gasping sobs. My own tears begin to fall on Karen's back. Her cousin, Ann, a nun, stands on the other side of the bed, stroking Karen's hair. The three of us are the only ones in the room with Ed.

Karen repeats her mantra over and over again, sure that Ed will eventually hear it and give over to what he can no longer fight. It is time to go home. The waiting is over.

Ed's breathing starts to slow. He seems less agitated, almost peaceful. Karen holds him tighter. "It's okay, Ed. Let go. We'll be fine. Close your eyes. I love you." His head is tilted to one side; his eyes remain open, staring intently, though seemingly at nothing.

Finally, the pause between each breath is longer, as if each inhalation will be the last. Then his stomach rises one final time, recedes, and he is gone. Karen's body heaves in sobs as she wraps her arms around his neck. I hold her from behind. The children slowly trickle into the room, sensing the end has come.

THEY SIT IN THE FRONT PEW dressed in white, just like the first time I saw them in the church on Martha's Vineyard. The casket, draped in a white pall with the Santa Fe crucifix atop it, rests in the aisle beside them. Over five hundred people are in the church for Ed's final send-off, a funeral Mass of joyous celebration of a life well lived, of a man well loved. Flowers enliven the Lenten sanctuary, voices lift in prayer and song, incense rises, as if to signify the final offering of Ed's spirit.

After communion, Erin, the eleven-year-old daughter, sings an a cappella rendition of "Dona Nobis Pacem," a fitting prayer. Yes, "give us peace." She flubs a note, stomps her foot with an echo-accentuated thud, and says, "Wait. I'll get it." The church erupts in laughter and applause. When she finishes, she says, "That's it. I'm done." More laughter and applause.

Patrick, the son, walks to the pulpit to give a eulogy, ending with the words, "My dad was the man I want to be someday." We all sense that in many ways, he already is. He returns to his spot in the pew beside his mother. Karen rests her head on his shoulder.

As we file out of the church, a bagpiper leads us to the cemetery, Ed's body's final resting place, not far from the church. We walk, a sea of people, causing construction workers to stop their work and place their hats over their hearts. The golfers on the green across the street do the same. They must intuit that this funeral is for one important man. As I say the prayers at the grave site and the birds sing in the cypress trees that provide a canopy of shelter, I pray about what lies ahead for this family. I ask for smooth sailing from here on in. They deserve it. I demand it. Enough already. I trust my prayerful edict rises to God as Ed's body is lowered into the ground.

CHAPTER NINE

Mercedes-Benz to Monastery Mazda

HE IS ONE OF THE MOST PLACID INDIVIDUALS I know, moving through a room with remarkable stealth for a large man. Though an admittedly unfortunate comparison, when I see him navigate a room with his light step and rhythmic pauses, I'm sometimes reminded of the dance of the hippopotami in the classic animation film *Fantasia*. The allusion is all the more apt when he trots to the dance floor at a wedding or church celebration to lead an eager group in the "electric slide." Dressed in impeccable, stylish attire that he has worked long and hard at coordinating, he moves with dignity and composure. His may not be the first image that comes to mind when you think "Catholic priest," but he's a damn good one.

Melvin was born in Baltimore in 1948, well before the civil rights movement and integration. He and his sister, Brenda, shared the same bed in a cramped railroad apartment until he was ten years old, when his family finally moved into their own modest row house in the shadow of Saint Joseph's Passionist

Monastery Church on Monastery Avenue. He recalls that time with mournful precision.

"I remember the stares we got from some of our new white neighbors," he says. "We were only the second black family to move onto the block, so the neighborhood hadn't really begun to change yet. I think they resented us because we were an unstoppable tide they couldn't push back anymore. They worried they were going to drown in a sea of black folk. They should've only known that we were the ones afraid."

His father, Big Melvin, as he was called, and mother, Edith, had been married in the church rectory because his mother wasn't Catholic at the time. The priest had performed a quiet ceremony without any fanfare because that's what one did at the time for people in "such situations."

"I found out later," says Melvin, "that there may have been another reason, too. It's funny that I never realized it until I was an adult, but my parents were married in December of 1947, and I was born in June of 1948. You do the math. So they had three strikes against them: my mother was black, a Baptist, and pregnant. They're lucky the priest married them at all. It's probably why my mother converted to Catholicism after they were married. The Catholic Church took them in when her church wouldn't even look at them. She never forgot it."

Melvin's father worked on the old B&O Railroad (Baltimore-Ohio line) as a dining car waiter, tending to the whims of the mostly white clientele who made the overnight runs. Big Melvin was what is called a "cradle Catholic," meaning baptized as an infant. His nondescript attire of black pants and button-down shirts simplified his life: when he went to work, he had only to change his shirt to the standard white with black bow tie. While his job may have been seen as menial by some, the Shorter family benefited by receiving free passes for the Pullman car on the overnight trip to Cleveland, which became the family vacation destination each year.

"We loved traveling on the train," says Melvin. His eyes look sleepy and distant, as if he can still hear the roar and whistle. "It made us feel important in some way. Most black folks only worked on the train, but here we were *riding* on it, and even *sleeping* on it. Nobody had to know that it was because my father worked on it. When we went on vacation, we forgot who we were, and enjoyed being somebody else. We lived high for a few days. Some of my happiest memories are of riding that train. I still like riding trains."

Melvin's happy memories are eclipsed by painful ones of a father who drank to the point of stupor most days. Melvin's earliest recollections are of going to his grandparents' house each Sunday after the nine o'clock Mass and Sunday school. By the time Melvin and his family arrived, the house smelled sweet with the aroma of ham hocks and collard greens that his grandmother had boiled in big steel pots. Gingerbread pies would be cooling on the rack next to the stove. The liquor would already be out and Aunt Bernice and Aunt Myrtle, in floral print dresses and church hats, would be holding court in the living room while Big Melvin and Edith got Melvin and his sister, Brenda, settled in the corner with dolls and picture books and the other cousins.

"It wouldn't be long before my father'd be parked in front of the liquor, pouring away, while my mother scowled at him from her perch on the couch. Usually they'd start fighting there, and just continue with worse fighting once we got home. I could never understand why she kept going back for more. I guess my mother figured it was better than him drinking alone at home. At least at my grandparents' she had someone to talk to."

It is clear in listening to Melvin that the malevolent tentacles of his father's drinking spread well beyond Sundays. Everything seemed to revolve around preventing his father from drinking; or dealing with him when he was drunk; or making sure he didn't spend his paycheck on alcohol. When Big Melvin finally lost his job in 1963 because of drinking, he was fortunate enough to collect a disability check. But someone had to be home with him every third of the month to intercept the check from the mailman so that he wouldn't get it and drink it away.

When his father was drinking, Melvin and his mother would hide Big Melvin's clothes so that he wouldn't go out of the house drunk. One time, after a two-day bender, Big Melvin was alone in the house while Edith was at work and Melvin and Brenda were in school. Melvin came home to find his father walking down Monastery Avenue in his underwear, looking for something to drink or someone to bum some money off.

"The one consolation," says Melvin, "was that Mr. Brown, who lived down the block, was also a drunk, and he had a wooden leg. Well, Mrs. Brown would hide his wooden leg when he was drunk to keep him from going out of the house. But every once in a while you'd see that man hopping down the street on one leg looking for something to drink. I don't know which was sadder: a man in his BVDs stumbling around, or a man with one leg looking like a strung out Hopalong Cassidy."

While attempting humor, Melvin also imagines a life without the disease of alcoholism that incapacitated his father—and his family. As we sit on a Central Park bench under a royal blue sky and unrelenting sun, Melvin grows pensive and looks into the distance beyond my shoulder. Fully absorbed in relaying the extreme actions he took in response to his father's drinking, it's almost as if he's reliving them.

"One time my mother was in the hospital with phlebitis and my father was too drunk to know or to care. And it really pissed me off. I came home from the hospital and I laid him out for not visiting my mother in the hospital. I told him he was a piece of shit.

"The next day I come home from the hospital and find that he's locked the screen door so that I couldn't get into the house. Well, let me tell you, I lost it. I ripped that screen off that door and went into that house seeing red. He was passed out on his bed. I went into the kitchen and heated water on the stove until it got nice and hot, and I poured that water right on him. He jumped up and came after me, and we went at it. I'm telling you, child, if I didn't kill that man that day, I never would have."

It was a few days after Christmas and Melvin's mother had bought Big Melvin some cigars that now sat in a box by the bed. Melvin picked up the cigars, crumpled them in his hand, and threw them in his father's face. His father lunged at Melvin again. "And I still can't believe I did this," said Melvin, "but I picked up a hammer and went back at him with it."

Miraculously, the head of the hammer was loose and flew off the handle and into the wall of the bedroom. "I thank God every day for that loose hammerhead. Because if it hadn't flown off, I would've put it in his head, sure as I'm sitting here. Only I wouldn't be sitting here. I'd be telling you this story from jail right now."

Melvin pauses and pushes his wire-rimmed glasses back up to the bridge of his nose. He seems embarrassed by the disclosure he has just made. "I walked into my room after it was all over," he finally says. "And I shut the door and turned on the TV. I remember that there was a show on about violence in America. I sat there not believing that people could be so violent. I was totally oblivious to what had just happened with my father. How's that for being out of touch with what's going on in your life?"

I wondered how Melvin had survived such upheaval and appeared seemingly unscathed on the outside. The inside was another matter. As he continued to talk about the injurious legacy of a father whose life was cut short by a disease he never conquered, the toll it had taken became apparent. But what also became apparent was that Melvin was destined to overcome that legacy.

HE REMEMBERS that as a young teenager he had tried to join the Catholic Youth Organization (CYO) at church. But since he and Brenda went to public school, there was a problem: the priests only admitted kids who were taking religion in the school. Melvin made an appointment to see Father Callistus Connelly, a tall, kindly old priest who was the moderator of the CYO, to discuss the possibilities. He remembers Father Connelly's hesitation because there were no blacks in the CYO and he feared Melvin might feel out of place. But the intuitive cleric also sensed Melvin's determination.

"Well, Melvin," he said. "I'll make a deal with you. If you go to religious instruction classes on Tuesday nights, you can join CYO."

Melvin relished this monumental victory and never forgot the acceptance the priest had shown him. When Father Connelly developed throat cancer later in life and was reduced to being able to say only two words, "yes" and "why," Melvin thought the scant words summed up how the priest had lived his life. As a tribute to the priest, Melvin later took "Callistus" as his confirmation name, and his sister, Brenda, took "Callista." It was obvious the taciturn man had made his mark.

Melvin joined not only CYO but also a "vocations club" at

the monastery church, which was moderated by Father Justin Brady, a short, balding priest renowned for his holiness. The priest invited young men considering a religious vocation to the monastery for a monthly meeting where they watched movies about life in the monastery and shared a meal afterward. He took Melvin to his first priestly ordination in Union City, New Jersey—quite a treat for a wide-eyed outsider enamored by the ecclesiastical pageantry. When Father Brady died not many years later, a contingent from the parish in Baltimore tried to introduce his cause for sainthood.

"I was suddenly surrounded with these holy, remarkable men," says Melvin. "I don't know what it was about the monastery, but I always felt accepted there. I was picked on in school because I wasn't exactly a fighter or an athlete. I was a *sensitive* boy, you might say. Well, sensitive didn't go over too well then. But at the monastery, it was okay to be sensitive. I was welcomed there—not only by the other kids, but by the priests and brothers, too. It became a kind of sanctuary in my life, from school *and* home."

Melvin found closeness to God there as well. He began to fantasize about being a priest like the holy monks he saw scurrying about in their long black habits and sandals. He pictured himself saving pagan babies in the foreign missions. There was mystery to the lives of these religious that intrigued him, and a peacefulness and contentment that made him envious. He wanted all of it.

His mother wanted none of it. She found the monastery cold and unwelcoming, and even a bit racist. "You don't see any priests your color parading around up there, do you?" she'd say.

Edith looked out for her children with the diligence of a mother who knew firsthand the harm a racist world could inflict.

She had experienced discrimination her whole life and was intent on shielding her children from whatever she could. When she enrolled Melvin and Brenda in PS 65, the school automatically put them in speech classes. When she learned that the school enrolled *all* of the black kids in speech class, she went up to the school and demanded that her children be taken out of the class. "There's nothing wrong with the way those children speak," she told the principal. "And if you think there is, then *you* need the classes." Melvin and Brenda were taken out the next day.

One of the reasons she had put them in public school was that the monastery Catholic school was slow to integrate. Blacks couldn't go to school on days when the children went to Gwynn Oaks Park on a field day, because the park wasn't integrated. Edith bristled at the thought of her children being excluded. She feared that Melvin's attraction to the monastery would only lead to his being excluded once again in what she perceived as a white world where blacks tidied up. And so when Melvin was offered an application for the Passionist Prep High School seminary by one of the priests, Edith said no. She didn't believe Melvin knew yet what he wanted to do with his life. And even if he did, she didn't agree.

After graduating from public high school, Melvin lived at home and went to Coppin State College and worked for the federal government in the evenings—Phi Beta Sigma fraternity member by day and peripheral computer equipment operator by night. It was a busy, full life, but the call of the monastery could not be hushed. Melvin would still go to Mass there and periodically show up for community celebrations. The imposing edifice sat on the hill like a beckoning grandfather who wouldn't take no for an answer.

"One day I showed up for a Vocations Day, which was for anyone who was considering joining the religious life or priesthood," says Melvin. "Brother James Johnson was giving the talk. He was really good. Very sincere. And he concluded by saying, 'Come and see.' I knew by the time he was done it's what I had to do."

Melvin went to speak to Father Fran Landry, the local vocations director at the monastery. Fran could tell that Melvin was conflicted about what to do and was feeling pressure from home and work to stay put. Fran proposed a compromise solution.

"Melvin, we can tailor a formation program for you," he said one day in his office. "I don't think you're quite ready to leave everything behind and move away, so how about moving, but staying here?"

"What do you mean?" Melvin said.

"I'd like you to move into the monastery here in Baltimore and share our life, but continue to live part of your other life as well. Keep your job, visit your family down the street, see your friends. But you'll eat, sleep, and pray here. It will serve two purposes: you'll get a better look at what this life is all about and you won't have to burn any bridges just yet."

It seemed like the perfect solution to everyone, except to Edith.

"You're just running away from me and your father," she said when Melvin told her. "You'll never be able to do that. You like the good life too much, and now that you've gotten a taste of it, you're not going to be able to give it up to live like that. You think you're better than everyone else, Melvin. And you can't live in there thinking like that."

But Melvin needed to find out for himself. On September 14, 1976, on the feast of the Triumph of the Cross, Melvin moved out of his parents' row house on Monastery Avenue and into the monastery down the street. His mother cried. His father was passed out on the couch. His sister, Brenda, asked if she could have his bedroom.

"They had a big meal at the monastery that night," says Melvin. "I was feeling so important and welcomed until I realized that the meal was because of the feast day, not me. But even so, everyone was so friendly. It felt like home from the very first day, maybe even more so than the home I'd just moved out of. I think I liked the peace and quiet most. No more yelling, no more fighting."

Melvin lived that year with both worlds pulling at him, unsure of which one he belonged in. He prayed morning prayer and Mass with the priests and brothers and then went to work for the federal government, by this time as a career counselor doing training and career development. He'd return to the monastery at the end of the day and pray evening prayer and have dinner with the priests and brothers. Afterward, he would recreate with the religious in the common area or read quietly in his spartan room. On weekends he would visit the sick at Saint Agnes Hospital and bring them communion.

"It was perfect for me," he says. "I wasn't ready to give up everything, yet I was able to get more than a peek at what this world was like. I guess it was my way of holding on while still looking back—one foot in, one foot out."

The foot *in* eventually started to feel more comfortable than the one *out*. At the end of that year, Melvin decided to go to the Passionist novitiate in West Hartford, Connecticut, to see definitively if he was being called to a religious life. While entrance into the novitiate is usually seen as a break from one's past, to literally "put on" a new way of life, Melvin still didn't seem ready to make that move. He was moving geographically, but part of his heart was staying behind.

"I didn't resign my job. I simply took a leave of absence. I kept my health insurance. I let my mother take care of my car. I gave her my bankbook to hold. Basically my life was waiting, ready for me to return to it whenever I wanted. I put my hand to the plow and kept looking back. In retrospect, it was probably the wrong way to do it, but it seemed best then."

Two friends, Mallory and Charles, drove Melvin to Holy Family Monastery on a sweltering August day. Awaiting him were his three classmates, Joe, Tim, and Mario, and the novice director, Father Raphael, and his assistant, Father Tom. Father Raphael escorted Melvin to his "cell."

After climbing the three flights with Raphael leading the way, Melvin arrived breathless in the novitiate wing of the monastery. Raphael led him down the long monastery corridor, which shone like a freshly buffed car. When they reached a room with a wooden door that already had Melvin's name hanging on it, Raphael said, "Here it is, Melvin." He pointed to the ten-by-fifteen-foot, lackluster beige room. "Anything you need?"

"Yeah," said Melvin, "a private bathroom, cable TV, and air conditioning would be nice." Raphael laughed. Melvin was only half kidding.

Melvin found that life as a novice at Holy Family Monastery was different from life as a layman living in the monastery in Baltimore. At the latter he was treated as an adult, with the same privileges as the priests and brothers in the monastery. In the novitiate he was seen as the beginner he was, needing to be indoctrinated into the ways of religious life by those who had lived it for years. He resented the demotion. He wasn't used to not doing anything all day. Reading books and waxing monastery corridors didn't quite cut it. He abhorred having to ask someone else for money to buy toiletries, or for permission to leave the grounds. The hallowed walls of the monastery closed in on him quickly, and while he tried to push them back, they wielded a strength he hadn't anticipated.

"I couldn't believe that we couldn't even go to the mall when we wanted," he says. "I just wasn't used to it. I'm so independent and private. I hate having to account for my every move. Suddenly, everyone knew my business."

The platonic honeymoon with his three classmates fizzled rather quickly as well. The novices had a separate recreation room from the professed priests and brothers, so the four of them depended upon each other for companionship and entertainment. During recreation time they played cards and board games, and sometimes watched TV together—when they could agree on a program to watch. But the pressures of being thrown together with people he didn't choose, and who didn't choose him, soon got to Melvin. The disapproval he was still getting from home didn't help either.

"My mother was writing me letters asking me to come home," he says. "She was telling me I didn't belong in a monastery, and that I was making a big mistake. Living alone with my father wasn't easy for her.

"To top it all off, Tim, my classmate, was driving me crazy with his Franciscan spirituality, planting things in the garden, keeping goldfish, wearing a winter coat with no buttons and claiming it was poverty. And the other two, Mario and Joe, were smoking pot on the monastery roof. I was so mad and confused, I didn't know what to do."

One day Melvin went to the monastery mailroom to see if he had gotten any letters, which he hadn't in almost a week. Tim was there thumbing through about *ten* letters that he had received that day from friends and family. He gave Melvin a sleepy, sloe-eyed grin and started to walk out of the mailroom, but before doing so, he patted Melvin sympathetically on his rear end.

"Well, child, I don't know why, but it just set me off," said Melvin. "I just think I was so fed up and angry at everyone and everything by that point, that Tim was there to receive it. I hauled back and I smacked that little farm boy across his face so hard that he didn't know what hit him. I don't know what came over me. He looked so shocked, like I had lost the little bit of my mind that I had left. He backed up slowly and practically ran down the corridor. And I walked straight into Raphael's room and sat in the chair and said, 'I think I have to leave.'"

That occurred on a Tuesday. By Friday, Melvin's bags were packed and he was on a train back to Baltimore. By Monday morning he was at his desk at his old job with the federal government. Although they had filled his previous position, they assigned him to the Department of Personnel, where he worked in an alcohol and drug abuse program, of all things. "How ironic is that?" he said. (Two weeks after Melvin left the novitiate, Tim left, too. And two weeks after him, Mario left as well, leaving only Joe. Melvin takes pride in being a trendsetter.)

Living at home again was not easy. Having experienced life away, Melvin was resolved to not get enmeshed in the perennial problems of a drunken father and a demanding mother. He realized that he could easily become a "surrogate husband" to his mother again if he wasn't careful. He decided to make the move he had always dreamed about. With the money he had squirreled away before leaving, and which his mother had safeguarded in his absence, he rented a luxury apartment in a tony section of downtown Baltimore, ten blocks from the inner harbor. It came with a white-gloved doorman, a twenty-four-hour answering service, and a private garage for his undependable white Chrysler

Cordova. He moved into a one-bedroom on the seventh floor and furnished it with a king-sized bed and modern pale-wood Scandinavian furniture. He felt like he had finally arrived—at least for a time.

Melvin took Father Raphael's sage advice and began to see a therapist to talk about issues he had long avoided. "I talked about my father for the first time in my life," Melvin says. "Dr. Sandy Unger got me to open up to stuff I had bottled up for so long. I had so much anger toward my father that I never knew what to do with. I started remembering things that I thought I'd let go, like the stupid little pencil sharpener that was gone one day from the basement cabinet because he'd sold it to get money to drink. Or never mind that, how about the dining room china cabinet itself that he hocked for drink money, or the alcohol that I brought back from the Virgin Islands with me that he found and drank in one night? It was like living in a prison. We had to put everything under lock and key or it would disappear."

But that wasn't the worst of it. All that violence had taken its toll. Melvin had some serious father issues. While he was talking about them one day in Sandy's office, Melvin remembered that when he was in high school there was a father-son banquet that he and his father had been scheduled to attend.

"But my father got drunk, of course, so we couldn't go," he said. "I got so angry that I said to him, 'You're not the damn father I always wanted.' And without hesitating, he turned around in his stupor and looked me straight in the eye and said, 'And what makes you think you're the damn son I always wanted?' It was like getting the wind knocked out of me. I couldn't believe he didn't think that I was the model son. I did well in school. I went to church. I helped my mother. What more could he want?

"But as I was telling the story to Sandy, it hit me that maybe he had needs that I didn't meet either. I *was* a bastard to him. I threw scalding water on him, for God's sake. And I never could get the hang of baseball, try though he did to teach me how to throw a ball. So I disappointed him, too. It was a revelation for me. It didn't make his drinking okay, but for the first time I felt some compassion for him. It was a beginning."

There were other beginnings as well. Melvin found that he enjoyed his newfound independence and his high-on-the-hog lifestyle. He went out dancing in clubs with friends, shopped at the trendiest stores downtown, and threw dinner parties with coordinated china in his chichi apartment. He began to feel like somebody, as everyone agreed he had certainly arrived. The image was complete the day his Chrysler Cordova broke down on Security Boulevard.

"I had just had it with that car by that point," he says. "I left it by the side of the road and marched right into an Audi dealership two blocks away. I stood there for five minutes, but no one came over to help me. They must've thought a black man wouldn't be in there to buy an Audi. So I walked out of there and across the street to a Mercedes-Benz dealership, where they were much more accommodating. After a call to my credit union, who approved a loan, the man sold me a pastel gray diesel 230 Mercedes-Benz with black leather interior."

Melvin pauses for a moment and shakes his head. "Do you want to hear something strange?" he finally says. "What I remember most about buying it was wondering if my father would be proud of me now. I kept hearing him say that the sandalwood Monte Carlo that I bought as my first car was 'a sissy color.' Funny that it still mattered to me what he thought."

What Melvin didn't know at the time was that there was little time left to impress his father. Shortly after buying the Mer-

cedes, Melvin and his mother went to the Catskills for the weekend with some of his aunts and cousins. He had been taking a
walk with one of his cousins and returned to find his mother sitting in the lobby of the hotel with a blank expression on her face.

"What's wrong?" he said.

"Daddy's dead," she said calmly. "Brenda called and said she
couldn't wake him up. We have to go home."

The night before they left for the Catskills his father had
been seriously ill, vomiting profusely in the bathroom. Melvin
had stood at the bathroom door witnessing a familiar scene. He
doesn't know why, but he felt something different this time—
sorry for the man, sorry for the waste of a life, sorry for the relationship that never was. Instead of his usual response—walking
away in disgust—he paused and said to his father, "Are you sick
enough to finally get some help?" For the first time, his father
answered, "Yes, I am." Two days later he was dead.

Melvin remembers the bus ride home from the Catskills as
being quiet and long. While sitting next to his mother, she and
Melvin hardly spoke. He stared out the window for the entire
trip, the lush scenery rushing past in a blurred wash. He realized
that he and his mother would be returning to a house where his
father would not be passed out on the couch anymore. Not
knowing what he felt, he didn't cry, but instead thought about
what he was going to do with his life now. The death of his father
and his therapy sessions with Sandy Unger had brought him to a
precipice from which he finally felt ready to leap.

He started visiting the monastery in Baltimore more frequently again and found himself lingering at the refectory table
long after the dishes had been cleared. He still enjoyed listening
to the stories of the older priests, who seemed so content with a
life that Melvin's worldly friends dismissed as dull. Only it didn't

seem dull to Melvin; it never had. It had always appeared noble and fulfilling, self-sacrificing and gratifying. It still did. He couldn't shake it—not even with a Mercedes-Benz parked in the church parking lot.

"Then one night I'm sitting in Morris Mechanic Theatre in downtown Baltimore," Melvin says. Having purchased a season's subscription, he enjoyed the concerts and Broadway touring companies that stopped there on their way to someplace else.

"I was alone that night, as I frequently was. I never mind going to the theater alone. And I'm paging through the playbill, waiting for the curtain to go up, when suddenly this ad jumps at me from the page. And it says: *Where do you go, and what do you do, when the party's over?* It hit me right between my eyes because it was *my* question. But I was always afraid to ask it because I didn't know the answer. I left the theater that night knowing I had to find out the answer."

Two weeks later Melvin called Father Raphael in West Hartford and told him he'd like to come back and give the novitiate another try, if the community would have him. He heard a few months later that he had been accepted again in the next novitiate class, but was informed that the novitiate would be moving to the Pittsburgh monastery of the Passionists, its first foundation in the United States. Melvin decided he could live with that, but he might *not* live after telling his mother that he was returning to the life he had left two and a half years before.

"I sat her down at the kitchen table and told her. She cried again. Told me she didn't think she could make it financially without me. Told me I'd be back again. And then she said, 'Melvin, you're thirty-three years old. You should have made up your mind what you're going to do with your life by now. Jesus was dead by now, for God's sake.'

"But I knew that she was wrong this time. At last, she was wrong. I realized that I couldn't live to make her, or anyone else, happy anymore. I had to be honest with myself and try to make myself happy. And that this time I had to leave totally, with no ties to the past, no looking back.

So he didn't take a leave of absence from his job. He quit it outright. He didn't give his mother the Mercedes to hold for him. He sold it. He also sold the furniture from the apartment and everything else, and gave his mother the money for herself.

"I had to do it honestly this time, no security blanket."

WE SIT IN CENTRAL PARK together some twenty years after that silent bus trip home with his mother. It is shortly after his mother has died after a long illness, during which Melvin was as present to her as one could be. "When I found out she was dying, I felt I had to be there for her and make her as comfortable as possible. Maybe I still carried around some guilt about leaving her, even though she did finally come around and was as proud as anyone the day I was ordained a priest. She walked down that church aisle in a black and yellow dress like she was the queen of England there to witness the coronation of her son."

I ask Melvin if her death is harder for him than the death of his father was. He seems unable to answer at first. His half-closed eyes fill with tears as he watches a squirrel scamper hesitantly up an old oak.

"I think with my father, it was kind of a relief when he finally died. He was just in so much pain for so long. At last, he was at peace. With my mother it was different. I somehow thought that she was always going to be around. She seemed invincible to me. I mean, look at all she survived. She never,

ever thought of divorcing my father. She said she married him for better or for worse, and that just because he got sick was no reason to leave him. She was this tower of strength, this source of faith for me.

"And except for when I was leaving for the novitiate, I never saw her depressed or thinking that tomorrow wouldn't come. She just never felt sorry for herself. And she never went on welfare, even when my father was drinking and there was no money coming into the house. Somehow she held it all together and never asked anyone for help—except Saint Jude, who she said a novena to every day. And I miss knowing I can pick up the phone and tap into that tower of strength. I just miss her being there. I don't think anyone has ever loved me that much."

We stand up to walk toward Central Park West as the sun now hangs low over the San Remo Towers, soon to disappear across the Hudson into the meadowlands of New Jersey. I realize how grateful I am for my eighteen-year friendship with Melvin and how much I have learned from him. I think that we are finished for the day, Melvin emotionally spent, and I sunburned, yet full of the beauty and grace of all that he has shared. But as we cross the street on our way to dinner, Melvin has one more story to tell.

"When I was chaplain for the 1996 Olympics in Atlanta, there was a marathon race on the last day," he says. "There was this black runner from some country in Africa . . . I think it was Somalia. And he was the only representative from his country who had made it to the Olympics. They had never had anybody get that far before. But he just wasn't up to the same level as the rest and he fell far behind during the race. Way behind. But, he never stopped running. He just kept on. He didn't give up.

"People had basically forgotten about him though," Melvin

continued. "They had locked up the stadium after everyone from the stands had gone home."

As it was getting dark, the Olympic orchestra was rehearsing for the closing ceremonies the next day. Melvin was getting ready to leave, after having spoken to some athletes who had wanted to see him.

Two hours after the last runner had entered the stadium from the marathon, the African runner finally made it to the arena and was running in position outside, pounding on the gates. When the workers finally saw him, they opened the gates to the stadium again and turned on the lights.

"And this guy, looking half dead, barely able to run, begins to take his own victory lap as the orchestra plays the Olympic theme song," said Melvin. "I was so touched, I didn't know what to do. And I've been thinking about that man all afternoon because all of the people who come to the Olympics are winners up to that point. But the majority leave as losers. And that's the way it is in life. For most people life is a struggle. It was for my father. It was for my mother. And it has been for me. Things weren't all rosy just because I went back to the novitiate. I've had some tough times since then, to say nothing about how much I miss that Mercedes. But I've learned not to give up, that the goal isn't necessarily winning, but participating and surviving. My parents did that. And they taught me how to. And I'm just gonna keep on—just like they taught me to."

And he has kept on. Despite periodic health concerns and an occasional lapse into self-pity, Melvin gets up every day and pushes himself to go on. He is currently the beloved pastor of one of the most prominent African-American parishes in Atlanta as well as valued consultor to the Provincial (head honcho) of the Passionist Community of the eastern United States. He has met

Maya Angelou, Bishop Desmond Tutu, Andrew Young, and Coretta Scott King. He remains a vocal spokesperson for justice in the African-American community and continues to toil for a day when the color of his skin—or anyone else's—won't matter. And he remembers well the lessons his mother taught him.

I SIT NEXT TO HIM at Edith Shorter's funeral Mass in the sanctuary of Saint Joseph's Monastery Church in Baltimore, the haven where it all began. I wonder what's going through his head as he stares at the coffin of his mother. There is a touching irony in the son she never wanted to be a priest now presiding at her funeral Mass. I doubt I would have the composure he has seemed to muster. As the "Alleluias" ring out, signaling the proclamation of the Gospel, Melvin slowly ascends the marble steps of the pulpit. At the end of his elegiac and inspired homily, he recites the Langston Hughes poem, "Mother to Son." It is his final tribute to her. It is also her ode to him.

> Well, son, I'll tell you:
> Life for me ain't been no crystal stair.
> It's had tacks in it,
> And splinters,
> And boards torn up,
> And places with no carpet on the floor—
> Bare.
> But all the time
> I'se been a-climbin' on,
> And reachin' landin's,
> And turnin' corners,
> And sometimes goin' in the dark,

Where there ain't been no light.
So boy, don't you turn back.
Don't you set down on the steps
'Cause you finds it's kinder hard.
Don't you fall now—
For I'se still goin', honey,
I'se still climbin',
And life for me ain't been no crystal stair.

A Love That Dares Speak Its Name

I NOTICED THEM A FEW TIMES at Saint Francis Xavier Church in the Chelsea section of New York City. They usually arrived just before Sunday Mass began, sat in the same pew, and afterward visited a side altar to light candles and kneel before the statues of the saints looming above in the alcove. They were obviously pious and, I thought, perhaps in love as well. As I was crossing Sixth Avenue one Sunday after Mass on a pristine spring day, when New York never looks better, they introduced themselves. It was then that I became a part of their story.

"Wow, *you're* a priest," said Norm, once we were across the street. "We never would have thought that. I told Héctor you were probably some professor at Columbia or something."

Norm appeared to be in his thirties, with sandy brown hair, an aquiline nose that seemed a bit large for his face, and green eyes, the color of sea moss.

"Yeah, but I told him you could just as easily be a writer or something," said Héctor.

I was glad they had at least chosen professions that indicated I seemed to be intelligent, though I wondered why I had become a topic of conversation in the first place.

"Well, I must admit," I said, not knowing quite what to say, "that I noticed you guys, too. You seem very devout in church. I don't see that too often, at least with two guys who appear to be together, I mean." (I wasn't sure what I meant.)

I had been on my way to my car, parked four blocks from the church. Intent on getting home to work on a talk I had to give, I was caught off guard. They seemed interested in continuing the conversation, though, and I guess I was, too.

"We live in this great house and spiritual center on the Hudson River," I said, as we stood beside my car after some minor chitchat en route. "The community has owned it for years. You can't believe the view we have. You'll have to come up and see it sometime."

Norm, never one to miss an opening, said, "Gee, we'd love to see it. Would you mind if we took a ride up with you?"

I hesitated, not sure if I was prepared to extend a mid–Sixth Avenue encounter into an afternoon commitment. I also wondered how they were going to get back to the city. Did they expect a round-trip ride?

Héctor, sensing my hesitancy, tried to come to the rescue. "Norm, maybe Edward has plans. We can always go up another time."

Héctor seemed a bit older than Norm—and not just chronologically. He was darkly handsome with curly, brown, closely cropped hair, which I later learned he colored to remove the gray. A few facial moles gave him a certain mystique.

"No, it's not that," I said. "I just wasn't sure you wanted to spend your Sunday afternoon looking at some retreat house."

"*I* think it'd be interesting," said Norm, turning to Héctor, waiting for confirmation.

Héctor rolled his eyes a bit, seemingly resigned to spending the afternoon with a priest he had just met in a spiritual center he knew nothing about.

We drove up the Westside Highway to Riverdale, with the Hudson River on our left reflecting the intense blue of a clear sky. Norm sat in the front, as if there was never a question that he belonged there. Héctor made conversation from the back, his slight accent giving him an interesting sound.

I learned that he was born in Santurce, Puerto Rico, a suburb of San Juan. He talked a bit about his grandmother Lola, who seemed a big influence in his early life.

"She became disaffected with the Catholic Church, though," said Héctor, playing with the seat-belt strap he had diligently secured. "She got really pissed off when the priest of the parish seemed to blame her when her husband abandoned her."

He went on to say that she made her own church in the house. Walking with a limp due to a botched operation, she would light candles scattered around the house and pray to her icons and statues, whose number rivaled those of her church. She presided in her own sanctuary, complete with holy water with which she blessed herself and which she placed in front of the statue of Saint Martin de Porres, a particular favorite.

"My mother wasn't too keen on my grandmother's way," said Héctor. "She thought her *espiritismo* wasn't Catholic enough and worried that her constant talking to the spirits might give people the wrong idea—a little *loquita*."

I could tell that Héctor, on the contrary, was charmed by his grandmother's eccentricities. Even more than that, he seemed impressed by her renowned hospitality. "She was always cooking something on the stove, just in case somebody should stop by. The smells in that house were always of food. I miss that."

In the house of olfactory delights, where "family" was as revered as the saints who lined the walls, Héctor learned the art of hospitality from a woman who cultivated it in her own domestic church.

Norm seemed bored by Héctor's "grandmother musings." He stared out the car window, occasionally commenting on a passing sailboat or about how gorgeous the day was. Perhaps feeling some pressure to clue the priest in on *his* "spiritual influences and upbringing," Norm finally said, "My mother has those statues too, but it's more the American version. No dead chickens or anything like that."

"*Norm*, there were no dead chickens," said Héctor from the backseat.

Norm evaluated his upbringing as less exotic, born in Astoria, Queens, and moving to a cookie-cutter house in Levittown, Long Island, when he was five years old. Norm hardly remembers his maternal grandmother, other than when she died. He had found his mother crying in the bathroom, the first time he had seen her so vulnerable.

"I spelled out 'I love you, Mommy' on a Fisher-Price magnetic blackboard and held it up for her to see." His attempt to cheer up his mother was a prescient moment that they would revisit many times through the years.

"No offense," said Norm, as we approached the George Washington Bridge, "but unlike my mother, I've had some real struggles with the Church."

While he was active in church as a teenager, teaching religion to grade school children and faithfully lecturing at Sunday masses, he became disenchanted later by the Church's seeming "hypocrisy and archaic notions about morality and sexuality. It was very hard for me to reconcile what I knew to be true from my experience, and what the Church was telling me was true." I had the sense I'd be hearing more about that as the day went on.

"But, you know," he continued, seemingly wanting to change the topic for now, "when I was younger, I was asked by some of the priests if I ever thought about becoming a priest. And actually I did think about it, but then puberty kicked in and there went any thoughts of celibacy and the priesthood."

"Lucky for me—and the people of God," said Héctor and smiled.

WHEN WE ARRIVED at the retreat center and residence where I live, Norm and Héctor seemed impressed by the serenity and bucolic surroundings.

"I can't believe we're less than twenty minutes from Manhattan," said Héctor.

"So this is what a vow of poverty looks like," Norm chimed in. "Not bad."

After showing them around (and getting a few unsolicited decorating suggestions from Norm), I got them some juice and water, and we retired to the glassed-in back porch, with magnificent views of the Hudson River and the adjacent Palisades.

"Gee, I don't know if I'd ever leave this place," said Héctor, as he stared out the glass door facing the river.

"Yeah, I could get used to this, too," said Norm, as he checked out each artifact in the room. "As long as I could get my fix of the city each week."

When we were finally seated, they were eager to share more of their story with me, and I was a willing listener. I learned that they had met at Binghamton University. Héctor had arrived there in 1989 from the University of Kentucky, where he had worked on a PhD in marketing. He had come to the States to pursue a better program than the University of Puerto Rico was offering. With only his dissertation left to finish, he moved into a two-bedroom apartment off the Binghamton University campus, overlooking the picturesque Susquehanna Valley, and got a job teaching marketing.

Unbeknownst to Héctor, Norm arrived at Binghamton that same fall of 1989 to begin his undergraduate studies with a double major in biology and political science, having recently graduated from Levittown's Division Avenue High School as valedictorian. A failure at sports, he had compensated for his athletic inability by excelling in academics and school politics. Winning over even his more churlish classmates, who had previously resented his intellectual acumen and designated him a "geek," by the time he graduated he was student class president and prom king.

While Norm and Héctor arrived at Binghamton the same year, they strolled the same terrain for four and a half years before finally meeting—not on campus, but in Splash, the only gay bar in Binghamton. It was January 1994, and neither one could have anticipated what awaited them.

Splash was the only game in town for young gay men in Binghamton hoping to connect. Héctor hardly remembers meeting Norm that first night. Norm was more taken with Héctor's roommate, Steve, a Cornell student with blond hair and "fake green eyes," as Norm says.

"He was very cute and preppy," said Norm. "Héctor was tired and wanted to leave, which was fine with me, because Steve and I went out to a diner alone. I was very giddy that night because I was so attracted to Steve. But I was really looking for a more serious relationship by that point, so when I drove him home, I simply shook his hand and said good night. I didn't want to ruin it with casual sex right away."

Norm had already gone that route and found it lacking. While he knew that he was gay from the time of puberty, he was conflicted about it growing up, feeling stranded in Levittown with few role models and no healthy outlets for sexual exploration.

"My first couple of years at Binghamton I tried to be straight, because I never thought I could live a happy, integrated gay life. I convinced myself that I wanted the wife, family, and white picket fence. And I think a part of me really did. That's what I'd been trained to believe was the only acceptable way."

So Norm dated a woman, Jennifer, for two years at college, but he was never able to overcome his homosexual feelings. By the time he met Steve at Splash he was ready for a serious relationship with a guy. Perhaps Steve could be the one.

What Norm didn't know was that Steve had broken up with a guy he found cheating on him that very day and casual sex was *exactly* what *he* wanted. Willing to give Norm one more chance, Steve called him to see if he wanted to go to Héctor's to watch a movie—a safe invitation. The three of them watched *Naked Gun* that night and then went to Wegman's Supermarket for Chinese food, but much to Steve's disappointment, Norm still refused to sleep with him.

"Now you have to understand," said Héctor, "that I still wasn't really interested in Norm." Norm shook his head with a slight smile, apparently having heard many times before how Héctor "wasn't really interested" in him.

"I mean, Norm was cute and all, with nice green eyes," Héctor continued, giving Norm his due, or risk hearing about it later, "but Steve was the one interested in Norm—and in one thing only, I might add." Héctor looked at Norm and nodded, emphasizing Steve's superficial designs. "So he tells me to hug Norm goodbye to see if he was well built, because Norm was wearing a bulky sweater and Steve couldn't tell. So there I was, feeling up Norm for Steve. It was a little ridiculous."

"Yeah, but you enjoyed every minute of it," said Norm.

"But, of course, Steve was so fickle," Héctor continued, "that he met someone else that night and moved on anyway, not giving Norm a second thought. And he left me with the mess to clean up. Story of my life."

"Yeah, you've had it so rough," said Norm.

Héctor felt sorry for Norm because Steve wouldn't return any of Norm's calls, so Héctor called Norm and invited him to lunch.

"And I ripped his head off," Norm interjected. "I blamed him for coming between Steve and me, and how dare he. And I'm going on like a crazy man until Héctor calmly tells me what really happened and then hangs up on me. Needless to say, I felt like a complete idiot. I called him back to apologize and invited him to dinner at a place called Hole in the Wall, which was an apt description. We wound up having a really nice time, and we went out four or five more times after that—strictly platonic. But we really enjoyed each other's company."

On a return visit to Splash some weeks later, Norm had a little too much to drink. "And I just leaned across the bar and kissed him. I don't know, something finally clicked. I felt this emotional connection. He seemed like such a good person. The beginning of love, I guess."

Héctor clearly felt the same way because that night Norm

stayed the night at Héctor's apartment and never left. "I was ready for something more serious at the time, too," said Héctor. "I had my first crush when I was twelve years old, so this was long in coming."

Héctor says he's always been comfortable with his homosexuality. Through most of his teens, he and his friends had hung out in large groups, so his sexual preference wasn't an issue. Since few of his friends dated seriously, it was easy to blend in with the larger group. It wasn't until he was seventeen years old and his cousin, Vanessa, came out as a lesbian that he began earnestly to explore his own sexuality.

"Just hanging out with her and being around her somehow gave me permission to be who I was. She took me to my first gay bar. I guess she was helping me to get ready to meet someone, which finally happened when I was nineteen."

In college Héctor met Pepito in French class. Héctor had noticed him early on, with his curly brown hair, beard, and thick lips. It was also obvious that Pepito was more experienced in the ways of dating than Héctor.

"He was definitely a smooth operator," said Héctor, as Norm looked at him, seemingly not wanting to hear about this guy again. "He had the art of seduction down. It began with him offering to give me a lift home from school, and then we started spending more and more time together."

The summer after they met, Héctor's family was given an apartment for a week at Luquillo Beach, which happened to be where Pepito and his family lived.

"I suppose there are no coincidences," said Héctor. "Anyway, he and I were on this secluded part of the beach one day and he finally made a move, and that was it. I was nervous and exhilarated, all at the same time. But I knew that it's what I'd been dreaming about for so long. It all finally felt right."

Héctor added that it was important to him that Pepito was a spiritual person. Although he too had been raised Catholic, Pepito had long ago given up on a Church that seemed to discriminate against him. But he did not give up on his faith, and like Héctor's grandmother, Pepito had statues of saints and his own prayer ritual. The ocean, not a church, served as his sanctuary. Héctor was more than familiar with the unconventional routine.

"Everything was great for a while," said Héctor. "We dated for about two years and then moved in together. But that's when it started to go downhill because he started drinking and drugging more. I always knew that he did drugs occasionally, but he went from pot to acid and cocaine. I just couldn't live that way."

They started fighting all the time. "The last straw was when Pepito started dating his drug pusher while we were still living together, and he didn't even try to hide it. I finally left and didn't date anyone for about a year. It was a tough time in my life."

"I can't believe you would be with someone like that," said Norm, apparently no longer able to restrain himself. "I know you've told me that it was part of your growing up, too, but it just seems so weird to me, knowing you now. I mean, he was dating his *drug pusher*? Good thing I came along or who knows where you'd have wound up."

"You never know," Héctor shot back. "Maybe I'd be living high on the hog in a Puerto Rican villa with minions catering to my every need."

"I think you're living pretty high on the hog right here in Nuevo York, thank you very much," Norm said.

By the time Héctor arrived at Binghamton some years after the end of his relationship with Pepito, he had dated a few other people briefly, but none seriously. His relationship with Pepito had made him skittish. Knowing he wanted more than the gay club scene had to offer, Héctor was finally ready to open himself to love again. The night Norm made a serious overture in Splash and later stayed over at Héctor's apartment was the beginning of something unchartered for both of them.

"I was so nervous that night," said Norm, standing up to watch a tanker float down the Hudson. "First of all, because Héctor had an extra toothbrush readily available, and he also had a huge block of knives displayed prominently on his kitchen counter."

"You're so ridiculous," said Héctor, shaking his head. "What did you think I was going to do, carve you up like Hannibal Lecter, and then brush your teeth?"

"Plus," said Norm, ignoring him and sitting down again, "this was the first serious relationship I had had, except for those two years with Jennifer, and we know how disastrous that turned out to be. The *one* time I did have sex with her—with the lights out, I might add, so that I could think about someone else—she thinks that she's pregnant a few weeks later. I couldn't believe it. When she told me, I thought I'd throw up. Thank God she wasn't pregnant, but we broke up not long after that."

"Gee, there's a surprise," said Héctor, smiling.

"Now, here I am with Héctor, who's twelve years older than me, and my parents know nothing about any of this. And when I'd told my mother the previous summer that I was gay, after which she cried for four months, she made me promise not to date anyone. And now I was basically *living* with someone already. It was a lot to handle right off, to say nothing of that fact that I was leaving that summer to go to NYU law school."

The setting sun over the Palisades told me that it was getting late. I was scheduled to cook dinner for the community that Sunday, a rarity, since I hardly know what to do with a frying pan.

"I'd love to hear more, but I need to start preparing dinner. Would you guys like to stay and eat with us?" I could sense that, even for Norm, this might be a bit much for a first get-together.

"No, thanks," he said. "We're actually meeting some friends back in the city for dinner." He looked to Héctor for confirmation. "But we'd love to get together again."

"And maybe we can hear some of *your* story, too," said Héctor. "We've done all of the talking."

"Oh, they'll be plenty of time for that," I said.

I drove them back to the city, despite their mild protestations.

A FEW WEEKS LATER, after Sunday Mass once again, we went to brunch at the Blue Water Grill in Union Square. After ordering our drinks I reminded Norm and Héctor that we'd left off with them finally getting together at Binghamton. No more prompting was needed.

Norm said that he left Binghamton to go home to Levittown for spring break that year with a lot of apprehensions. He wondered whether he could continue a long-distance relationship with Héctor and was comforted in knowing his move to New York City for law school would make a breakup easier, if it came to that.

"I was basically a mess," said Norm. "And it only got worse when I was talking to Héctor on the phone that week—from a gas station pay phone, by the way, since I didn't want my parents to know—and he tells me that he has a chance to come to New York with me, because he's been granted a year's scholarship to study wherever he wants. Honestly, I wasn't really sure whether or not I wanted him to come. It suddenly all seemed so complicated."

On Tuesday of Holy Week during that spring break, Norm's mother, Maria, asked him to go to church with her, sensing that he was conflicted about something. While his mother went to church every day, Norm was hesitant because he usually loathed the masses at his local parish. He had grown accustomed to the more progressive liturgies at the Newman House at Binghamton, which he called a "bastion of liberal thinking." He resented the more conservative preaching of his home-parish priests, including that of a monsignor he had already had a run in with when the priest preached, in 1992, that Catholics could not in good conscience vote for Bill Clinton, since he would be an "anti-life president."

Norm had challenged him on the comment after the Mass and wound up engaging in a dialectic with the cleric about abortion, women in the Church, and gay issues. Norm ended the session with the comment: "Gay youth suicide is a *life issue* too, you know." He was honing lawyerly skills well before he took the bar.

"I told my mother that I would go to Mass with her," said Norm, "but I was grateful that she picked Saint Bridget's. It was a more progressive church than ours, by Long Island standards anyway."

As Norm and his mother sat in church, a young priest gave a riveting homily about social justice and the failure of the United States to take a more active role in aiding poor and struggling countries. Norm began to cry uncontrollably. "I don't know what brought it on," he said. "The whole Mass I felt like I had to speak with this priest."

Coincidentally, the church was offering confession after the

Mass, and Norm spied this priest making his way to the confessional. Norm entered nervously, not sure what he was going to say. After some initial hedging, the floodgates opened.

"I just told him everything, crying the whole time. I told him about being gay, about Héctor, about moving to New York City, the whole thing. Oh yeah, and then I said, 'By the way, I'd like to do some social justice work this summer, too.' After all, I wanted him to feel that I had heard *something* of what he said in the homily."

The priest was welcoming and sympathetic, saying to Norm, "God loves you, just as you are." He also gave Norm the name of a priest to call who could lead him toward some social justice ministry. Norm left the confessional feeling "cleansed and wonderful."

During the ride home from church with his mother, he felt he had to make inroads there, as well. He said to her, "You know you've made all of this very difficult for me by asking me not to date or get involved with anyone."

She turned to Norm and said, "What's his name?"

"Héctor," said Norm. They drove the rest of the way home in silence.

When he contacted the "social justice" priest, Norm discovered that the priest was openly gay and ministering to AIDS patients. He became Norm's therapist that summer and gave him an icon of two saints, Sergius and Bachus, purported to be gay.

"But even more important than that," said Norm, "he told me about Saint Francis Xavier Church and said I'd be comfortable worshipping there. I didn't realize it then, but that was a great gift."

*   *   *

THE NEWLY FORMED COUPLE planned that Norm would live in student housing at NYU, since he didn't feel ready to live together full-time, and that Héctor would try to get an apartment close by, so they could see each other as much as possible.

At this point in telling the story, Héctor became more animated and wanted to take over. He leaned across the table, making sure I was paying attention. "I found this beautiful apartment across the street from Barney's downtown," said Héctor, his index finger making an exclamation point. "But Norm was afraid he was going to get murdered crossing Washington Square Park to see me, so I took this dive on Thompson Street instead."

"You are such a drama queen," said Norm, shaking his head.

"Three hundred square feet," continued Héctor, ingoring him, "and a slanted floor. It looked like the villain's lair in the old *Batman* TV series. There was also no closet space and enough cockroaches to choke a horse. And, to top it all off, it shared a wall with a jazz club, the Mondo Cane, I think was its name."

"That wasn't the name of it," Norm said.

"Whatever. All I know is that, after about a day of living there, I was on the hunt for some expensive earplugs. The things we do for love."

"Yes, you're so chivalrous."

Norm admitted that he didn't spend even one night in his room in dorm housing. In effect, he had a seven-hundred-dollar-a-month office that he worked in during his first year of law school, and three-hundred-square-foot slanted hovel that he lived in with a man he felt secure with from the beginning.

"Getting back to the point," said Norm, "in all seriousness, I've always felt like Héctor is my soul mate. I still feel closest to him when we are in church together. Just today at Mass, I reached over and held his hand, feeling so grateful for what we have."

"Yeah, that's true," Héctor said. "That is the main point. But it took a while before we found a place to share that."

Norm and Héctor had begun going to Mass together at Dignity, a gay Catholic organization, not officially recognized by the Church. The organization was told some years ago that it couldn't celebrate masses in a Catholic church. Many Dignity chapters moved their worship to Protestant churches, which were more welcoming, and imported Catholic priests willing to celebrate Mass for the banished group.

"We didn't like it that much though," said Héctor. "We felt like a group of outcasts—separate and not equal. St. John's Episcopal Church was fine, but it wasn't home, and I missed my Church and so did Norm."

While Norm and Héctor were at the beach one weekend, some guys they met happened to mention Saint Francis Xavier Church. Norm remembered that it was the same church that the social justice priest had recommended as well, but Norm was scheduled to stay over at his parents' house that weekend. Héctor showed up at the church on Sixteenth Street on Sunday morning, to see what this supposedly inclusive and progressive Catholic church had to offer.

Arriving late, he took a seat in back, taken with the magnificent architecture, high, vaulted arches and dulled marble. He realized that a woman was preaching the homily, not an everyday occurrence in a Catholic church, where women are forbidden from doing so.

"I could hardly see her in the pulpit from the back, because she was so tiny, but she had this resonant voice, strong, yet soothing at the same time. She wasn't reading anything either. It was coming straight from her heart. She spoke about the kind of inclusive Church we are called to be and how we have a moral obligation and Gospel mandate to be so. She blew me away."

Héctor called up Norm once the Mass had ended and told him that they had found their church.

Meanwhile, on Long Island, Anna, a friend of Norm's mother visiting the house that weekend, told Norm that she had received "words" for him and Héctor. Norm's mother had shared with Anna some of the details of Norm and Héctor's relationship. A religious woman, steeped in the Catholic tradition and prayer, Anna often feels that she receives prophetic words directly from God.

"I always thought that Anna was a little *out there*, to tell you the truth," said Norm. "But she's a good person and very religious, so I listened. She said that she got *words* that Héctor and I have these two guardian angels, and that Aloysius was my angel and Stanislaus was Héctor's. She said that somehow we were to be connected to them."

I must have seemed a bit incredulous hearing this, because Norm looked at me and said, "You don't believe me, do you?"

I put down my fork, taken aback. "No, it's not that at all," I said. "It's just not my kind of spirituality. God doesn't seem to work in my life like that. But I respect what you're saying." After all, it wouldn't have been seemly for the priest to be the doubting Thomas.

"I can't blame you," said Norm. "I didn't put much stock in it either. Anna's always getting these 'words' about something, and quite frankly, it didn't mean anything to me."

Norm and Héctor attended Mass the following Sunday at Saint Francis Xavier Church, and Norm felt the same way about the church as Héctor did. The soaring arches, the melodious choir, the high concentration of gay people, and the welcoming environment all contributed to making them feel that here, at last, was a place where they could publicly share the most important aspect of their relationship, their faith.

Norm was also grateful that he had found a church to help heal some of the residual anger he held toward the oppressive policies of the institution. He felt at home at Xavier—so much so that he decided to become a lector, harkening back to his days as a high school student when he read at masses in his home parish.

While they were standing in back of the church, waiting for a meeting for new lectors to begin, Héctor and Norm noticed a printed schematic of the church on the bulletin board. They saw that the altar on the front right side was named the "AIDS Memorial Altar: An Altar of Hope and Remembrance," dedicated to those who had died from AIDS. But what really caught their attention was the names of the saints whose statues garnished that altar: Aloysius and Stanislaus. They rushed to the altar.

"I just couldn't believe it," said Norm. "There they were. The two saints Anna had talked about, standing side by side."

"Yeah, even I became an immediate convert," said Héctor.

"But wait, I'm not finished," said Norm. The name of the mural behind these two saints was *My Guardian Angel*. Now, how freaky is that?" I had to admit that either this was indeed one strange coincidence or God was making a move.

Norm called his mother on his cell phone once they were on the street, and she confirmed that Anna had told her she knew nothing about Saint Francis Xavier Church and nothing more about Aloysius and Stanislaus, other than that they were two saints.

Héctor and Norm pondered if this could be a confirmation

from God that they were meant to be together and that God was blessing their relationship, even if their Church wouldn't.

"What Aloysius and Stanislaus said to me was that we were exactly where we belonged," said Héctor. "Although the Church is pretty hard-line about homosexuality, I never got too hung up, as some gay people do, on the teaching. I've never felt excluded or denigrated in any way. I've experienced welcoming people and sympathetic priests."

Upon researching the lives of these Jesuit saints, Norm and Héctor discovered that the saints were contemporaries who were canonized the same day in 1726, though Aloysius was younger, born the same year that Stanislaus died, at age eighteen. (Norm is fond of reminding Héctor that, although Norm's patron, Aloysius, was considerably younger than Stanislaus, it took Aloysius less time to be canonized.)

WITH ALL THIS SAINTLY INTERVENTION, it seems natural that Norm picked Rome to visit for his celebratory, post-bar-exam jaunt two and a half years later. He had always wanted to visit Rome, especially after hearing Héctor talk about his travels there before they met. In the summer of 1997, they set out for two weeks of a Roman holiday that neither one would ever forget.

They fell in love with Rome almost immediately, savoring the fine cuisine and the warmth of the people, and they saw just about every church in the city.

"Norm felt compelled to see as many as we could," Héctor said, a trace of weariness still evident.

Near the end of their stay in Rome, they had decided to visit one church they had passed by previously, Saint Ignatius Loyola, named for the founder of the Jesuits. Since Saint Francis Xavier was also a Jesuit, it was a connection that intrigued them. When they arrived however, it was closed for lunch, as just about everything in Italy is during the early afternoon. So they decided to get some cappuccinos and wait for the church to open.

"When we finally went back," said Héctor, "we walked into this beautiful, soaring, dark church and began to look around. By this time, it took a lot to impress me because I was all churched out. I mean, you've seen one Roman church and you've seen them all."

As they were walking down a side aisle, they both stopped at the same time. At an altar to their right a sign said "Burial Site of Saint Aloysius Gonzaga."

"I couldn't believe it," said Norm. "What are the chances of that? We had no idea he was even buried in Rome, and here we are, *per chance*, stumbling upon his burial site?"

There was a beautiful lapis lazuli marble casket cover and candles illumining the holy shrine. They knelt down to pray, and they lit their own candle to add to the multitude, thanking God for another sign.

"I know, Edward," said Norm. "I can tell by your expression what you're thinking."

Was my poker face giving me away again?

"That we're not supposed to need all these *signs*. But sometimes I really do. They just confirm for me that we're not alone in all of this."

"They also confirm," said Héctor, "that God is part of us, despite what the official Church or others might say."

"Look, you have no argument from me," I said. "I have my own signs. We get what we need. And I'm really happy that you two felt such confirmation." I did feel that, but maybe I was a bit envious, since I don't usually get such tangible confirmation.

On their last day in Rome, Norm decided that he wanted to buy a statue of his patron, Aloysius, as a remembrance of the trip. They consulted *Frommer's* guide and discovered that the Quirinale area of the city was the best place to look for statues and other religious objects. They set out to find Norm's statue, but for some reason, this time Héctor suggested another route.

"I just was sick of seeing the same stuff and I thought it would be good to walk another way and see something new," said Héctor.

While walking down a street they had never been on, they noticed an imposing church with a Jesuit symbol on it. They debated whether or not they were up to seeing one more church.

"My first instinct," said Héctor, "was to just go get the damn statue and be done with it. No more churches. I must admit that maybe I was feeling a little envious because Norm had found Aloysius's church and now we were looking for his statue, too. I had nothing of Stanislaus because he was a Polish Jesuit."

"God, it's always competition with you," said Norm, slightly annoyed. "But finally I said, 'Oh, what the hell. One more church can't hurt.'"

They crossed the street and saw the sign for the church that said "San Andreas a Quirinale," and underneath that, it said "Masses in Polish."

"It was the sign under that," said Héctor, "that was the real killer. It said, big as life 'Burial Site of Stanislaus Kostka.'"

"I almost passed out," Norm said.

"It really was a little spooky," added Héctor. "I mean, who'd believe this? I'd just figured that Stanislaus was buried in Poland since he was Polish. But here he was. It was then that I noticed that Stanislaus died the year that Aloysius was born."

"Yeah, he was the older man, too," Norm quipped.

They ran into a Jesuit novice from Naples in the gift shop who offered to show them the room where Stanislaus stayed and eventually died.

"That's when I finally had one up on him," Héctor said with a self-righteous nod toward Norm. "Seeing the room where the saint died was better than any old statue." Héctor smiled and Norm rolled his eyes.

They left Italy without buying any statues, both feeling that they'd encountered something mere statues could never capture.

BY THE TIME we got to the end of their mystical tale, we were sharing dessert. The waiter was hovering, clearly ready for us to pay our bill. As we sat ignoring him in our booth by the front window, I realized how impressed I was with the faithfulness of these two men who were so committed to making God part of their union. While the story of the saints was intriguing, it didn't entice me half as much as the love that was evident across the table—even amidst the playful bickering. I said, "It must make it easier to know that you're meant to be together, almost as if it had been preordained."

"I don't know if 'easier' is the right word," said Héctor. "We're still working to find a place where we belong. It's not *easy* in our culture. Society, the Church, even *gay* culture, make it difficult for gay couples to survive. You're always working against other people's expectations of what you should be."

"To say nothing of the fact," added Norm, "of how hard it is to remain monogamous in the midst of a sex-saturated and very physically oriented society—especially in the heavily gay neighborhood that we live in.

"But even more than all that stuff, I worry about being left alone when he dies. He *is* twelve years older than I am, and who knows . . ."

Héctor, visibly moved, began to tear up, demonstrating one of his more charming qualities, his emotional immediacy. "Just remember," he said, with the wave of a finger, "I was the one frantically calling *you* on the phone on September 11, crazy out of my mind that you were in a high-rise office building uptown while they were flying planes into buildings downtown. Age has nothing to do with it. It comes down to wanting to be together. *I* also worry about anything that might prevent that."

Norm put his arm around Héctor and kissed him gently on the cheek. "The Latin melodrama," said Norm. "But I love you for feeling that way."

A FEW YEARS AGO Héctor and Norm attended a mass at Saint Francis Xavier Church where a fiftieth wedding anniversary was celebrated. It was a beautiful Mass, with friends and family applauding the faithful commitment of the elderly couple who sat beaming in the front pew. By the end of the Mass, Norm was feeling a little depressed.

"I kept thinking," he said, "that we'll never have this. We'll never be able to celebrate our love and commitment in the Church that means so much to both of us. At the end of the Mass, we went to the side altar of Aloysius and Stainslaus to light our candles and we were kneeling, praying. I was feeling so bad, so empty.

"Suddenly this elderly Chilean priest who was visiting Xavier was standing behind Héctor and me. And he asks us if we were a couple. I didn't know what to make of it. I was afraid he was going to chew us out for being in a sinful relationship or something, but I mustered my courage and said a bit defiantly, 'Yes, we are a couple.' And this old priest looks at us and says, 'I can see your love. It's obvious that God has blessed you.' Then he walked away. I hold on to that moment. It gets me through a lot."

"It gets *us* through a lot," added Héctor, "and even more than that, it helps us to remember that God is still in charge. Who knows, maybe someday if God wins out, we will be able to kneel at that altar and profess our love. That would really be something."

CHAPTER ELEVEN

Topless in Seattle

HOW CAN I SAY THAT THE FIRST THING I noticed were her breasts? Yet, God forgive me, it's true. When she strolled through the back doors of the church, ample chest leading the way, I wondered if she was lost. She didn't look like any of the others who had gathered for the evening retreat service, many of whom were elderly couples craning their necks around the ends of the pews to watch her saunter to a seat in the second row in her tight jeans and open (by necessity), wooly, white jacket—a walking snowball from the back. As I watched her take off the jacket and glide her fingers through her long platinum hair, I thought she could have easily passed for one of Tony Soprano's molls—chewing gum, filing her nails, and pressuring Tony to leave his wife, Carmela, or this chick would blow it all wide open.

But then two kids walked in, a teenage girl with long ash-blond hair and a younger boy with a baseball cap and hip-hop jeans that dragged along the tiled floor. The girl held his hand like a protective sister as she surveyed the pews, obviously looking for someone already seated. The now melted snowball turned around, spotted the kids, and waved her long, seemingly fake, silver nails, which glittered under the dull church lights like Vegas stardust. When the kids slid into the pew, she kissed them as only a mother would and wrapped her arms around their shoulders. I knew then that there was a story here.

GISELLE GREW UP IN NEW JERSEY and sounded like it. When she first came to speak to me, two days into the parish retreat, I was distracted by her stereotypical accent—a Jersey girl who Bruce Springsteen would have been proud of. But as she began to share her story with me, the initial impressions faded.

She began by recalling a day in the fifth grade at a strict, nondenominational Christian school that her parents had struggled to afford. In the daily Bible class the students had to recite verses they had memorized the night before. Most days Giselle got a gold star, having practiced the verses ad nauseam before class and driving her mother to distraction with the repetitive drills. "One more time, Mommy," she would say. "Giselle," her mother would respond, "it's okay if you don't get *every* word exactly right. So long as you know the gist of the story." Not good enough for Giselle. The word of God was at stake.

She rose from her chair, stood next to her desk, and began reciting, "The Lord is my shepherd. There is nothing I shall want." Before Giselle could continue, she felt the hand of the boy who sat behind her on her thigh, beneath her plaid dress. She froze as the children behind her began to giggle.

"Giselle, what is it?" the teacher asked from her desk in front. "Please continue. Didn't you study this passage?"

Giselle couldn't respond. She felt her face grow flush and her knees begin to shake. By this time the boy had removed his hand and was dutifully writing in his notebook.

"Giselle?"

No response.

"Well, you can just come up here to the front of the class and sit in the corner while you learn this Bible verse. I'm surprised at you, Giselle."

"I DON'T THINK I'LL EVER FORGET the feeling I had that day," Giselle said to me in the church office. "I don't know why he would do such a thing, except that he was being a show-off, but it really affected me. Why *me*? And while I was reciting the Bible, no less. I remember crying in my bedroom that afternoon and asking God why He let me be embarrassed like that in front of everyone. I thought He was supposed to be my shepherd."

GISELLE DREAMED about being a ballet dancer. She began taking classes in the sixth grade, smitten with the dancers' attire and the gracefulness of the acrobatic moves that seemed so effortless.

"It was wonderful," she said. "Every time I put on that tutu and those dancing shoes, I felt like I was someone else, somehow magical. I could be a princess, or the girlfriend, or even the left-behind lover. It didn't matter. I was someone else."

Giselle spent a lot of her adolescence wishing she was someone else. Her father unwittingly encouraged that desire. He drove a bus, often late into the night, but when home, he may as well have not been there.

"I wanted him to love me, but he didn't seem to know how. I kept trying to make myself prettier or smarter, just so he would notice me more. But it was my sister he doted on, and she didn't even have to try. He once said, 'Giselle, if you could only be more like Emily, your life would be so much better.' Can you imagine saying that to a thirteen-year-old who was already filled with self-loathing and doubt? Geez, the things parents can say."

One night Giselle's parents came to a ballet recital she had worked on for months. She was in high school by then and was dancing a lead part in *Swan Lake*. The performance had gone beautifully the whole evening, and she was dancing in the last scene of the ballet. She leapt into the air confident that her partner would catch her, as he had done hundreds of times before—but not this time. His arm folded in front of her stomach instead of behind her back and he dropped her to the floor with a loud thud. The audience gasped while the dancers onstage locked in position. Giselle lay there unhurt, but afraid to move, feeling every eye on her, as the curtain dropped and technicians and other dancers rushed from the wings.

Her parents and sister waited for her in the lobby after the performance. When Giselle emerged from the backstage door, her mother rushed to her.

"Gissy, sweetheart, are you okay? You were wonderful tonight." She stroked her hair and pushed aside the tears falling down Giselle's cheeks. "Don't let that one fall ruin your whole night. You danced beautifully, sweetheart."

Her father called from his leaning position by the exit door, "Hey, Giselle, maybe if you lost a few pounds, that poor kid could've held you up." He laughed and looked around for company, but there were no takers.

Giselle's sister, Emily, said, "Daddy, sometimes you can be such a jerk." She walked over and hugged Giselle, whose head was buried in her mother's coat.

"Oh, come on," her father said. "I was only kiddin'. Geez,

you're all so serious. You have to admit though that Gissy is a bit heftier than those other waifs up there tonight."

Giselle's mother tried to fill the lacuna left by her often absent, boorish husband, but parenting wasn't her strong suit either. She cleaned houses all day to supplement his bus driver's salary and often returned home with limited energy to cook dinner, watch the evening news, and go to bed—leaving Giselle to fend for herself much of the time.

"I used to pray at night that I could have the same kind of loving family that I saw my friends had," said Giselle. "Of course, I know that they had their own stuff. No one gets off scot-free, huh? I guess we find love where we can, but then that became part of my problem."

One Thanksgiving, Giselle and her family were having dinner at her aunt and uncle's house on Long Island. Giselle was a sophomore in high school and had begun to turn heads in the lunch line, though she continued to see in herself more flaws than assets. Her cousin, Tommy, then twenty years old, was visiting his parents for the Thanksgiving holiday, and, after dinner, asked Giselle if she'd like to see some of the sketches he'd been working on for his design class.

"Sure," she said, "go get them."

"Well, I have them organized in my old room here in the house because I've been working on them while I've been home. It'd be easier if we just looked at them there."

"Okay," said Giselle. "Emily, you want to see?" Emily was sprawled out in front of the television on the living room floor, half dozing.

"Not right now," said Emily. "I want to watch a bit more of the parade. Maybe later. No offense, cousin."

"None taken," said Tommy.

Giselle and Tommy walked to the back wing of the house where Tommy's old room was. Giselle remembered playing there many times when they were children, with Tommy always getting his way as the older cousin. He made the rules and always won. Some things never change.

Tommy closed the door of his room and locked it. "Why are you doing that?" Giselle asked.

"Give us a little privacy."

"Privacy, for what?"

"For us."

"Tommy, what are you talking about? I thought we were going to look at your designs."

"We will, cuz, but be patient." He moved toward Giselle, put his arms around her waist, and kissed her hard on the lips. She pulled back, pushing him away.

"Tommy, don't. What are you doing?" she whispered. "Are you crazy?" She wasn't sure why she was whispering instead of screaming.

"Come on. You know we've both wanted this," said Tommy. "Give it up, cuz. Who better than with me, someone you know and can trust?"

Giselle turned to unlock the door, but he grabbed her by the shoulder and pushed her onto the bed. He laid on top of her and put his hand up her shirt.

"Tommy, please don't."

"Don't worry. We'll just do a little. Nothing too drastic. Don't want you having retarded kids, cuz."

"THE FUNNY THING IS," Giselle said, "that I finally just kind of went with it. I didn't really put up much of a struggle. Part of it was that it felt good just to be wanted, even if it was by my sick cousin. I remember hearing the voices of our parents in the kitchen, laughing, and the TV blaring marching bands. And I started staring at a decorative border by the ceiling, all different kinds of airplanes. I focused on those airplanes and prayed, 'God help me, and forgive me.' And then I started kissing Tommy back."

Giselle never spoke to anyone about the incident with her cousin. She avoided him at subsequent family gatherings and was never alone in a room with him again. Her mother once asked, "Why are you so rude to Tommy?"

"Maybe you should ask Tommy," was all Giselle said. Her mother dropped it.

"BUT THAT INCIDENT really affected me," said Giselle, "because from then on I began to sleep around. I was only in high school, but I guess I figured that, since I was damaged goods now, I couldn't get any more damaged. I became the most popular cheerleader of the football team, and it had nothing to do with my high kicks or pom-pom waving. The other girls began to hate me. It was the loneliest time in my life. And each time that I was with a boy, I thought he might be the one to take that ache away. But the ache just kept getting bigger. When I finally got out of high school, I wanted to begin again. I felt like it was my second chance."

WHILE GISELLE HAD NOT BEEN RAISED Catholic, she had met a friend, Penny, at a part-time job after high school. She was religious and used to take Giselle to church with her; on Monday evenings they would leave work early from A&S department store to attend a weekly novena at Saint James Church in downtown Brooklyn. The church was dark with candles burning in every corner of the massive space and the smell of incense permeating the sanctuary. Two altar boys with lighted candles would lead a priest in a shiny gold cope holding the monstrance that contained the Blessed Sacrament down the center aisle. He held the stem of the monstrance with a humeral veil that provided a barrier between his skin and the holy receptacle.

"I never quite understood it all," said Giselle, "but it was magical and very comforting. Much more so than any of the dry Protestant services I had attended. There was real mystery there, even if it didn't all make sense. I remember asking Penny why the priest couldn't touch the gold starburst, but then he *could* touch the host inside it to give out communion. 'It's a mystery,' she said, as if I was dumb to even ask such a question."

Soon Giselle began going to church without Penny. Novenas three times a week and Mass on Sunday. Her father began to call her a Holy Roller. Her mother figured it was "a phase" and better than her hanging out on the street corners with her friends. Giselle was drawn to the comfort she felt while seated in the uncomfortable pews. She savored her anonymity in a sea of worshipers, "all praying for something else but ultimately wanting the same thing."

"I know they all wanted to be loved by something, someone outside of themselves. I could see it. That's what I wanted. And since it didn't seem to be happening with my family or friends— or with the football team—it was a place where I felt accepted and even a little loved, not only by the strangers around me, but by God. I got to ask Him things, too, like why I felt so sad sometimes."

It was around that time that Giselle began to wonder if a

non-Catholic could be a nun. Most evenings at the devotions she noticed a group of five sisters who huddled together in a pew, separate, yet somehow united. Giselle imagined them leaving the church after the service, and, once home, discussing what God had revealed to each of them in their mystical reveries. They would then retire to their simple cells for an evening of quiet reading and numinous ecstasies. "It seemed to simple, so pure, just like the movies with Ingrid Bergman and Audrey Hepburn that I loved to watch." Not like Giselle's life at all.

"But that didn't last too long," she said. "When I tentatively broached the topic with my mother, she told me to forget such nonsense. She said, 'No one who wears as much mascara as you do could ever wrap her head in a veil.' So much for that. I guess a part of me knew she was right, though. I could never do it. But what I really wanted her to say was, 'Giselle, you can do anything you want. And you'll be good at it.'"

Giselle had little aspiration or encouragement to attend college. Her father had said it was a waste of time for a girl, especially for Giselle. "What do you need that for?" he had said. "You're a pretty girl now that you've lost some weight. You'll meet a guy, have kids, and stay at home. He'll take care of you. Why waste your time, to say nothing of my money, with college? Doesn't make any sense."

Giselle did convince him, however, to spring for beauty school tuition for nine months. "Now, there's something I can see you doing until the right guy comes along," he had said.

Giselle attended a beauty school in lower Manhattan, learning how to cut hair and apply makeup, receiving the title of "full-service stylist." At the end of the day she would take the Path train to Hoboken, New Jersey, and often stop in a church on Washington Street before catching the commuter bus home. She said some scenes from *On the Waterfront* were filmed at the church.

One night she decided to go to the San Gennaro feast in Little Italy after hearing that it was a religious festival and eating soirée all rolled into one. "Right up my alley," she said. San Gennaro was a bishop who became the patron saint of Naples. Each year, on Mulberry Street between Canal and Houston Streets, about three million people gather over eleven days in September (12–22) to gamble, eat, and pray—usually in that order. The National Shrine of San Gennaro is located in the Most Precious Blood Church, staffed by the Franciscan Fathers, and the famous statue sits surrounded by ever-burning candles lit by a constant throng of worshipers. The statue gets paraded through the streets on the feast day, and the people pin dollar bills to every inch of it.

Giselle was supposed to meet Penny on Houston Street, but she never showed up. Giselle waited on the corner for a half hour, getting propositioned by two men, "one young and cute with curly blond hair, and the other fat, with a comb-over."

"Talk about attracting all kinds," she said.

Hordes of people scurried past her into the popular restaurants that lined the streets, their owners benefiting from the eclectic piety that made the cash registers ring. After waiting a half hour for Penny, Giselle decided to go to the festival for a while, just to see what the fuss was about, and then make her way across the Hudson River to New Jersey.

She walked toward the Mulberry Street address that she had scribbled down from that morning's *Daily News*. When she reached the street, a sea of people loomed before her, some of them shouting at spinning wheels, others reverently blessing themselves, as the statue of San Gennaro, covered with dollar bills that fluttered in the wind like fringe on a flapper's dress, was paraded past on a platform. The candlelight procession marched past Pete's Zeppole and Calzone stand, where sausage and peppers were being grilled on open flames, and past a fat man who Giselle said looked like her uncle Tony, weighing figs that people were buying up like gold.

"I'd never seen anything like it," said Giselle. She stood under the red, green, and white garlanded Christmas lights that were strung across the street and marveled at the curious mix of the sacred and profane. "I mean, people were gambling in the booths as the dollar-bill statue passed by. They'd stop to bless themselves, and then go right back to spinning the wheels and throwing balls for stuffed dogs. It was a riot."

It was rumored that a guy known as Tony Waterguns, of the Genovese crime family, controlled the booths and most of the profits. No one could run a booth without his approval. He was put in jail for racketeering and fraud, so it's unclear who runs them now—hopefully, not the Franciscan friars who parade in their habits and sandals through the crowds of partyers and prayers.

Giselle watched the scene from the front of Ferraro's Restaurant, an institution since 1892. "I wondered what any of this had to do with God or the Catholic Church, but I didn't care. I figured that, if people could have this much fun and make this much money in the name of God, it couldn't be all bad."

Having had her fill of sausage and peppers and seductive glances, Giselle decided to make the trek back to Jersey. As she turned to walk toward Houston Street, a man with ink-black hair and luminous green eyes blocked her way.

"Excuse me," she said. "I'm sorry." She turned to walk around him while he sidestepped in front of her.

"Not at all. It's me who's sorry. Sorry it took me so long to see you standing there." He smiled a Hollywood smile, which slightly expanded his cleft chin.

"All I could think," said Giselle, "was what a lame line that was. I mean, really. But I have to admit, he was so handsome that he practically took my breath away."

"I'd love to buy you a drink," he said.

"No, thank you," said Giselle. "I'm actually just on my way home. It's kind of late for me."

"Late? The night's still young, sweet thing. C'mon. You have your choice, strawberry daiquiris from that stand over there, or cappuccino and biscotti from Café Palermo just down the street. Your call. I am your obedient servant."

"It was as if I couldn't say no," said Giselle. "Like he wielded some kind of power over me from the very beginning. It took a long time to break it."

They sat at Café Palermo until 2 a.m., with Giselle laughing most of the time at Mario's quick wit and trenchant observations of the passersby.

"Look at that guy," he said. "That rug he's wearing looks like it was deep-fried in the calzone pit, doesn't it?" With Mario's black, wavy hair, a toupee was something he'd never had to worry about.

"Mario, that's not nice," said Giselle, whispering and laughing. "He probably paid a lot of money for that hair."

"Yeah? Well, he should have pinned it on that baby-doll statue that they're carrying around like King Tut. At least then he'd have a prayer."

Although Giselle was taken aback by Mario's gruff candor, she relished feeling comfortable with a stranger who seemed to worship her from the start. She wondered what was different

246 / UNLIKELY WAYS HOME

about him that made her feel so happy. It had been a long time. She wanted more.

Before getting on the commuter bus in New Jersey that night, she stopped by the church on Washington Street. It was locked, of course, but she stood outside and made her prayer. "Let this guy be better than the others. I'm ready. Please, God, show me if he might be the one."

SEVEN MONTHS AFTER THEY MET, on a stopover in Las Vegas while driving cross-country to Seattle, a justice of the peace married Giselle and Mario in an Elvis Presley chapel, of all things.

"At the time, it seemed like a lot of fun. Just keep it light and breezy. After all, it was only marriage, right?" Giselle paused. Her eyes began to fill up. She reached in her bag for tissues. "I think that's what I thought, though. I knew a church wedding was out with Mario. He'd never go for it. And what church? I wasn't Catholic, and didn't go to any other church. And God knows, I didn't want to deal with my parents and all of that, so it seemed like the best way. Keep it fun. Marriage lite. It was the theme of our relationship in the beginning. Nothing too deep. No real feelings. Until the real feelings hit so hard I thought I'd never get through it."

THEY WERE ON THEIR WAY to Seattle because Mario wanted to get in on the ground level of some new dot-com ventures springing up there. Some friends had made a killing in a short period of time. It was Mario's idea of work: easy, fast, high gain. Only none of that materialized once he and Giselle had settled in a one-bedroom apartment not far from Pike Place Market in downtown

Seattle. Unfortunately, the boom had crested and was on the wane. Each of Mario's attempts at grasping the golden ring ended in failure. He was let go from three different jobs within six weeks. Most interviews never even garnered a call back. His moods grew black and his increasingly angry outbursts made Giselle wonder what she had gotten into. The fun-loving guy on Mulberry Street with the green eyes that seemed to promise the moon was nowhere to be found. Nor was any money to pay the rent and food bills.

Giselle was planting flowers in a flower box outside the bedroom window when Mario came home unusually early one day, even for him. They had been in Seattle for six months.

"What are you doing home already?" said Giselle. "I thought you were interviewing with the Columbia guys this afternoon."

"Yeah, for what?" said Mario. "So they can tell me I'm one year too late and five years too old. Forget it. I'm done with this shit. We need to do something else. Emphasis on *we*." He put down his briefcase, grabbed her by her elbow, and spun her around to face him. "You can't just stay home all day planting pansies while I'm out breaking my ass trying to make a living for us. I thought we could swing this with just me working, but we can't."

"Mario, let go of my arm. You're hurting me." Giselle pulled away, rubbing her elbow, surprised at his eruption. "What's the matter with you?" She paused and consciously changed her tone of voice. "Look, maybe we should just go back east. Our families are there. You'll have more contacts. You can go back to the construction company for a while until you find out what you want to do. Please don't blame this on me. You're the one who wanted to come out here."

"No, I'm not leaving this soon. We'll be a laughingstock. All those assholes who said we should never come out here would

be right, including your parents. I'm not giving them that satisfaction. Not yet, anyway."

"Well, what are we supposed to do then? I have bills on that
table that need to be paid, Mario. I can't keep putting these people off."

"I just told you. *You* have to work, too. I'm out there every day
trying. You haven't done shit."

"And what more would you like me to do? I put in applica-
tions at salons, and they never called me. I'm cutting some people's hair here in the apartment. I'm doing facials without even
having the right materials to do them. What more do you want
me to do?"

Mario paused and looked out the window where the flower
box sat, half planted. Giselle said it was as if he couldn't look at
her.

"I was at a place today where I think you could make some
good money. Seems like a nice respectable place. I talked to the
owner and they're looking for some people."

"What kind of place?"

"Like a club, a dance club."

"You were at a dance club yesterday? With who?"

"Giselle, I stopped in for a drink. I was thirsty."

"Mario, I haven't waitressed for years. I hated it when I did."

"You wouldn't be a waitress," had said, lowering his voice.
"You'd be a dancer. They're looking for dancers. And you're a good
dancer."

Giselle needed a moment for it to settle in.

"A dancer? What kind of dancer?"

"A club dancer. They have girls who dance. It's a men's club.
Though there were some women there too, well dressed. It's
really a high-class place. I want you to see it."

"What kind of dancer, Mario?" Giselle moved toward him. He was silent, still staring out the window. "Mario, what *kind* of dancer?" She was practically in his face.

"Giselle, so it's topless dancing. Big shit. Girls do it all the time. Girls who look as great as you do." He turned toward her, putting his hands on her shoulders. "Honey, why not use your assets right now? Just to help see us through this rough patch. It wouldn't be for long. I promise. No one touches you. It's nothing like that. They simply get to admire your beauty as I do."

"And you wouldn't mind that?" She pushed his arms off her shoulders. "All those men looking at me up there, dancing with nothing on. That wouldn't bother you, Mario? I can't believe you're saying this. Who are you?"

"Giselle, you *would* have something on. You'd only be topless, like on a beach in France for christssakes. Maybe we can even talk them into letting you wear pasties or something. Honey, just for a month or so, until I can figure this all out." He stroked her hair. "Please. Help me out here."

They didn't speak for two days. But within two weeks, Giselle was dancing at Silverado's Men's Club, and making fifteen hundred dollars a week doing it.

"HE JUST FINALLY CONVINCED ME that he was right," said Giselle. "There was no way we were going to make it without money. And if *he* was telling me to do it, how bad could it be? I mean, he was my husband, and I did like to dance. So, I started. I thought I was going to throw up that first night when I went out there."

The club had a chrome-and-glass exterior with a black awning that extended to the street, protecting the gentlemen being dropped off by their drivers from getting wet if it was raining. It was as Mario had said, a high-class place, as those places go. Inside it was dark and smoky, nicotine still allowed, with a wraparound mahogany bar on which the dancers strutted their stuff. Pink and blue lights illumined sections of the bar while pin-light strobes pulsed on other parts. Adjacent to a side wall was a small stage with poles that the more accomplished dancers wrapped themselves around like coiling snakes. The beginners started on the bar, though, as Giselle did her first night.

"When I came out of the sleazy dressing room, or rather *undressing* room, I was wearing a T-shirt. I just couldn't bring myself to go out there without it. But when I got up on the bar, one of the guys sitting there said, 'Okay, honey, it doesn't say "topless" out there for nothing.' Some of the other men started to laugh. It was like something out of *Gypsy*. So I took off the T-shirt and closed my eyes, trying to let my hair cover my breasts at first. I started moving to the music, pretending I was someplace else. I imagined I was dancing on a beach, all alone by the water. Just me, the sun, and the water. All the smoke I was inhaling didn't help the fantasy though, and then it was broken completely."

A man touched the back of Giselle's leg, brushing it from her knee to her thigh. Touching was supposed to be off-limits, but obviously this guy hadn't read the rules. Giselle stopped dancing, freezing momentarily, and then lost her balance and fell onto the sticky wooden bar.

"I swear I was back in that classroom when I was reading Psalm 23 and that kid touched my thigh. Same feeling, shaking inside. But this time, it was like I was asking for it. I'd put myself there, or Mario had. And then, I don't know how I did it, but I picked up a drink from the bar, threw it in his face, and got up and kept dancing."

The guy bolted up, cursing at Giselle, "You lousy whore," but a bouncer escorted him outside. This place took care of their girls, just as Mario had said. Giselle got through the first night spending most of the time on the beach, nearly falling off of the bar twice because of her closed eyes and shaky footing. But soon, she got better—much better. Within weeks she became one of the most popular and requested dancers at the club.

"It actually was easy after a while. In some ways, it was as if I'd always done it. After all, I'd wanted to be a dancer my whole life. And even though it wasn't *Swan Lake*, I guess we can get used to anything.

"But I always had to put myself somewhere else in order to do it. I could never be in that bar in my head. The only thing that made it bearable was if I imagined myself on a beach, or in a garden, or in my room as a little girl, or even in the clouds sometimes . . . heaven, maybe, I don't know. Sometimes I just prayed the whole night. And I'd wonder, did God hear the prayers of a topless dancer?"

PERHAPS GOD DID, because the dancing lasted for only six months, though for Giselle it was six months too long. Something had changed in her and in Mario. She knew there was no going back to before. Mario began getting angry at her seeming popularity with the patrons at Silverado's, though he never went there when she was dancing. He had spared them both that humiliation. But he had heard from friends who went there that there was a new girl who was really cutting up the bar. They never knew it was his wife.

One Friday afternoon he came home from yet one more firing just as Giselle was getting dressed to go to work, and said, "Pack up your stuff. We're going back to New York. I'm through with this place." He already had plane tickets in his jacket pocket.

"Just like that, we're leaving?" said Giselle.

"Yeah, just like that. Unless of course, you can't bear to part with your new dancing career and your admiring customers."

"Just remember, Mario, you're the pimp here. Don't put it on me."

"Whatever. Just get ready. It's over. We'll move on from here."

The next evening they left everything in the apartment, including the meager furniture they had acquired. Carrying only the luggage they could handle, they took a taxi to the airport with Mario holding Giselle's hand. "As if everything was okay now," she says. Giselle stared at Mount Rainier as the taxi sped on the expressway and she wondered how they could "move on from here." By the time they landed at JFK in New York City the next morning, Giselle was convinced that Seattle, and Silverado's, had changed them forever.

They lived with Giselle's mother and father for three weeks in an upstairs apartment that happened to be vacant, and then rented a house in Rockaway, four blocks from the ocean. Mario went back to construction work and Giselle to a job in a Supercuts hair salon, after some training on how *they* cut hair.

For a while things seemed to get better, with Mario seeming more his old self and Giselle trying to forget her recent self. She got pregnant, and a few years later, pregnant again, hoping that children might help finally to create a real marriage. Perhaps Mario would stay home more, she thought. Perhaps kids would give her someplace to channel her love, and maybe even get some in return.

* * *

"THE KIDS WERE A GREAT ADDITION to my life," said Giselle. "They filled something in me that nothing else had. But they didn't do the same for Mario. After a while he seemed to get worse again. He was short-tempered and hostile all the time, even with the kids. He started spending more time at work, or so he said.

"I think he never forgave himself for what he asked me to do. And I guess I never forgave him, either. We never talked about it, just pretended it didn't happen. I finally came to a point where I knew we couldn't be together anymore. The past was just too painful, and the present wasn't much better. I didn't see a future. I didn't want a future, at least not with him."

Around this time Giselle began attending a Catholic church regularly and participating in a Bible study group once a week. She felt drawn to the liturgy and desired to receive the sacraments. "I had never taken Catholic Holy Communion before, and I'd sit at Mass and just hunger for it." The feelings she'd had when she attended church with Penny years before returned. She felt safe, comforted, "somehow at home."

"In Bible study, I began to learn about the Scriptures I had heard my whole life but never really knew. They finally were making sense to me."

She talked to a priest about the tenuous state of her marriage, and he told her to "work harder, offer up the difficulty of it. You have two children to think of." And when she told him that she thought she wanted to become a Catholic, he said, "Well then, you *must* stay married." When he said those words, it sounded like a "death sentence" to Giselle.

"But, Father, we weren't even married in a church," she said. "It was an Elvis Presley chapel, for God's sake."

"Yes, but you're not Catholic," he said, "so we recognize that marriage as valid. Once you become Catholic, then we can bless the marriage in the Church."

"It made no sense to me whatsoever," said Giselle. "I didn't want it blessed. I wanted it ended. I knew that day in the priest's office that I *would* be a Catholic, and that I *wouldn't* stay married, despite what he said. The marriage had somehow died, and I wasn't going to sacrifice the rest of my life living that way. I couldn't do that to my kids, either. Mario would still be their father, but it'd be better for all of us if he lived someplace else. I left the priest's office and went home and told Mario that he had to leave or that I would. One week later, he moved out. And one year after that, I was baptized a Catholic."

WHEN GISELLE CAME TO SPEAK TO ME, she had been divorced for three years. Mario had remarried six months after the divorce. Aside from wanting to tell me her story, she wanted advice. She had fallen in love with a man, but he was married. Although he was separated and planning to divorce when he and Giselle met, "technically" he wasn't free to date, yet they had done so for eight months. She was also sleeping with him. She would sneak him in and out of the house so that his wife didn't find out about their relationship until the divorce was final. They feared the wife might make things ugly if she knew he was already involved with another woman. He also had three children.

"I know that I'm not playing according to the rules," she said. "But the rules don't make sense for me right now. I'm working toward making all this right, and it will be soon, but I feel like I have to live in this in-between for a while. I think God understands. I hope you can, too. I hope the Church can. I'm finally on the verge of my life being what I always dreamed it would be.

I love Paul more than I've ever loved anyone, and the kids love him, too. It's all right here. Finally. I just have to hang on, and I know God's hanging on with me. I can feel it."

I told her I could quote Church teaching to her about what she "should" do, but she already knew that. It wouldn't make a difference. She was convinced she was living according to a deeper Church teaching, her informed conscience. I hoped that conviction would lead her ultimately to a place of peace and resolution. I could tell she was on the way, and I knew that I couldn't deter her, even if I wanted to, which I wasn't sure I did.

"And there's something else, too," she finally said, smiling. "I'm still dancing."

My heart sank. I was prepared to give her some leeway, but not this much. I turned into "Our Miss Brooks."

"Giselle, I think I've been very understanding and patient with everything you've said, and I've cut you a lot of slack, but I can't go along with this. There *must* be a job that you can get that doesn't demean you and your children. You're too good for that. I just think it's unacceptable. You've come too far."

She paused for a moment, tilted her head at me, as if to say, "What language are you speaking?" and wrinkled her nose. Then she got it.

"Oh, no," she said with a chuckle. "I don't mean *topless* dancing. I'm dancing for God now—in church, as a ministry. I dance for prayer services and special liturgies, you know, *liturgical* dance."

"What?" I said.

"Yeah, I started about five months ago, and it's been great. As a matter of fact, I'm dancing this Saturday evening for the opening of a religious education conference and I'd love for you to come. My parents are coming, too."

Three days later I sat in an auditorium that had been transformed into a worship space with looming palm trees, colorful banners, and an altar, lecturn, and ten musicians. About five hundred people had gathered, forming a circle around the central focus, a platform upon which the altar and lecturn sat. Four aisles divided the sectioned participants of the conference.

I sat about halfway back, directly across from Giselle's parents who sat in the front row with Giselle's two children. I assumed that the man seated with them was Paul. People were chatting, creating a din that reverberated off the shiny, tiled floor. As the lights dimmed, the crowd quieted and the musicians began to play the first notes of a familiar song. A soloist began singing, "The Lord, He will be my shepherd. Nothing more shall I want . . ."

A spotlight found Giselle, who had begun to dance down one of the aisles on her toes, her arms raised, her face turned upward toward the ceiling, and beyond. She wore a beautiful white, flowing dress, with the sleeves and hem cut to points that moved as freely as she did.

"He lets me rest in rich green meadows. He leads me to quiet pools of fresh water. He revives my soul . . ."

Her arms formed a circle above her head and she moved her torso from side to side in rhythm to the music. A quick leap. A reverent bow. Then running with short steps, arms in front of her, reaching out, fingers extended toward the platform in the center. Running the race. Grasping the prize. Not "someone else" anymore. Just herself.

"You prepare a banquet for me, a table full . . . You anoint my head with rich oil, you have welcomed me, and filled my cup to the brim."

A long leap, legs fully extended to the top of the platform.

"Your love and goodness follow me, all the days of my life."

She teeters as she lands, off balance, tilting backward, looking as though she is about to fall. The audience gasps. Her father bolts from his seat and extends his arms toward her, too far away to be of any help. But none is needed. Giselle somehow balances herself with her arms, which seem to be pulled toward the ceiling by some magical force, and then, once hitting the platform, she takes our breath away as she moves into a full spin, arms raised, face gazing heavenward.

"Your house, O Lord, shall be my home, for as long as I live."

CHAPTER TWELVE

Can a Mother Forget
Her Child?

IT'S NOT EVERYONE WHO GETS TO LIVE under a roller coaster. I remember in the movie *Annie Hall*, the character played by Woody Allen lived under The Cyclone roller coaster in Coney Island as a child. Every time the snaking carts would whiz by, the windows of "young Alvy's" apartment would rattle menacingly and his mother's dishes and table lamps would shake like a 6.5 earthquake was rolling through Brooklyn. Later I realized that it wasn't such an outlandish sight gag when I learned that, at the time *Annie Hall* was made, there was still a seventy-three-year-old woman living in an apartment that had been built right into the side of The Cyclone.

So it didn't sound too far-fetched when Geraldine McGuiness told me about the day she was riding the LA Thompson roller coaster in Coney Island, which just happened to fly by *her* apartment window on West Eighth Street countless times a day. But this was no ordinary roller-coaster-riding day. The temperature was about twenty degrees; the skies were overcast, dispensing an icy drizzle; and the wind was whipping with a howling cry. While most kids were ice skating on a pond or building snowmen with charcoal eyes, Geraldine and her friends were sleigh riding—not down some snow-covered grassy knoll, but down the iced tracks of the towering LA Thompson.

"I know it sounds crazy," she says, "but we did it all the time. The roller coaster would shut down for the winter. And when it snowed and the tracks iced, me and my friends would climb up to the top of it with our sleds. The blades of the sleds would fit right into the tracks, and we'd go down the hills of the roller coaster on our sleds."

Twelve-year-old Geraldine was tough, a tomboy with long braids that she tucked up under her backward driver's cap. Bowing to the warning of winds that were moving objects heavier than sleds, some of the other kids passed on the ride this particular day, but not Geraldine. She refused to let a little air keep her from having a good time. She began her climb with the bravado of a shark in a guppy tank. With the rope of the sled wrapped around her waist, she clawed her way to the top with both gloved hands. A few of the braver (or dumber) kids followed behind her while the others watched from the ground like gawking spectators at a bridge jumping. By the time she reached the top, the winds seemed even more ferocious at the higher altitude. She swung the sled onto the launching platform of the roller coaster, placed the blades in the metal tracks, and quickly lay down on the wooden sled.

"Go, Gerri!" shouted Phil, one of her acrophobic buddies on the ground.

Some of the other kids chimed in, "Gerri, let it loose!"

By this time Carol, Gerri's older sister, had come into the backyard and looked up to see Gerri about to make her launch.

"Gerri, get down from there," she shouted into the sound-robbing wind. "Gerri, Momma's going to kill you!"

Too late. Geraldine pushed off and began her descent on tracks that were as glazed as dipped donuts. It all happened quickly. As the sled neared the bottom of the breathtaking dip, the blades jolted loose from the track, lurching Geraldine forward over the front of the sled. Somehow she reached her hand out and grabbed hold of the side of the track. As she hung from the LA Thompson with only air between her and the hundred-and-fifty-foot drop, she began to pray.

"Please God, don't let my mother come out now. Please God, don't let her see me." It was the first of many unanswered prayers.

"Gerri! What are you doing up there?" her mother, Caroline, shouted from the backyard, as her daughter Carol stood beside her crying. "Get down from there, you stupid ass. You want to kill yourself?"

It was more than enough incentive for Geraldine to marshal strength even *she* didn't know she had. She pulled herself up until her stomach was adjacent with the track and swung one leg over it, straddling the track as she hung on its side. Then with one final push, she lifted her body until she was lying, stomach down, on the track, with both legs securely resting on the wooden cross beams. She inched her way to a safety ladder and slowly climbed down it.

"My mother grabbed me by my braids and pulled me into the apartment," says Geraldine. "My head ached for two days. But a part of me was almost glad to see her so upset, because at least it meant she cared. I wasn't always sure of that."

*   *   *

GERALDINE'S MOTHER, Caroline McGuiness, had two children, but perhaps she had never wanted them. Michael McGuiness, her husband, died of bleeding ulcers when their young daughters were only five and seven years old. Geraldine, the younger of the two, remembers an arrestingly handsome man with thick, wavy, black hair and incandescent blue eyes that shone with life. He had a large looming frame, chiseled by work as a shipbuilder at Bethlehem Steel in Hoboken, New Jersey, a town known for its corrupt politics and a skinny crooner named Frank Sinatra, who happened to be a neighbor.

Geraldine's memories of her father, Michael, though vivid, are few. She remembers him walking in the apartment door in the evenings after long days at work and playfully searching for her and her sister Carol.

"We'd hide from him, and he'd roam the apartment pretending not to know where we were," says Geraldine. "When he'd find us, he'd start tickling us, and we'd laugh so hard. Then he'd pick us up in those big arms of his, where I felt so safe, and kiss us on each cheek and say, 'So, did my girls miss me today?' I couldn't begin to tell him how much."

They would miss him the rest of their lives. When he died at age forty-two, Caroline went back to work out of necessity and boredom while her mother, Delia, helped care for Geraldine and Carol. Some nights after work Caroline just couldn't bear to go home, and she'd escape to a local pub where she discovered that she could still attract the glances of admirers.

Geraldine remembers her mother speaking many times about the night she met the next important man in her life. It was at the Brass Rail Bar on Washington Street in Hoboken, where Caroline must have looked particularly beguiling, her red hair piled high and her perfect teeth flashing an alluring smile.

Seated not far from her was a man with a Rudy Vallee part in his hair and a gentle face. Christopher Taraboch, a Hoboken native of Austrian descent, saw Caroline seated at the end of the bar looking like she didn't belong, and he slowly moved toward her.

"Hi, my name's Chris. And you are a lovely lady. May I buy you a drink?"

"Why not?" said Caroline. "No one else has offered."

That night they sat at the end of the bar for three hours, with Caroline telling him as much of her life story as she thought he could bear. Chris Taraboch became the first and only man that Caroline dated after the death of her husband.

Although an unlikely pair, with Caroline appearing older, they seemed perfectly suited in temperament. Even their vices were compatible. Their shared penchant for drinking too much whiskey soon became legendary, and it was not uncommon for them to drink themselves into a stupor before getting thrown out of pubs where bartenders grew tired of their raucous fights and requests to run tabs.

While Caroline and Chris were frequenting the bars of Hoboken, Geraldine remembers that her grandmother grew impatient with her daughter's shirking of her maternal responsibilities. They fought violently about Caroline's nighttime jaunts, often with Delia threatening to do something drastic if Caroline didn't stay home more.

"I don't care if you are lonely," Delia bellowed from the top of the stairs one night. "You have two daughters and they're *your* responsibility now. I'm done raising my children, and I'm not about to start raising yours." Caroline sauntered out the door.

"Then one night everything changed," says Geraldine. "My mother didn't come home. I found out later that she and Pop

(Chris) got drunk and fell asleep on a bus headed for Coney Island. They woke up at the last stop and checked into a hotel room for the night near the amusement park. My mother got a job at Feldman's Restaurant on Mortman Street, and Pop hustled a spot running the carousel in the amusement park. My sister Carol and I were left behind in Hoboken with my seething grandmother, who soon realized that my mother wasn't coming back for us."

Intent on honoring her statement that she "was done raising children," Delia ushered the girls to Saint Mary's Home for Children in Hoboken and dropped them at the doorstep of the nuns who had a reputation for taking in abandoned children—no questions asked. Perhaps it was simply a ploy to get her daughter to come to her senses, but whatever Delia's motivation, suddenly two young girls felt the sting of being abandoned by everyone they knew and loved.

The orphanage is the setting for some of Geraldine's earliest and most painful memories. "We went from living in a home to being in a dormitory with fifty other girls. I was only six years old and didn't understand what was happening. There were these women in long black-and-white dresses and stiff veils who ordered us around. The food was awful. The beds were hard. We used to have to go to chapel, and I remember refusing to pray until God got me out of there. I'd cry and ask the nuns if I'd ever see my mother or grandmother again. They'd tell me they didn't know."

A few months later Delia got word that Caroline was in Coney Island and sent another of her daughters, Mary, to take the two girls from the orphanage to her delinquent daughter. Mary showed up with the girls one Friday afternoon at Feldman's while Caroline was working the day shift. She walked into the restaurant as Caroline was serving hamburgers and shakes to a table and brought the girls to her side.

"I'm sorry, Carrie, but Momma sent me," said Mary. "She said they're your children and your responsibility. She told me to bring them here and leave them. She said they belong with you." She handed the girls over and left.

Caroline set the girls up at the counter with ice cream sodas while she continued to work. The wide-eyed daughters watched for hours as their mother served burgers and wiped down tables; and they wondered what would happen when the workday was over.

"I remember sitting at that counter petrified that she was going to bring us back to the nuns when she got out of work," says Geraldine. "My knees were literally shaking. And I thought my sister Carol was going to throw up."

But they needn't have feared. When Caroline finished her shift, she gathered the girls beneath both arms like a repentant mother bird and walked them home to the small apartment she and Chris had rented under the LA Thompson roller coaster. Acting as though the girls had been with her all along, that evening Caroline made grilled cheese sandwiches and rice with tomato sauce for them. And the few months spent in the orphanage were never spoken of again—at least in her presence.

Caroline decided to enroll the girls in Catholic school in Coney Island. Though she wasn't religious in any kind of formal way, her new "husband" Chris was a weekly churchgoer and convinced her of the quality of Catholic education and that the discipline of the nuns would be good for her daughters. After their experience at the orphanage, her daughters weren't as convinced.

Despite their mild protestations, they were enrolled in Our Lady of Solace Catholic Elementary School, but not until Caroline had a contentious initial meeting with the principal.

"Why is your name 'Taraboch' on this form and the girls' name 'McGuiness'?" asked the principal, Sister Imelda, a Dominican nun in a perfectly ironed white habit and black veil. Caroline had gone to her office to enroll the girls in the school, never anticipating any difficulty.

"I've remarried," said Caroline. "McGuiness was their father's name."

"Were you remarried in the Church?" asked the nun.

"That's none of your business," said Caroline. "We're married, and he's a good father. That's what matters."

"I'm afraid that's not correct," said Sister Imelda. "You need to set the right example for these children and bring them up according to the laws of the Church."

"Look, Sister, I'm here trying to get them a good education and put them in your school. That's the example I'm setting. Now I wish you'd stick to the teaching, and let me do the mothering."

"Very well," said the nun after a brief pause, "but I think you should have them take your *husband's* name," saying the word "husband" as if it was a dirty word. "There'll be too many questions if you all have different names. The other kids make fun of such things. You will all be 'Taraboch' or you can find another school for them."

It was a standoff, with Sister having the upper hand.

"*Very well*, Sister," said Caroline finally. "But you explain to them why they have a new name, and why their real father's name is no longer good enough for them."

"Happily," said the nun. "Tell them to report to my office Monday morning. Oh, and Mrs. Taraboch, they are here only on a trial basis."

"I WASN'T PLEASED about the name change," says Geraldine. "I went from Geraldine Maureen McGuiness, with the map of Ireland on my face, to Geraldine Taraboch. I had all these Irish friends with Irish names and now I had to say that I was half Austrian. I loved my stepfather and all, but I really didn't care for the name."

Geraldine wasn't a good student, barely getting by in arithmetic and reading, though excelling in schoolyard kickball. By the time she reached third grade, she was convinced that the nuns had pretty much given up on her.

Sister Michael, the third-grade teacher, was moderating a classroom spelling bee one fall day. Geraldine was the first student eliminated, and she had to sit for the whole hour watching her less phonetically challenged classmates throw letters around with the ease of seals tossing beach balls. She couldn't understand why she lacked their effortless facility.

"I was feeling pretty discouraged, like I'd never get this stuff," says Geraldine. "And then Sister Michael told us to open our history books. I was happy because I was better at history, but the spelling thing was still bothering me."

Sister Michael began speaking about the majestic Mississippi River and its long path from Canada to Louisiana. With her Irish brogue, she made it sound almost mystical.

"I remembered that Pop used to play around with the word 'Mississippi,'" says Geraldine. "He'd spell it out in a song. 'M-i-s-s-i-s-s-i-p-p-i,' he'd sing. It struck me that it was a really long word that I could actually spell."

Excited by her realization, Geraldine picked up her pen, dipped it into the indelible black ink in the well on her desk, and in clear, bold letters began to write MISSISSIPPI across both pages of the opened history book. Since no one else was writing, Sister Michael didn't miss this display of writer's flourish.

"Geraldine Taraboch, what are you writing?" said Sister Michael from her place at the blackboard.

Geraldine felt her face grow hot. "Nothing, Sister," she said.

"Nothing? Well let me see *nothing*."

The tall nun walked quickly down the aisle, her long dress moving like sheets in a gentle breeze and her rosary beads hitting against the sides of the perfectly aligned wooden desks. When she reached Geraldine's desk and saw the large, perfectly formed capital letters splashed across a page that recounted Lewis and Clark's expedition, she slowly folded her arms.

"Well, Miss Taraboch, penmanship is *one* thing you haven't failed. But I still think there is room for some improvement."

The nun grabbed Geraldine by the ear and pulled her to the front of the classroom. "Now practice writing that one word you *can* spell on this blackboard. Write it five hundred times. And don't let me see you stop."

Geraldine was still writing long after the other students had gone home for the day. Sister Michael sat at her desk correcting papers while Geraldine's hand grew sore. By the time she left school that late afternoon, she never wanted to hear Pop sing about that river again.

When Geraldine told her mother why she was so late returning from school, Caroline thought the punishment excessive. "That nun has some nerve," she said. "I'm going up to see her."

"Momma, don't do that," Geraldine pleaded. "It's okay. You'll just make it worse."

Caroline arrived at the school just as Sister Michael was packing up her desk to leave for the day. "I'm Geraldine Taraboch's mother," said Caroline, "and I think you have some nerve making my daughter stay so late and write that word five hundred times. She is home soaking her hand in ice."

"And I think you have some nerve telling me how I should run my classroom," said the undaunted nun.

"You have a brogue," said Caroline, her tone suddenly changing. "What part of Ireland are you from?"

"County Cork," said the nun, "but what does that have to do with anything?"

"County Cork? That's where my family is from. A friend of ours, Jim O'Shea, just came back from home there, too."

"Jim O'Shea, Molly O'Shea's son?" said the nun, obviously surprised and changing her tone as well. "You know him?"

"Yeah, he's our neighbor," said Caroline. "He's over at our house all the time."

And from then on, so was Sister Michael. She would arrive in the evenings after dinner, in full habit, with a black cape wrapped around her. She'd hike up her dress, and she and Mr. O'Shea would dance an Irish jig and knock back some Irish whiskey to the amazement of Geraldine and her sister Carol. Sister Michael also began taking extra time to tutor Geraldine, that is, until one night the Irish dancing nun ran away with the Italian school janitor.

"But I would have forgiven her anything," says Geraldine, "because she was so real. I had always been petrified and in awe of nuns, but she was a real person. It felt like God used to visit our house when she'd come over. And even though she'd dance and drink, she did it with such dignity and class, never too much. She was holy. And I think it's the first time I began to think, what kind of woman gives herself to God the way she did? Even though she left to marry the janitor, to me she was always Sister Michael. To this day, when I see the word 'Mississippi,' I think of her."

THE NUN IN FOURTH GRADE was just as memorable, but, unfortunately, for not as benevolent reasons. Sister Mary Louise never smiled and had a reputation for using her hands to get her point across. One afternoon, Geraldine was playing during recess with her classmates in the schoolyard. The bell rang to signal the end to playtime and the kids started running to take their last kick of the ball before being herded into line. Geraldine was standing behind Sister Mary Louise when a classmate, Jack Lutter, ran behind the nun and accidentally pulled her tightly pinned veil halfway off her head, exposing the shortest hair Geraldine had ever seen on a woman. The nun turned with her hand already opened and smacked Geraldine across the face with a blow so powerful that it echoed in the hushed schoolyard. Geraldine started crying and ran home to Caroline, who was sitting in the kitchen half drunk.

"Are you home from school already?" said Caroline, as she checked the clock in the kitchen, wondering how she could've frittered the whole day away.

Geraldine stood in the kitchen, looking at the floor.

"What happened to your face?" asked Caroline, as she got up from the chair. "Why is one side of your face so red? Geraldine, answer me."

"Sister Mary Louise hit me."

"She *hit* you? Why?"

"She thought I pulled her veil in the schoolyard because I

was standing behind her, but it was really Jack Lutter." Geraldine began crying again.

"That son of a bitch," said Caroline. "Gerri, go wash your face, and don't worry about it. I'll take care of her."

Caroline was at the school within fifteen minutes. Sister Mary Louise was in the middle of teaching a class when Caroline opened the classroom door and walked up to the nun, who stood silent at the blackboard.

"You, out in the hallway," said Caroline, as she pointed at the nun and then the door.

"Madam, you cannot disturb me in the middle of my class."

"Oh, I'll do more than disturb you if you don't get out in that hallway."

The nun reluctantly followed Caroline into the hallway and closed the door.

"If you ever put your hands on my daughter again, it will be the last kid you touch."

"She's a ruffian. She needs to be put in line."

"I'm warning you. If she needs anything, I'll give it to her. Not you. Do you understand me?" The nun stood silent. "Do you *understand* me?"

"Yes, but one more incident with her, and she's out of this school."

"One more incident with *you*, and *you'll* be out of this school," Caroline shot back.

That night Geraldine sat in the kitchen on a chair with a white towel wrapped around her shoulder, feeling good that her mother was now fighting nuns for her rather than turning her over to them. Caroline poured kerosene in her daughter's hair and let it set for a few minutes. Geraldine's scalp began to burn.

"Momma, it hurts," she said.

"I know, but it's the only way to kill the lice. We don't want that nun having anything else to yell at you about."

Caroline then began combing Geraldine's hair with a fine-tooth comb as the dead lice fell onto the towel. Those that weren't yet dead, Caroline squished against the table with her thumbnail.

"Momma, I don't want to go back to that school. I don't like it."

"Well, you have to. We've already paid for your books. Give it another chance. You won't have any more trouble from her."

"But most of my friends go to public school."

"I don't care what most of your friends do. You do as I say, not as they do."

The next morning Geraldine got dressed as if she was going to school, but instead she went to her friend Jane Murphy's house and convinced her to play hooky. They went to Luna Park, an abandoned amusement park, where they fished for water rats in the dilapidated Shoot the Shute water ride that still collected abundant rainwater in its corroding labyrinth of slides. The rats were as big as the ones Geraldine's stepfather caught each night at home and placed in shoeboxes until he could discard them in the morning. That was if he hadn't come home too drunk to hear the traps snap shut at night.

After tiring of fishing for the rats, Geraldine and Jane found some grown-up dressing gowns and sequined shoes left behind by one of the amusement park shows, and they dressed up, pretending they were richer than they could ever imagine.

"You want to go see if the gypsies are around?" said Geraldine, her gold gown dragging along the littered floor.

The park was also a settling spot for gypsies, and Geraldine and her friends would often sit around their campfire as the gypsies told stories that made the kids' eyes wide as silver dollars. The kids were amazed at how dirty the gypsies were and sometimes sickened by their penchant for eating whole sticks of butter with their hands.

"Sure," said Jane, "but it's getting late, so we better not stay too long."

They found the gypsies encamped nearby and joined their circle as evening fell. Although the gypsies were comprised of different ethnic groups with no formal religion, Geraldine got a mini-tutorial in their religious practices from an elderly woman with large hoop earrings and stringy hair that dangled from beneath a red bandana. She was crying.

"What's the matter?" asked Geraldine.

"My grandson. He die yesterday. I'm sad. We pray to Jesus for him."

"You pray to Jesus?" said Geraldine, surprised that the gypsies believed in God. She had always assumed they had no real belief. Her mother had always referred to them as "lying thieves."

"Yes, sure," the old woman said. "His soul now goes back over his life for year. His body must stay whole for soul."

"Wow," said Geraldine. "I had no idea you believed all that. Do you go to church, too?"

"No, no church," said the gypsy. "We pray here and in house. God is everywhere. We don't need church. World is our church."

"Hey, Jane," said Geraldine, "do you hear this? They believe in the same God we do, but they don't have to go to church. Pretty neat."

When Caroline got the call that Geraldine wasn't in school, she went looking for her at Luna Park, based on a tip that someone had seen Geraldine and Jane there. Not able to find them, Caroline was convinced that the gypsies had stolen her daughter and went to the police to report her as missing. The girls had simply gone back to Jane's house after singing some songs for the dead boy with the gypsies.

"I got the worst beating that night," says Geraldine. "It was the last time I ever sat with the gypsies. I went back to school the next day. Though Sister Mary Louise didn't lay a hand on me, she treated me like dirt because she'd heard I'd played hooky. I remember going to the nine o'clock Mass that morning, which we did every morning as a class, and asking God how a woman so devoted to Him could be so mean. The gypsies' religion was looking better and better to me."

The following year, when Geraldine was in fifth grade, her family's dog, Lucky, got lost. Her stepfather, Chris, had come home drunk the night before, causing Lucky to cower under the kitchen table and then bolt out the door when Chris failed to close it properly. The hunt for the black mutt was on the next day. Geraldine was in Brighton Beach looking for Lucky when she decided to stop in a drugstore and help herself to some trinkets without paying. As she was crossing the street after coming out, she found herself trapped in oncoming traffic from both directions. When she turned to go back to the sidewalk, a black sedan hit her, sending her flying a few feet and causing her to land on her face, breaking her nose. When the police arrived, to Geraldine's horror they carried her into the drugstore to await the ambulance. Geraldine began to pray. "Please God, don't let the bobby pins fall out of my pocket in this store. Please God, don't let them fall out."

That prayer was answered, as well as another one Geraldine had been praying for for some time. Because Geraldine was afraid to go back to Our Lady of Solace after being out of school for one month because of the accident, Caroline finally gave her daughter permission to transfer to public school. "I guess you can go to PS 100," she said to Geraldine. "But I'm still going to have to go up to Our Lady of Solace because your sister wants to stay there. You kids love to make more work for me."

"But it was *so* much better for me," says Geraldine. "Catholic school was just books, books, books. But in public school they had stuff that I was good at, like cooking and gym and shop. And no more nuns, though I missed them in a strange way. I stopped going to church then, too. Pop went every week, but Momma never did, probably because she couldn't stop smoking for the hour, so I couldn't see why I had to go. I guess I figured, if the gypsies could pray to God without church, so could I. I took a little break from religion until I was about sixteen, and then everything changed for me."

GERALDINE DROPPED OUT of Lincoln High School and went to work at Martin's Department Store selling hats in the millinery department, giving her total pay each week to Caroline, who by that time had stopped drinking but had been unable to convince Chris to do the same. He still staggered home a few nights a week, much to the embarrassment of his daughters, who used to run and hide when they saw him coming down the street. Caroline would punch his head when he walked in the door, furious that he had drunk away the paycheck she was waiting for to pay bills.

"He was a wonderful man, but a terrible drunk," says Geraldine. "I'm not sure why Momma stopped drinking. She just did one day. Maybe she saw that things couldn't go on as they were. We were thrown out of our apartment on West Eighth Street by marshals who put all our furniture on the street because my parents hadn't paid the rent. They'd lost a lot of money on dice games that they used to have on the floor of our apartment.

"So Momma went across the street and got a two-room apartment for us at 3 Kister Court. It only had a kitchen and living room, so we all slept in the same room in two double beds. At night we could feel the mice tugging at the bottom of the blankets. Terrible. We didn't even have a television. On Tuesday nights we'd go across the street to neighbors to watch *Texaco Star Theater* with Milton Berle. That was our big night out. They were pretty tough times."

After work Geraldine would hang out on Avenue W and McDonald Avenue near Coney Island, where a friend's father owned a candy store. Rosemary was a heavyset blond, known to be a little loose with the boys, who worked in the Montgomery Ward department store, where she later got Geraldine a job as well, invoicing merchandise. But it was the other teenagers who hung out at the candy store who caused the change in Geraldine's life. They happened to be a devoutly religious bunch who attended novenas at Little Flower Church on Tuesday and Friday nights.

Geraldine liked one of the guys, Dominic, whom they called "Flip," a tall, good-looking Italian with black hair and a killer smile. If he was going to the novena, so was Geraldine. She rode on the back of his motorcycle to church one Tuesday night, feeling like Marlon Brando's chick in *The Wild One*.

"When I walked into the church, it was as if I was going for the first time. It seemed so beautiful and peaceful. Candles were lit, a choir was chanting, and it smelled so nice. I'd never seen anything like it. Believe it or not, I even forgot about Flip for the hour and really prayed, maybe for the first time. I cried, too, because my life had been so hard up to that point. I was sick of being poor, sick of Poppa getting drunk, sick of having to hand all my money over to Momma and then have her tell me on Monday morning that she didn't have carfare to give me so that I could go to work.

"So I told God I wanted things to change. I told Him I'd forget about all the stuff with the orphanage and the nuns and how bad we had it, and that I'd come back to Him, but He had to come through, too. And I eventually really felt peace as I knelt there. I felt God say I was going to be okay. I left the church somehow stronger that night. It was a real turning point for me."

When Flip dropped her off at home after the novena, the night became even more magical.

"Hey, Gerri, how about you and me go to a movie tomorrow night?" asked Flip, as he sat on his motorcycle and combed his DA.

Geraldine's stomach dropped. She didn't think prayers worked that quickly. And while she was excited at the prospect of dating the most coveted guy on Avenue W, Flip had a reputation with the ladies, part of which was not showing up when he was supposed to.

"Sure," said Geraldine, a bit hesitantly. "What time?"

"I'll pick you up at seven," said Flip, as he gunned the engine of the motorcycle.

"Okay, I'll be ready," said Geraldine. She rushed into the apartment, her heart thumping with excitement as Flip roared down Kister Court.

Geraldine was unable to sleep much that night. She returned to the praying she had begun at the novena hours earlier, with a slight shift in subject matter.

"Please God, let him show up tomorrow night," she prayed. "Please God. I'll do whatever you want. Anything. Just please let him show up. I'll fast all day and night. Not even water, if you let him come. Please God."

Geraldine fasted the next day, not even water. Flip showed up at 7:10 that evening in a black leather jacket and white pegged pants in time for a 7:30 showing of *The King and I* with Yul Brynner and Deborah Kerr at a local movie theater. And although it turned out to be the only date they ever had, it was enough to convince Geraldine that there was something to this prayer stuff. It was the beginning of a deeper shift in her perception of and relationship with God.

"I realize now," says Geraldine, "that it wasn't exactly the most mature religious perspective. But to be honest, I have to say that my relationship with God did begin because I felt He answered my prayers. I started going to Mass regularly and praying all the time, about everything. And I always seemed to get what I asked for. And if I didn't, I just figured I'd done something wrong and God was mad at me that day. But that didn't happen too often. Still doesn't. But now I do pray more for other people than I did back then, in fact, *mostly* for other people now."

The day after her *King and I* dream date, Geraldine told her mother that she was no longer giving her full salary to her.

"I'll give you twenty-five dollars a week, Momma, and that's it. I can't live like this anymore."

"Well, your sister Carol still gives me her full pay and she's two years older than you. Who do you think *you* are?"

"I don't care what Carol does. She's better than me. Twenty-five dollars. That's it. And another thing, we're not going with you to Atlantic City this weekend if we can't smoke in front of you."

Geraldine and her sister were supposed to go to the shore with their mother and stepfather for the weekend, and though Geraldine and Carol had been smoking for a couple of years, they had never dared smoke in the house or in front of their mother.

"Fine, do what you want," Caroline finally said, as she lit up a cigarette. "I know you've been smoking anyway. But remember, you should do as I *say*, not as I *do*."

"You got that right, Momma," said Geraldine.

I SIT ON A DIMINUTIVE roller coaster at Buddy's Kiddie Amusement Park on Flatbush Avenue in Brooklyn. The hills rise barely five feet from the ground, with one killer that maybe goes eight feet high. I am six years old, ashen-faced, and holding on for dear life. I don't want to do this. My mother stands outside the gate with a cigarette hanging out of her mouth and a green kerchief tied around her bobby-pinned set hair.

"What's the matter with you?" she says. "Do you know I used to ride down the LA Thompson in Coney Island on my sled with no safety belt or anything, and the hills were ten times as high as these?"

Though it was scant consolation, I tried to picture my mother freely looping the gleaming tracks of a much bigger roller coaster on her unfettered sled as my little red cart pulled out from the safety of the canopied entrance. As we chugged up the eight-foot-high hill, I thought I was going to throw up. Good thing she waited years to tell me about hanging off the side of that "ten times as high" roller coaster.

I've listened to my mother's stories most of my life: how poor she was, needing to put cardboard in her shoes to walk to school, the lice infestations in her hair, getting hit by the car after stealing from the drugstore, bonding with the dirty, butter-eating gypsies, sitting on her family's furniture on the street after being evicted, rats as big as cats scratching at the walls at night, the Nazi nuns, the harrowing orphanage, demanding Nanny and drunken Poppa, and on and on. I used to think she embellished her stories as a parental pedagogy to make her point and to force my brother Chris and me to appreciate what we had. "You wouldn't have survived my childhood," was a mantra drilled into our heads until we were sick of hearing it.

But now I don't think she embellished any of it. Perhaps some of the particulars have become more grandiose with time, but they are surely as she remembers them. And through her telling, I remember them, too. I believe I am a priest today partly because of her and those memories, especially the "spiritual" ones. I couldn't imagine how anyone who had come from such dire circumstances had retained such a strong faith. I watched her never miss a Sunday Mass my whole life. I noticed her bless herself with holy water in a font nailed to the doorpost each time she came in or out the front door. I saw her lips move in silent prayer before every meal as the rest of us were already slicing into our entrées. I observed her hands still clasped together many nights as she drifted off to sleep, not yet finished with her litany of supplication. And I wanted what she had. I wanted whatever had happened to her at the novena when she was a teenager to happen to me. And so I went in search of it.

After the Stories

IT IS HARD TO SAY GOOD-BYE to the people in the preceding pages. Now that their stories have been told, they have a life of their own. And the stories continue. But one story felt unresolved and unfinished. When I handed in this manuscript to my editor, he said, "But what about the cocktail waitress in the beginning? You never *did* find out if she had a spiritual story. You kind of left the reader hanging." And so, lest I be accused of being a tease of a writer, I set out to remedy the situation. Months after my pre-theater drink with my goading friend, I returned alone to that trendy bar in the theater district.

When I took the elevator to the seventh floor, the door opened to a deafening cacophony of sound as imbibing and chatting patrons filled the dimly yet professionally lit bar space. Pink accent lights splashed against Venetian-plastered white walls. It was just after Thanksgiving, and already ultramodern Christmas decorations—oversized silver and blue balls on stainless-steel branches—hovered over the twenties-to-thirties-something crowd, many of whom were sitting low to the ground on white leather couches and chairs from which some needed help to stand up.

Couples were huddled in side alcoves encased by what looked like giant venetian blinds that gave an Eastern, almost Zenlike feel to the room. Black-clad young men with earpieces milled about, seemingly talking into space.

I scanned the room looking for my waitress, but I didn't see her. I had no idea if she even worked here anymore. Maybe I could just talk to a different cocktail waitress and ask the same questions and pretend it was the girl I'd met before. No one would know the difference. Feeling conspicuously alone, I found a free seat on a couch in the back of the bar area.

A smiling waitress peered down at me on the low settee.

"May I get you something?" she said, as she crouched down to put a napkin on the table, careful to not let her black, slits-up-the-side miniskirt reveal more than was seemly.

"Just a glass of sauvignon blanc, please . . . Oh, and can I ask you something?"

"Uh-huh."

"I'm kind of looking for someone. A waitress I met here a while ago."

"What's her name?"

"I'm not really sure."

"What does she look like?"

"Well, I kind of remember long blond hair and a very pretty smile."

"That describes about half of the girls who work here. Why do you want her?"

"I just want to ask her something."

"Look, you know we're not really permitted to socialize with the patrons, so it might not be a good idea . . ."

"Oh, no, it's nothing like that," I interrupted, somewhat defensively. "I really do just want to ask her a few things."

"Uh-huh. Well, with no name, I really can't help you. Sorry. I'll be back with your drink in a sec."

Gee, a little snippy, I thought. *I won't overtip* her.

I plunged my hand into the oversalted mini-pretzels that a busboy had set before me while I continued to scrutinize the girls who balanced serving trays with the skill of circus performers. Some guy in the chair next to me began talking on a cell phone in a voice that attempted to compete with the rising decibels of the rapidly filling room. I wanted to get out of there.

I gulped at the wine that the waitress had set before me, thinking this wasn't a great idea after all. As I was fishing for my scarf from the sleeve of my jacket, I spotted my elusive muse *behind* the bar serving a drink to an overweight man in a business suit. Funny, I hadn't thought to look there. Even from a distance I was sure it was she—same hair, same smile.

I parked myself on the only free hard plastic seat at the end of the bar. *Gee, could they make these things any more uncomfortable?* I thought. I waved to get her attention, but she didn't see me. The other bartender, a bicep-bulging Calvin Klein–like model in a black stretch-polyester shirt, came over to me.

"Can I get you something?" he said.

"Um, no, I actually just wanted to speak with the girl down there."

"Well, I can take your order."

"I don't really want to place an order. I've already had something to drink. I just want to ask her something." He looked at me with slight disdain.

"Adrienne," he yelled to the other end of the bar, "someone here wants to see you."

He went back to cleaning glasses. She served one more drink and slowly made her way toward me. My stomach jumped a little as I suddenly realized I hadn't rehearsed what I would say.

"Hi, may I help you?" she said, and smiled.

"Um, I hope so," I said. "I was in here a number of months ago with a friend of mine and you waited on us."

"Uh-huh."

"You mean you remember us?"

"No, I mean, I just take your word for it."

"Oh. Well, my friend and I were talking, and he had an interesting theory about you."

"I see. You know, I have customers here that I have to serve," she said, as if to say, "I've heard so many better lines before."

"Yes, of course you do," I said. "Could I maybe just have a few minutes of your time when you go off duty?"

"You mean at 2 a.m.? I don't think so."

"Oh, that late, huh? Well, actually my question is really a simple one. Do you consider yourself a spiritual person?"

"That's a *simple* question?" she said, as her eyes widened. I could hardly believe myself that I was asking her this. It just kind of came out, almost desperately.

"Well, you see, I'm a priest, and my friend and I were having this discussion when we were here. And he used you to make a point. He thought you were spiritual and . . ."

"You're a priest?"

"Yes."

"Prove it," she said, and tilted her head.

"Well, how can I prove it? You just have to take my word for it, like you did about my being here before. I really am."

"Even if you are a priest, why would you care about whether or not *I'm* spiritual?"

Someone started waving a ten-dollar bill at her from halfway down the bar.

"I think he's looking for you," I said, and pointed.

"One second," she said, and walked over to him to make change.

When she returned, I thought it was time to come totally clean.

"Look," I said, "I should also tell you that I'm just finishing a book about people's unlikely spiritual journeys and I thought you might be a good person to end with."

"What makes you think my journey is unlikely or that I even have one?"

"Well, I don't know. That's why I'm asking."

"And you don't know anything else about me?" she said, skeptically. "No one has told you anything?"

"No, promise."

She paused, as if weighing whether or not I was psychotic.

"And you're going to write this in a book?" she finally said.

"Well, yes, but not using your name or anything. And it wouldn't be a chapter like the others. Just kind of a conclusion. Oh, and you're kind of in the beginning, too."

"Before you've even talked to me?"

"Well, I told you my friend and I talked about you months ago. I mean, all nice things. My friend was especially complimentary."

She started to smile. I began to feel relieved. A minor breakthrough.

"Well, to answer your question, I would say, yes, I am spiritual. At least, I think that I am."

She walked away for a few minutes to tend to a few mildly

perturbed patrons and then came back to me. For the next hour, in between serving her customers, she talked to me about her "spiritual life." I sat amazed at how on the mark my unwitting friend had been.

"YOU HAVE ACTUALLY BEEN TO LOURDES?" I said, after we had been chatting for about fifteen minutes. *I* haven't even been there. (Lourdes is a shrine in France where miracles are purported to occur.)

"Yes, when I was diagnosed with the pure red cell aplasia (a rare bone marrow disorder). That was after they found the tumor in my thymus gland."

"And what happened?"

"I was cured. No tumor. No aplasia. They can't quite explain it, but so far I'm doing fine."

"And no treatment?" I was finding what she was telling me hard to believe.

"Nope. I went before they were going to start."

"And why Lourdes?"

"I found it on the Internet and thought France might be nice." *Nice?*

"So you're Catholic then, right?"

"Nope. Quaker."

"Quaker?" I sputtered. Now I was sure she was putting me on.

"You say it like it's a dirty word or something."

"No, it's just that . . . you don't meet many Quakers today. And one who's been to Lourdes, no less."

"My parents were very big in the Quaker movement. I've never really been that active, but I like the whole peace thing and the lack of rules. It always felt kind of avant-garde, actually."

"Did being cured at Lourdes make you want to be a Catholic?"

"No. Should it have?"

"Well, I just mean that with Mary and all . . ."

"God healed me as a Quaker, so I think it's okay with God if I stay one. I do pray more now though. And I've even gone to a few Quaker meetings with my parents in California. It was nice. I liked it."

"Wow. I'd say that's pretty dramatic. You seem so matter-of-fact about it all."

I began to wonder if someone had put her up to this, but no one had known of my plans to go there.

"No, not matter-of-fact. Just really grateful. And I actually want to learn more about my own spiritual place in the universe, if that doesn't sound too Oprah. George Fox, who was the founder of the Quakers, claimed that everyone could have a personal relationship with Jesus without having to depend on a priest or minister. No offense, or anything."

"None taken." She finally had me convinced.

"And that the Bible isn't the final revelation of God. We have to keep listening to what the Spirit is speaking in our hearts today. And that's what I want to do. I want to experience God more for myself. To listen. And I think my illness and my cure has given me a great start."

I called my friend on my cell phone as soon as the elevator reached the lobby.

"You are *not* going to believe this," I said.

I DIDN'T QUITE BELIEVE IT MYSELF, but the experience (and that of the people in the preceding pages) has encouraged me to continue to push the boundaries of what I believe about religion and Spirit and God. I've been formed in a Church with a lot of rules and regulations. It was implied that there was one true way to go to God. I was taught to believe that there are things about God that we know *absolutely and unequivocally*. I'm not sure there are as many as I once thought. *God is Love.* I can buy that one. It seems to ring true with my and others' experience of God. Everything else may be up for grabs, I think. People find their way to the source of that Love in their own way, albeit with help and guidance—which is the boon of religious traditions—but ultimately alone.

And yet we make the journey *together*, as individuals inextricably connected to one another. Therein is the power of the faith stories of others' lives. They can inspire us to be more than we are alone, to reach further than might be our initial instincts to do. They can lead the way when the path seems uncertain, or treacherous, or unlikely. If others have made it, maybe we can, too. Thus the trodden paths of those who have "run the race," as Saint Paul says, assure us that we are not alone in our, at times, meandering journeys. We may come to see that the detours have been taken before; that the unlikely is not always so; and that home is a place that we arrive at together.

✺ ACKNOWLEDGMENTS ✺

In writing this book I realized that *I* wasn't really writing it. The Spirit of the people whose stories are told in the preceding pages wrote the book. That Spirit was my muse. Others also helped by their loving care and support, always believing that a book celebrating Spirit was worth writing—and reading. I thank them for their encouragement and for making a significant contribution to this book coming to fruition. Special thanks to:

Geraldine and Edward Beck, for being powerhouse parents

Christopher and Jayne Beck, for being a supportive brother and sagacious sister-in-law

Alexandra Beatty Morris and Kate Harris, my publicists at Doubleday, for their untiring work in making sure this book got noticed

Augusten Burroughs, for remembering where he came from, even in the midst of his staggering success

Andrew Corbin, my editor at Doubleday, for his sharp wit and perspicacious eye, and to his assistant, Joan Schadt, for her fine work in helping to prepare the manuscript

Bob and Maurie Flanagan, for their generosity and open home

Peter Friedman, teacher and editor extraordinaire, and the writing group that he so lovingly guides, for being honest and usually right

Monsignor Thomas P. Leonard of Holy Trinity Church in Manhattan, for providing me with "a room of my own" in which to write this book

Denise McManamon, for still riding the waves with me

Karen O'Neill, for her cherished friendship, bravery, and unparalleled generosity

The Passionist Community, my religious family, for their unwavering support

Denise Marcil, my literary agent, and her able staff of assistants, for going to bat for me even when I don't ask

Huguette J. McKenzie, for her generosity and wild ideas

Michelle Rapkin, publisher at Doubleday, for her encouragement and joy

Columkille Regan, C.P., for maturing the way I want to